THE MAXIMUS POEMS

THE MAXIMUS POEMS

CHARLES OLSON

Edited by George F. Butterick

University of California Press / *Berkeley*   *Los Angeles*   *London*

University of California Press
Berkeley and Los Angeles, California

University of California Press, Ltd.
London, England

This complete edition of *The Maximus Poems* brings together the volumes of Charles Olson's long poem
(begun in 1950 and completed shortly before his death in 1970) with corrections and alterations where
necessary and appropriate. The first volume, *The Maximus Poems* (New York: Jargon/Corinth, 1960), is
©1960 by Charles Olson and reprinted by permission of Corinth Books. The second volume,
Maximus Poems IV, V, VI (London: Cape Goliard, 1968), is ©1968 by the Estate of Charles Olson.
The Maximus Poems: Volume Three (New York: Viking/Grossman, 1975) is ©1975 by the Estate of
Charles Olson and the University of Connecticut; the poems added to this volume in the present edition
are ©1983 by the University of Connecticut. The emended texts and editorial apparatus are ©1983
by The Regents of the University of California.

Library of Congress Cataloging in Publication Data
Olson, Charles, 1910–1970.
  The Maximus poems.

  Includes index.
  I. Butterick, George F.   II. Title.
PS3529.L655M3   1983   811'.54   79-65759
ISBN 0-520-04015-5   AACR2

Printed in the United States of America

1 2 3 4 5 6 7 8 9

CONTENTS

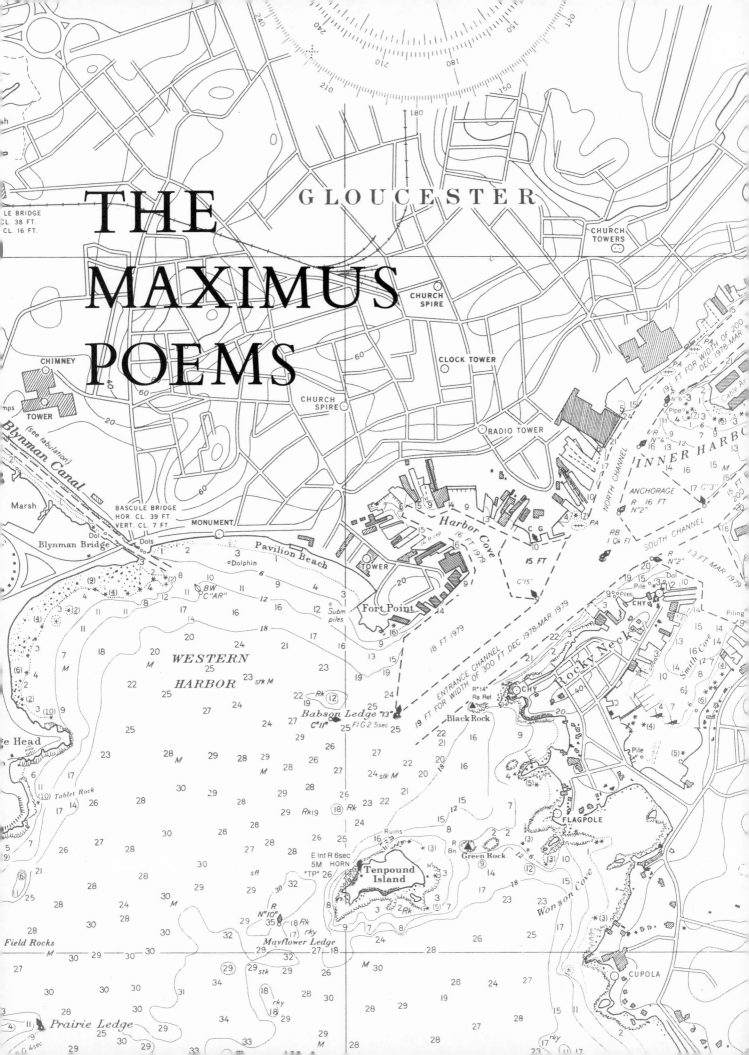

THE MAXIMUS POEMS

for ROBERT CREELEY
—the Figure of Outward

*All my life I've heard
one makes many*

I, Maximus of Gloucester, to You

> Off-shore, by islands hidden in the blood
> jewels & miracles, I, Maximus
> a metal hot from boiling water, tell you
> what is a lance, who obeys the figures of
> the present dance

1

the thing you're after
may lie around the bend
of the nest (second, time slain, the bird! the bird!

And there! (strong) thrust, the mast! flight
                              (of the bird
                               o kylix, o
                               Antony of Padua
                               sweep low, o bless

the roofs, the old ones, the gentle steep ones
on whose ridge-poles the gulls sit, from which they depart,

                              And the flake-racks
of my city!

2

love is form, and cannot be without
important substance (the weight
say, 58 carats each one of us, perforce
our goldsmith's scale

                    feather to feather added
                    (and what is mineral, what
                    is curling hair, the string
                    you carry in your nervous beak, these

                    make bulk, these, in the end, are
                    the sum

(o my lady of good voyage
                    in whose arm, whose left arm rests
no boy but a carefully carved wood, a painted face, a schooner!
a delicate mast, as bow-sprit for

                              forwarding

      3

      the underpart is, though stemmed, uncertain
      is, as sex is, as moneys are, facts!
      facts, to be dealt with, as the sea is, the demand
      that they be played by, that they only can be, that they must
      be played by, said he, coldly, the
      ear!

      By ear, he sd.
      But that which matters, that which insists, that which will last,
      that! o my people, where shall you find it, how, where, where shall you listen
      when all is become billboards, when, all, even silence, is spray-gunned?

      when even our bird, my roofs,
      cannot be heard

      when even you, when sound itself is neoned in?

      when, on the hill, over the water
      where she who used to sing,
      when the water glowed,
      black, gold, the tide
      outward, at evening

      when bells came like boats
      over the oil-slicks, milkweed
      hulls

      And a man slumped,
      attentionless,
      against pink shingles

      o sea city)

4

one loves only form,
and form only comes
into existence when
the thing is born

       born of yourself, born
       of hay and cotton struts,
       of street-pickings, wharves, weeds
       you carry in, my bird

              of a bone of a fish
              of a straw, or will
              of a color, of a bell
              of yourself, torn

5

love is not easy
but how shall you know,
New England, now
that pejorocracy is here, how
that street-cars, o Oregon, twitter
in the afternoon, offend
a black-gold loin?

       how shall you strike,
       o swordsman, the blue-red back
       when, last night, your aim
       was mu-sick, mu-sick, mu-sick
       And not the cribbage game?

             (o Gloucester-man,
             weave
             your birds and fingers
             new, your roof-tops,
             clean shit upon racks
             sunned on
             American

braid
with others like you, such
extricable surface
as faun and oral,
satyr lesbos vase

o kill kill kill kill kill
those
who advertise you
out)

6

in! in! the bow-sprit, bird, the beak
in, the bend is, in, goes in, the form
that which you make, what holds, which is
the law of object, strut after strut, what you are, what you must be, what
the force can throw up, can, right now hereinafter erect,
the mast, the mast, the tender
mast!

The nest, I say, to you, I Maximus, say
under the hand, as I see it, over the waters
from this place where I am, where I hear,
can still hear

from where I carry you a feather
as though, sharp, I picked up,
in the afternoon delivered you
a jewel,
          it flashing more than a wing,
than any old romantic thing,
than memory, than place,
than anything other than that which you carry

than that which is,
call it a nest, around the head of, call it
the next second

than that which you
can do!

Maximus, to Gloucester

LETTER 2

..... tell you? ha! who
can tell another how
to manage the swimming?

he was right: people

don't change. They only stand more
revealed. I,
likewise

1

the light, there, at the corner (because of the big elm
and the reflecting houses) winter or summer stays
as it was when they lived there, in the house the street cuts off
as though it were a fault,
the side's so sheer

they hid, or tried to hide, the fact the cargo their ships brought back
was black (the Library, too, possibly so founded). The point is

the light does go one way toward the post office,
and quite another way down to Main Street. Nor is that all:

coming from the sea, up Middle, it is more white, very white
as it passes the grey of the Unitarian church. But at Pleasant Street,
it is abruptly
black

(hidden
city

2

Or now, when such houses are not built,
or such trees planted, it's the doctor knows
what the parents don't know. Or the wife doesn't,
of the husband, or the husband, of the other. Sins,

they still call them, and let
pejorocracy thrive. Only the lady

has got it straight. She looks
as the best of my people look
in one direction, her direction, they know

it is elements men stand in the midst of,
not these names supported by that false future she,
precisely she,
has her foot upon

                    (He
made the coast, and though he lost his feet for it,
and the hands he'd purposely allowed to freeze to the oars,
I knew him, drank
with my elders, in his own bar, a toast to him

Or my other, the top of whose head a bollard clean took away.
It was four days before they could get him to Chelsea Marine.
This spring I listened to him as good as new, as fresh as it's always been
to hear him talk of the sea. He was puttering in his garden when I came up,
looking over his Santa Fe rose. And he took off his hat to show me,
how it is all skin where his skull was,
too much of a hole for even the newest metal
to cover

Or the quiet one, who's died since (died as deck-watchman, on his vessel, in port).
Years ago I heard from others
how he'd pulled two men out of the sea one night
off Eastern Point. They'd not been able to shed their jacks
when the ship went over, and when he caught them
they were going down too. He hauled them into Brace's Cove,
even though the shore wasn't there, it was such a storm and the sea so big
it had turned the Lily Pond
into an arm of itself.

Last, he with muscle as big as his voice, the strength of him
in that blizzard
to have pulled the trawl slack from the very bottom and released
his mate from the cod-hook had him out, and almost off,
into the snow. It wasn't that there was so much sea. It was the cold,
and that white, until over the dory went and the two of them,
one still,
were in. The wild thing was, he made the vessel, three miles, and fetched her,
found that vessel in all that weather, with his fellow dead weight
on him. The sort of eye
which later knew the Peak of Brown's
as though it were his own garden (as Bowditch brought the Eppie Sawyer
spot to her wharf a Christmas morning)

3

Which is the cream of the milk, of course. And the milk
also of the matter, the most of it, those
who do no more than drink it in a cup of tea alone of such a night, holding
(as she)
a certain schooner

What still is, in other words. And the remarkable part of it,
that it still goes on, still is
what counts:

          the lad from the Fort
who recently bought the small white house on Lower Middle
(the one diagonally across from the handsome brick with the Bullfinch doors)
He stood with me one Sunday
and eyed (with a like eye) a curious ship
we'd both come on, tied to the Gas Company wharf.
She had raked masts, and they were unstepped,
fitted loose in her deck, like a neck in a collar.
He was looking idly, as I was, saying nothing.
When suddenly, he turned to a Gloucesterman, a big one,
berthed alongside this queer one, and said:
"I'll own her, one day"

4

While she stares, out of her painted face,
no matter the deathly mu-sick, the demand
will arouse
some of these men and women

LETTER 3

Tansy buttons, tansy
for my city
Tansy for their noses

Tansy for them,
tansy for Gloucester to take the smell
of all owners,
the smell

Tansy
for all of us

      Let those who use words cheap, who use us cheap
      take themselves out of the way
      Let them not talk of what is good for the city

      Let them free the way for me, for the men of the Fort
      who are not hired, who buy the white houses

      Let them cease putting out words in the public print
      so that any of us have to leave, so that my Portuguese leave,
      leave the Lady they gave us, sell their schooners
      with the greyhounds aft, the long Diesels
      they put their money in, leave Gloucester
      in the present shame of,
      the wondership stolen by,
      ownership

Tansy from Cressy's
I rolled in as a boy
and didn't know it was
tansy

1

Did you know, she sd, growing up there,
how rare it was? And it turned out later she meant exactly the long field
drops down from Ravenswood where the land abrupts,
this side of Fresh Water Cove, and throws out
that wonder of my childhood, the descending green does run
so,
by the beach

                    where they held the muster Labor Day, and the engine teams
                    threw such arcs of water

                                        runs with summer with
tansy

2

I was not born there, came, as so many of the people came,
from elsewhere. That is, my father did. And not from the Provinces,
not from Newfoundland. But we came early enough. When he came,
there were three hundred sail could fill the harbor,
if they were all in, as for the Races, say
Or as now the Italians are in, for San Pietro,
and the way it is from Town Landing, all band-concert,
and fireworks

So I answered her: Yes,
I knew (I had that to compare to it,
was Worcester)

As the people of the earth are now, Gloucester
is heterogeneous, and so can know polis
not as localism, not that mu-sick (the trick
of corporations, newspapers, slick magazines, movie houses,
the ships, even the wharves, absentee-owned

they whine to my people, these entertainers, sellers

they play upon their bigotries (upon their fears

these   they have the nerve
to speak of that lovely hour
the Waiting Station, 5 o'clock, the Magnolia bus, Al Levy
on duty (the difference
from 1 o'clock, all the women getting off
the Annisquam-Lanesville,
and the letter carriers

5:40, and only the lollers
in front of the shoe-shine parlor

these, right in the people's faces (and not at all as the gulls do it,
who do it straight, do it all over the "Times" blowing
the day after, or the "Summer Sun" catching on pilings, floating
off the Landing, the slime
the low tide reveals, the smell
then

3

The word does intimidate. The pay-check does.
But to use either, as cheap men

o tansy city, root city
let them not make you
as the nation is

I speak to any of you, not to you all, to no group, not to you as citizens
as my Tyrian might have. Polis now
is a few, is a coherence not even yet new (the island of this city
is a mainland now of who? who can say who are
citizens?

Only a man or a girl who hear a word
and that word meant to mean not a single thing the least more than
what it does mean (not at all to sell any one anything, to keep them anywhere,
not even
in this rare place

Root person in root place, hear one tansy-covered boy tell you
what any knowing man of your city might, a letter carrier, say,
or that doctor—if they dared afford to take the risk, if they reminded themselves
that you should not be played with, that you deserve . . . they'd tell you
the condition of the under-water, the cut-water of anyone, including those
who take on themselves
to give you advice,
to tell you, for example,
what not to read

       They'd tell you, because they know (know as the house knows,
wearing its white face, its clapboard mask) who there is will not outrage you
in the next edition, who'll not seek, even knowingly, to make you
slave

as he is slave
whom you read
as the bus starts off

                  whose slaver
                  would keep you off the sea, would keep you local,
                  my Nova Scotians,
                  Newfoundlanders,
                  Sicilianos,
                  Isolatos

4

Isolated person in Gloucester, Massachusetts, I, Maximus, address you
you islands
of men and girls

The Songs of Maximus

SONG 1

           colored pictures
of all things to eat: dirty
postcards
        And words, words, words
all over everything
             No eyes or ears left
to do their own doings (all

invaded, appropriated, outraged, all senses

including the mind, that worker on what is
             And that other sense
made to give even the most wretched, or any of us, wretched,
that consolation (greased
           lulled
even the street-cars

song

SONG 2

     all
wrong
     And I am asked—ask myself (I, too, covered
with the gurry of it) where
shall we go from here, what can we do
when even the public conveyances
sing?
     how can we go anywhere,
even cross-town
         how get out of anywhere (the bodies
all buried
in shallow graves?

Song 3

　　　This morning of the small snow
I count the blessings, the leak in the faucet
which makes of the sink time, the drop
of the water on water as sweet
as the Seth Thomas
in the old kitchen
my father stood in his drawers to wind (always
he forgot the 30th day, as I don't want to remember
the rent
　　　　a house these days
so much somebody else's,
especially,
Congoleum's

　　　　Or the plumbing,
that it doesn't work, this I like, have even used paper clips
as well as string to hold the ball up And flush it
with my hand
　　　　　　But that the car doesn't, that no moving thing moves
without that song I'd void my ear of, the musickracket
of all ownership . . .
　　　　　Holes
in my shoes, that's all right, my fly
gaping, me out
at the elbows, the blessing
　　　　　　　that difficulties are once more

　　　　"In the midst of plenty, walk
　　as close to
　　bare
　　　　In the face of sweetness,
　piss
　　　　In the time of goodness,
　go side, go
　smashing, beat them, go as
　(as near as you can

　tear

In the land of plenty, have
nothing to do with it
                    take the way of
the lowest,
including
your legs, go
contrary, go

    sing

SONG 4

I know a house made of mud & wattles,
I know a dress just sewed
                    (saw the wind
blow its cotton
against her body
from the ankle
            so!
it was Nike

        And her feet: such bones
I could have had the tears
that lovely pedant had
who couldn't unwrap it himself, had to ask them to, on the schooner's deck

and he looked,
the first human eyes to look again
at the start of human motion (just last week
300,000,000 years ago

            She
was going fast
across the square, the water
this time of year, that
scarce

And the fish

SONG 5

I have seen faces of want,
and have not wanted the FAO: Appleseed
's gone back to
what any of us
New England

SONG 6

you sing, you

who also

wants

LETTER 5

            (as, in summer, a newspaper, now, in spring, a magazine)

though how Gloucester will know what damage . . . only Brown's window . . . This quarterly
will not be read

The habit of newsprint
(plus possibly the National Geographic)
are the limits of
literacy

                (tho that the many want any more than, who died
                what scrod brought the Boston market,
                what movies, Gorin's sales, the queer doings
                Rockport—or Squib's coynesses
                about the Antigonish man was pulled out, 3 AM,
                from under Chisholm's Wharf, mumbling

I am not at all aware
that anything more than that
is called for. Limits
are what any of us
are inside of

And there is nothing less applicable
than the complaints of the culture mongers
about what the people don't know but oh!
how beautiful they are, how infinite!
And think how it will be when
                                        (Saint Santa

Claus! how they need
is the latest for oh!
how they bleed, the poor
children

1

Editor of a Gloucester quarterly: the eyes which watch you
do not look in the plate glass of Brown's (that display);
or idly, waiting for the bus, stare at yr cover in the Waiting Station
(if Lufkin has got over his scare, last summer,
when you were so sillily reviewed
in the local press

                    as sillily as you now show yourself
                    bringing such an issue as this
                    into the public domain

Helen Stein's eyes, and those others, Gloucester, who look, who can still look,
look right straight down into yr pages, into the pages of this sheet you've had the nerve
(no different from their nerve)
to put upon the public street

2

It is not the many but the few who care
who keep alive what you set out to do:
to offer Gloucester poems and stories
the High School Flicker's not the end of

                    but what you here bring in
                    is no such young thing
                    such as you, perhaps (I did,
                    and Helen Stein,
                    and Herman Melville)
                    as who does not,
                    when one begins?

Nor is it something else,
what it ought to seek to be: as much
as one Carl Olsen used to bring to port
from another Brown's than merchandise

        a peak of the ocean's floor he knew so well (the care
        he gave his trade, his listening
        at 17 to Callaghan (as Callaghan,
        at 17, to Bohlen,
        Bohlen to Smith) Olsen

could set his dories out
as a landsman sows his fields

and reap such halibut
it was to walk the streets of Gloucester different
to have a sight aboard the Raymonde

        As you should walk it,
        had you done your job

3

I do not know that Four Winds has a place
or I a sight in it
in a city where highliners breed,
if it is not as good as fish is

        as knowing as a halibut knows its grounds (as Olsen knows
        those grounds)

        its stories
        as good as any of us are
        stories (as even Squibs knows
        what men have done in dories)

        as women have had it, raising kids
        in such an unsteady economy

Nor assuage yrself I use the local as a stick to beat you. Such pages
as you now have published twice, do not need one small Gloucester thing
to be a Gloucester magazine. The point of the fix of your cover
is otherwise (I prefer it, in fact, to the rhetoric of your title):
North 42° 37', West 70° 40' It is enough Gloucester,
to say where it is,
had you also the will to be as fine as

        as fine as fins are

              as firm as

        as firm as a mackerel is
        (fresh out of water)

                  as sure

        as sure as no owner is
        (or he'd be to sea)

              as vulnerable

        (as vulnerable as I am
        brought home to Main St
        in such negligible company)

You have had a broken trip, Mr. Ferrini. And you should go hide in your cellar
(as a Portuguese skipper once had to, he'd so scared before a storm, and run for it,
leaving two of his men on the sea in a dory)

4

Or take it as I know you have to take it,
landwise. Making frames over East Main St,
the wife tutoring, the two of you
with children to bring up, you
are more like Gloucester now is
than I who hark back to an older polis,
who has this tie to a time when the port

        (I am not named Maximus
        for no cause

when blueberries

        (if you go, for highbush,
        to Dogtown, or, July,
        with pails, up Old Salem Rd,
        I'll not be there

              as I used to
        chase butterflies, or,
        bitten all day, cut brush
        at the new Alewife

That day was a sign, Ferrini.
The C & R Construction Company
had hired us Gloucester help
because the contract read "local"

and fired us, after 12 hours,
had tricked the city's lawyers,
had covered, by one day's cash,
the letter of the law

The new way does promote
cleverness, the main chance is
its law

        And you who come after,
        who've not known the ones
        had to crawl up out of Brace's Cove
        (even in red jacks)

        will not so easily know
        the grey-eyed one it does take
        to make a man's chest shine

        and he shake off the salt,
        the muck of the in-shore sea, the sludge
        of all shallows

5

I'd not urge anyone back. Back is no value as better. That sentimentality
has no place, least of all Gloucester,
where polis
still thrives

Back is only for those who do not move (as future is,
you in particular need to be warned,
any of you who have the habit of
"the people"–as though there were anything / the equal of / the context of / now!

I'll put care where you are, on those streets I know as well as (or better:
I have the advantage
I was a letter carrier, read postcards, lamped checks, talked
at the back doors

I'll meet you anywhere you say (the beer's best–the pipes are kept cleaner–
at the Anchor Inn (as the old captain called his bar,
with an old name.
You know it (at the head of the Atlantic Supply wharf, "Piney's wharf",
it got called, from Ben's magazine fame, Collier's and all those

        (though I was never convinced
        he was the best choice
        to race the Bluenose,
        dating back as I do to the first Race,
        to the Puritan, and the Elizabeth Howard,
        and Marty Callaghan fouling the boom of the Henry Ford
        just inside the Breakwater

You see I can't get away from the old measure of care: how your magazine don't raise me,
not even Hugh Hill, whose triangles
are so nicely made but the course he's running
doesn't strike me as good enough
to come home a winner (as the Bluenose so often did
after the Columbia was lost

            (did you know, by the way,

that it was off Sable
that she did go down?
that a trawler, a few years back,
caught her nose,
and she came up long enough,
before the beam broke,
for the letters to be read, gold
on black?   COLUMBIA

6

I'll try once more to meet you (what about Sterling's Drug,
is that where you are? Surely, not at the Library,
or you'd at least show that correction
which so many of the other little magazines now so show,
the school-boy Renaissance

(as you are differently adither, with that future
so many of your pieces show, the looseness
of "The Search", the Steiner
mystique

       The mind, Ferrini,
       is as much of a labor
       as to lift an arm
       flawlessly

       Or to read sand in the butter on the end of a lead,
       and be precise about what sort of bottom your vessel's over

7

I begin to be damned to figure out where we can meet. I liked your own house,
that first day I sought you out (you will recall that I came to your door
just because I had read a poem by you in just such a little magazine
as you now purport to edit

A magazine does have this "life" to it (proper to it), does have streets,
can show lights, movie houses, bars, and, occasionally,

       for those of us who do live our life quite properly in print

       as properly, say, as Gloucester people live in Gloucester

you do meet someone

as I met you

on a printed page

8

You get my drift: 4 Winds

       (or let me call it "Island",
       or something more exact—
       "Gloucester", just that flat,
       making my polis yours

       or if you have to be romantic,
       why not call it "The Three Turks Heads"
       and have something at least which belongs to the truth of the place
       as John Smith so strikingly did?

your magazine might excuse itself
if it walked on those legs all live things walk on,
their own

that is, it might,
if you knew that a literary magazine is not,
for example,
politics
       (even a man's own personal politics—
       what sticks out in this issue is verse
       from at least four other editors
       of literary magazines

       do you think such scratch-me-back
       gets by our eyes, the few of us there are
       who read?

nor is it life,
with a capital F

        the shocking play you publish
        with God as the Master of
        a Ship! In Gloucester-town
        you publish it, where men
        have cause to know where god is
        when wooden ships or steel ships,
        with sail or power,
        are out on men's business

        on waters which are tides, Ferrini,
        are not gods

        on waves (and waves
        are not the same as deep water)

        and themselves, and their vessel,
        in the hands of winds: winds, Ferrini,
        which are never 4, which have their grave dangers (as writing does)
        just because weather
        is very precise to
        the quarter it comes from (as writing is,
                        if it is as good as

9

It's no use.
There is no place we can meet.
You have left Gloucester.
You are not there, you are anywhere
where there are little magazines
will publish you

LETTER 6

polis is
eyes

          (Moulton cried up that day,
          "Where'd you get those glasses?"
          after, like a greenhorn,
          I'd picked three swordfish out of the sun-blaze
          where no regular could afford to look,
          to waste his eyes seeking a fin in that place

I have suffered since,
from that enthusiasm

          as my heart has never been so good
          as the day I'd be damned if that Englishman,
          and mountain-climber,
          would beat me
          up the Bright Angel trail
                              I'd been the cannier
          in the descent, had a chocolate bar we all ate
          as we cooled our feet in the Colorado
                                        It was coming up
          I spent myself, falling face-flat each step I managed,
          flopping in the fine dust which mules,
          wiser & wealthier persons rode,
          had ground the sandstone to)

It is just such folly is not necessary, yet I have not noticed
that those who are sharp haven't got that way
by pushing their limits
                    (above me,
          when Moulton hollered from the wheel,
          was Burke, humped over the masthead like the ball
          on top of a weather-pole, he squatting in the canvas strap,
          the rest of us standing in the whale-rope rigging, all of us
          like birds in a cote, and he the leader

as he well was, he was that good a professional, his eyes
as a gull's are, or any Portygee's,
and the long visor of his cap more of a beak
than even the same we all wore

It is of the matter that this Burke on land was a drunk (though, one Sunday,
I did see him on the wharf with his kids, showing them the vessel, he
in a blue suit, and the old stiff straw, the only time I did see him so,
like the oval portrait hangs
in so many living rooms
                              not at all the same grace of a man
came up on deck at sea in oilskins (as Olsen, two days out, would appear
in a new white shirt and new fedora, Hyperion
to the lump his men would have wheeled aboard,
at sailing time,
in a barrow)

It makes sense that these men

            Burke was raising his family
            in a shack out over the marsh;
            and Olsen, they now tell me,
            is carting fish, for Gorton-Pew,
            the lowest job, Gloucester,
            the job we all started with

            young Douglas, who never went to sea,
            he's different, is in the front office
            at Gorton-Pew, was so good a ball player
            he got moved up, and fast:

            he gave me cans of cooked mackerel,
            the last time I was home, "for the ride back"
            he said, and I couldn't tell him I hate
            picnics
                    ("pick-nicks", Pound roared
            when Con suggested we have fried chicken,
            and get him out of S'Liz for the afternoon,
            eat alongside the tennis courts
            out over the Anacostia

                              I was against it
               for another reason, because of the Navy planes
               roar in just there, and the chatter of the patients
               was more to my liking as background
               for the great man, in his black coat and wide hat, the whole man
               wagging, the swag
               of Pound

Eyes,
& polis,
fishermen,
& poets
              or in every human head I've known is
              busy
both:
the attention, and
the care
              however much each of us
              chooses our own
              kin and
              concentration

2

And the few—that goes, even inside the major
economics. It is not true that the many,
even in fishing, say, Gloucester,
are the gauge
              (where Ferrini, as so many,
              go wrong
so few
have the polis
in their eye
              The brilliant Portuguese owners,
              they do. They pour the money back
              into engines, into their ships,
              whole families do, put it back
              in. They are but extensions of their own careers
              as mastheadsmen—as Burkes

(the day we all stood around on the wharf examining the Laura Dysart,
the gash in her bow, and her foremast snapped off, where the Magellan
had piled into her. And Dysart himself telling about it, the thing still right
in front of him, how neither he nor Captain Rose would give way, both of
them coming up on the same fish. What struck me was, Dysart's admira-
tion, how the Magellan had overtaken him, from the speed of her Diesels,
and he saying he was sure Rose had sighted the fish as soon as he had, aft
of him though she was, those island eyes that very damned good, and he,
Dysart, and his ship, witness to it

So few need to,
to make the many
share (to have it,
too)

but those few . . .

          What kills me is, how do these others think
          the eyes are
          sharp? by gift? bah   by love of self? try it   by god? ask
          the bean sandwich

There are no hierarchies, no infinite, no such many as mass, there are only
eyes in all heads,
to be looked out of

LETTER 7

(Marsden Hartley's
eyes—as Stein's
eyes

       Or that carpenter's,
       who left Plymouth Plantation,
       and came to Gloucester,
       to build boats

       and who owned the land of "the Cut",
       until Gloucester, too, got too proper
       and he left, fended for himself
       (as Morton had, as there were several
       such as the Maverick Winthrop found,
       when Boston finally got to be
       the Massachusetts Bay
       settlement)

This carpenter
must have been the first to see the tansy
take root, the fishing stages then at Cressy's,
and the boats beaching
at Half Moon

(it was only later
the town moved up to Dogtown,
or at least the women were moved,
to be safe from the French,
and piracy—maybe even,
to be safe from Miles Standish

1

That carpenter is much on my mind:
I think he was the first Maximus

Anyhow, he was the first to make things,
not just live off nature

And he displays,
in the record, some of those traits
goes with that difference, traits present circumstances
keep my eye on

                    for example, necessities the practice of the self,
                    that matter, that wood

Commerce with you, any of you who have tried to bend,
any of you,
not just the old few who wore beards,
and culture – or the clean-shaven, the condottiere

                    (if I let any of that time in,
                    it is Verrocchio's cracked wood
                    of Lorenzo, with a head like a Minnesota back
                    or any worked schooner

                    "Why did you give him a black hat,
                     and a brim?" she queried,
                    "when he wore tennis shoes,
                     and held his pants up
                     with a rope?"

                              (as Al Gorman held his up, cadging fish
                              all those years, and kept a lock on the sugar bowl
                              so his sister . . . left $60,000 from the butts
                              he'd salted down, of begged mackerel,
                              pollock, halibut, cod
                              was thrown to him)

Or Mason Andrews, lived in a hogshead
over Concord Avenue, Harvard graduate
who used to scare people (I scared,
the first time) popping his basket
around the Bank corner of Duncan St: cat-nip,
shoelaces, oranges, gum
                              his great kind face
the Idiot, to Gorman's rodency, "the Wharf-Rat",
I heard his name was, when I first worked for Gorton-Pew

> How much the cracks matter, or seams in a ship, the absolutes
> of swelling (the mother), of weather (as even in machine parts,
> tolerance
>
> Only: no latitude, any more than any, elite. The exactness
> caulking, or "play", calls for, those
> millimeters
>
> No where in man is there room for carelessnesses
> Or those arrogations I gave him the costume of
>
> > (as he used to wear a turquoise
> > in one ear, London,
> > to let them know, here
> > was an American savage)

2

(As hands are put to the eyes' commands

> > There is this rock breaches
> > the earth: the Whale's Jaw
> > my father stood inside of
> >
> > I have a photograph, him
> > a smiling Jonah forcing back those teeth
> > Or more Jehovah, he looks that strong
> > he could have split the rock
> > as it is split, and not
> > as Marsden Hartley painted it
> > **so it's a canvas glove**

                    (such gloves
          as fish–handlers—as Olsen, say,
          or gardeners wear—or Ferrini ought to,
          handling trash:

          a man's hands,
          as his eyes,
          can get sores)

Hartley had so many courages,
and such defeats,
who used to stay too long at Dogtown,
getting that rock in paint,
he who was so afraid of night, and loons

But what he did with that bald jaw of stone,

          (my father differently usurped it,
          took it as he took nature, took himself
          until all bosses struck him down)

such cloth he turned all things to,
made palms of hands of gulls,
Maine monoliths apostles,
a meal of fish a final supper
—made Crane a Marseilles matelot

Such transubstantiations

          as I am not permitted,
          nor my father,
          who'd never have turned the Whale Jaw back
          to such humanness neither he nor I, as workers,
          are infatuated with

                    (as you are not either permitted, Ferrini,
                    friend I was too kind to,
                    in other letters)

What Hartley did was done according to his lights

                              (lungs, Ferrini, lungs:
                              you need no other friends than us,
                              you need not waste evenings, beers,
                              seeking too ready ears

The men of the matter of this city
(who was it did carve the Lady?)
are never
doctrinaires

3

(I only knew one such other pair of hands as Hartley's. Jake, his name
was, mate aboard the Lafond's gill-netters.
                              When I knew him his nails
were all gone, peeled away from the brine they'd been in all the days of
his life.

              Hartley's fingers gave this sense of soaking, the ends as stubbed
as Jake's, and each finger so thick and independent of the other, his own
hands were like gloves.
                              But not cloth. They stayed such salt rock as Jake's
were—or as marshmallow is, if the trope will stand, as Hartley's hands
did stand, they were so much (each finger) their own lives' acts

as Jake's did,
from baiting hooks for sixty years,
as Hartley's,
refusing woman's flesh

Tyrian Businesses

1

The waist of a lion,
for a man to move properly

And for a woman,
who should move lazily,
the weight of breasts

This is the exercise for this morning

2

how to dance
sitting down

3

or the one so far back she craves to be scalped,
and dragged over the ground
                              And because nobody has dragged her,
she has everybody do it. She does it. She wants clean sheets,
each night
                as that other, that international doll,
has to have silk, when she is put up
                                        (why is she put up with?)
in the white house

4

Or there are those sing ditties, that dead reason
of personality, the will of, like a seal
of a mealy justice: the body a shell, the mind also
an apparatus
                There are so many, children,
who want to go back, who want to lie down
in Tiamat. They sing:
euphoria

5

You can tell them this: the land-spout's
put all the diapers
up in trees (what musicians call
the middle voice, to command it
is to be in business.
                    There may be no more names than there are objects
                    There can be no more verbs than there are actions

It is still
morning

                              II

a hollow muscular organ which, by contracting vigorously, keeps up the

              (to have the heart

                        (a whorl of green bracts at the base

                                                        (ling,
she is known as

                  Weather
comes generally
                  under the
                        metaphrast.

                              (When M is above G, all's
                              well. When below, there's
                              upset. When M and G are coincident,
                              it is not very interesting)

1

                  (peltate
is my nose-twist, my beloved, my
trophy
              tropical American diffuse and climbing pungent
              with lobed or dissected
              And showy, e.g. so variously colored, a garden species, the

2

totipalmate
is the toc   And so vain
it plucks its tail to free the handsome green eye from
redundant feathers Which, then, it switches
to admire itself, as any Egyptian lady
must have looked fixing herself
by polished stone
                              (The farmer whose nephew we knew
was so exasperated
he used to heave anything at the bird, swearing
if his face got reflected in that burnished tail
he'd die,
right then & there

3

The seedling
of morning: to move, the problems (after the night's presences) the first hours of

          He had noticed,
          the cotton picks easiest

                              As my flower,
                              after rain, wears
                              such diadem

                                        As a man is a necklace
                                        strung of his own teeth (the caries
                                        of 'em

He sd: Notice
the whiteness, not
the odor of
the dead night

4

(the honey in the lion, the honey
in woman

5

"felicity
resulting from life of activity in accordance with"

Which is the question: in accordance with what?

Ukase: "the vertical
            through the center of buoyancy of a
floating body
            intersects
the vertical through the new
center made . . .

when the wind,

or the nature of the cargo

or a rip

        (so much it was the rain and the wind when we were running
to eastward before it. I had stood the third watch, and when I came below
they say I was that pale. For cause: the lightning had stepped along the
sea straight at us, so that I at the wheel could calculate whether the next
one would hit us fore, or aft, or strike us amidships.

        For three days the glass had read 29.2, and we had, you might
say, eat our cigarettes, there seemed no reason to think the "Hawes"
would weather that one, she being so small, and her screws no damned
good anyway. Moulton had been that greedy, he wanted to pick up all
the lumber we see floating ahead of us on the sea, had broke off the deck
of some schooner had lost her lashings. For the garage he was building,
Rockport.

It was crazy, coming up on those dead sticks cross-wise in the seas, not at all like coming up on those fish would scare the moment the iron, or the shadow of it, came at them. Or, once hit, how they'd run for it. And any of us, out over into a dory to battle them, for how many hours, alone, on the sea.

This, was no game at all, though none of us thought of the danger, even the skipper himself. He just wanted this windfall, and he ordered the striker out on the pulpit and the rest of us along the starboard side, the usual side to take up the slack of the line when the sword was making his first run away with it.

We gaffed a half a dozen of those planks, and it was party stuff —even the cook had gone below, he was so bored, was in the galley when it happened, told us afterward how it sounded, there. What happened was, Moulton fetched the vessel straight on one plank plunk in its middle, and it stayed there, right in its center, even when it swayed below water: you could hear it passing the length of the keel, bumping, bumping, but never losing, from the forward speed of the vessel, the center of her Moulton had hit her by.

Then there was the noise—and the ship suddenly acting as no ship ever did, as the blades of the screw bit into that wood, and as that wood chewed them up!

We watched the mess of it astern going off in the wake as the vessel fell off so she felt like dead in the water.

It was a caution, the rest of that trip was—63 fish, and most of them babies. And a lot of the big ones spoiled, we had to stay out so long to try to make up for our losses, not just to the fast Portygees, but to any schooner of the swordfishing fleet that July. Even the Little David, out of Edgartown, could get there ahead of us.

We were five weeks, from Moulton's folly—and that storm drove us four days before it, trying to get out of its path. The whole fleet scattered, but we had the worst of it, from no power. The last week, we had to have cod to eat, from Olsen's Raymonde, he roaring, in that voice of his, "Come aboard, Cece—come aboard, and get some cod!", it sounding, over the water, like the barrel of god.

I rowed the skipper over.

6

Definition: (in this instance,
and in what others, what
felicities?

       "The crooked timbers
scarfed together to form the lower part of the compound rib are

futtocks,
we call 'em

       But a fylfot,
she look like,
       who calls herself

           (luck

LETTER 9

> "I had to clobber him.
>
> Hold his hand (though I can't see he deserves
> forgiveness. There are these necessities
> are bigger than we are.
>   Only hate it,
> that he had to go and get himself caught
> in the wringer."

1

the flowering plum
out the front door window
sends whiteness
inside my house

> as the news that the almond
> was in bloom Mallorca
> accompanied the news
> that that book was in print
> which I wish might stop
> the workings of my city
> where so much of it
> was bred

                                        (as, in another spring,
                                        I learned
                                        the world does not stop
                                        for flowers

2

it puts a man back
to find out how much
he is busy, this way,
not as his fellows are
but as flowering trees
turn several greens
(as many greens as there are greys
of their several trunks

                    it was the reds of buds
                    sent me this spring,
                    lighting up the valleys

                                        as now the fruits do,
                                        and these pages have come in,
                                        of a white so right
                                        the print is brown

                                                    I, dazzled

as one is, until one discovers
there is no other issue than
the moment of
                    the pleasure of
                                this plum,

these things
which don't carry their end any further than
their reality in
themselves

3

It's the condition in men
(we know what spring is)
brings such self-things about
which interests me
as I loll today
where I used to,
atop Bond's Hill

        with both the inner, and the outer, harbor,
        the Atlantic, back of the back-shore,
        the Annisquam and her marshes, Ipswich Bay
        all out before me in one view

And all such colors as spring is, plus
the colors men's buildings are, the differences
his whitenesses are,
the tidinesses
he uses greens for, the bricks
he lights his city up with

As of myself
I'd pose it,
today,
as Alfred at Ashdown, a wild boar
        (*aprino more*, Asser says)
versus
my own wrists and all my joints, versus speech's connectives, versus the tasks
I obey to,
not to a nation's,
or at all to history,
or to building

      Flowers, like I say.

           And I feel that way,
           that the likeness is to nature's,
           not to these tempestuous
           events,

that those self-acts which have no end no more than their own
are more as plums are
than they are as Alfreds
who so advance
men's affairs

        (who threw Guthrum back
        even when he held Glow-ceastre

        and he himself was holed up
        in the Athelney swamp)

4

I measure my song,
measure the sources of my song,
measure me, measure
my forces

        (And I buzz,
        as the bee does,
        who's missed
        the plum tree,
        and gone and got himself caught
        in my window

        And the whirring of whose wings
        blots out the rattle of
        my machine)

LETTER 10

on John White / on cod, ling, and poor-john

on founding: was it puritanism,
or was it fish?

And how, now, to found, with the sacred & the profane—both of them—
wore out

      The beak's
there. And the pectoral.
The fins,
for forwarding.

      But to do it anew, now that even fishing . . .

1

It was fishing was first. Only after (Naumkeag) was it the other thing, and Conant
would have nothing to do with it, went over to Beverly, to Bass River, to keep clear
(as a later Conant I know has done the opposite, has not
kept clear)

It is a sign, that first house, Roger Conant's, there, Stage Fort. One of Endecott's first acts
was to have it dragged to Salem for his own mansion, for the big house,
the frame of it was that sound, that handsome, the old carpentry

      (not the house-making I feel closest to, what followed, so close
      I'd sing, today, of Anne Bradstreet's,
      or any of them, Georgetown, Rowley, Ipswich,
      how private they are in their clapboards
      and yet how they thrust, sit there
      as strong as any building)

                          Conant's
was Tudor

               Gloucester, your first house was as Elizabeth's
England

(and that that Endecott, the "New", should have used it
inside of which to smile, and bless that covenant Higginson and the others...

It sat
where my own house has been (where I am
founded

by racks so poor of fish there was not take enough to pay the Adventurers back. Three years,
and their 3000 £ gone. And as much more again (where I have picked coins up,
after circuses, slid out of men's trousers they so twisted in the bleacher seats
from the tricks Clyde Beatty made lions do,
keeping them under his eye and under his whip

3

Elizabeth dead,
and Tudor went to James
(as quick as Conant's house
was snatched to Salem

As you did not go,
Gloucester: you tipped, you were our
scales

        (as I have been witness,
        in my time,
        to all slide
        national, international,
        even learning slide

        by the acts of another Conant than he who left his Tudor house, left fishing,
and lost everything to Endecott, lost the colony
to the first of,
the shrinkers

4

Now all things
are true by inverse:
religion
shrank Elizabeth's, money
dilates ours. Harvard
owns too much

      and so its President
      after destroying its localism ("meatballs",
      they called the city fellers, the public school
      graduates) Conant destroyed Harvard
      by asking Oregon
      to send its brightest

Roger Conant did not destroy, was, in fact, himself destroyed, as was the city, 1626

      and is paid off by those he served (State St., Washington), is made High Commissioner
      (Endecott, of a stooge State

my Conant
only removed to "Beggarly",
as the smug of Salem—the victors!—
called that place still is, for me
(when I go down 1 A or take the train
the opening out
of my countree

Maximus, to Gloucester, Letter 11

The rock reads

        the rock I know by my belly and torn nails, the letters on it
        big enough I sat in triumph arriving,
        by a head start,
        run up the face, grab the stone emboss
        anchor rope
        carved from it) get onto
        the bronze plaque:

                        "In the Early History of,
A Notable Exemplification of
Arbitration"

        And the Short Chimney
wld have died right there, been plugged by a fisherman if
Conant had not ordered Capt Hewes to lower his gun, to listen
to what the little man from Plymouth had to squawk about

Mister Standish
wld have been the first to lie in the cemetery where my father does,

        at least where I say he does,
        where I wanted him to, either that
        or load him in a dory, row him
        beyond the Breakwater, and set fire to it, let him go, so,
        to sea

That a man's life
(his, anyway)
is what there is
that tradition is

at least is where I find it,
how I got to
what I say

1

"Tragabigzanda"
was what I heard,
right off the top of it. And we dropped,
trained Indians that we were, came up on the bush
we knew better than even the couples
we'd also sometimes be surprised by, parted it
as surely as we'd get each other
with wooden guns

and by god if there wasn't John Smith
all got up in ruff and armor, repeating
shouting:
"TragabigZAND-ah" (more Capt Shrimpe
from the loudness of him, quondam Drummer,
than the Admiral of New England Smith proudly
took himself to be, rightly, who sounded
her bays, ran her coast, and wrote down
Algonquin so scrupulously Massachusetts
And I know who lived where I lived
before the small-pox took them all away
and the Pilgrims
had such an easy time of it
to land

What further wowed us was
he had a swooning Turkish Princess
in his arms:
                    Historie

come bang into the midst of

our game! Actors,

where I have learned another sort of

play

2

Smith also got shoved aside. By 1622

(Stage Fort occupied 1623 and above squabble "fit"
end of same year, Plymouth irked
fishermen had come) Smith was writing such things as:

"for all their discoveries I can yet heare of,
are but pigs of my owne sowe"

"pardon me though it passionate me beyond the bounds of modestie,
to have been sufficiently able to foresee . . .

"they (the settlers) have been my wife, my hawks, my hounds,
my cards, my dice, in totall my best content"

       Or, to make altogether evident his femininities, this,
from his *Sea-Grammar*, 1626:

       "For when a man is ill sicke,
or at the point of death, I would know
whether a dish of buttered Rice,
with a little Cinnamon and Sugar,
a can of fresh water brewed of these,
a little minced meate, or roast Beefe,
a few stewed Prunes, a race of greene-ginger,
a flap Jacke,

be not better than a little poore John,
or salt fish
with oil and mustard,
or brisket, butter cheese or oatmeale pottage
on fish days,
salt beefe, porke and pease,
sixe shillings beare.
                This
is your ordinary ships allowance."

    3

      The Capteyne
he was, the eye he had
for what New England offered,
what we are other than
theocratic, why we are
not at all what the Mediterraneans
think we are, how we are
oxyacetylene, we come in that close

when we do come in.

"The quarter Maisters", he declares,

"hath charge of the hold
for stowage,
rummageing, and trimming
the ship;
and of their squadrons
for the Watch. A Sayne,
a Fisgigg, a Harping Iron,
Fish-hookes for Pogos,
Bonatos or Dorados Etc
And rayling lines
for Mackerell"

Maximus, to himself

I have had to learn the simplest things
last. Which made for difficulties.
Even at sea I was slow, to get the hand out, or to cross
a wet deck.
            The sea was not, finally, my trade.
But even my trade, at it, I stood estranged
from that which was most familiar. Was delayed,
and not content with the man's argument
that such postponement
is now the nature of
obedience,
            that we are all late
            in a slow time,
            that we grow up many
            And the single
            is not easily
            known

It could be, though the sharpness (the *achiote*)
I note in others,
makes more sense
than my own distances. The agilities

            they show daily
            who do the world's
            businesses
            And who do nature's
            as I have no sense
            I have done either

I have made dialogues,
have discussed ancient texts,
have thrown what light I could, offered
what pleasures
doceat allows

            But the known?
This, I have had to be given,
a life, love, and from one man
the world.

Tokens.
But sitting here
I look out as a wind
and water man, testing
And missing
some proof

I know the quarters
of the weather, where it comes from,
where it goes. But the stem of me,
this I took from their welcome,
or their rejection, of me

           And my arrogance
           was neither diminished
           nor increased,
           by the communication

2

It is undone business
I speak of, this morning,
with the sea
stretching out
from my feet

The Song and Dance of

I

In the present go
nor right nor left;
       nor stay
in the middle, where they'll get you, the "Germans"
will, if you use it for social purposes, the wild
clementine, the coarse hair in the middle, and the rest of the bundle
half a peyote bean

      Altschuler
taught us how to fight Indians, but Barbour,
Ralph Henry, that is, warned us
what sports are, how they breed only
blondes.
And tin horns.

I mean merchandise men,
who get to be President
after winning, age 12,
cereal ad
prizes

      As wars stooge
      for the left,
      all that appetite for thick-necks,
      and refrigerators,
      for An-yan
      steel

And for flowers, always
it's flowers, presented
by little girls
to killers (the killers not smiling
as the photographer does

      as it used to be only
      dead gangsters
      who were buried
      in banks of

1   The upshot is
(and this the books did not tell us) the race
does not advance, it is only
better preserved

            Now all lie
            as Miss Harlow

            as Sunday supplement mammoths
            in ice, as there used to be
            waxworks

            as ugly as Jericho's
            First Citizens, kept there

            as skulls, the pink semblance

            painted back on, as though they were once,
            and they were, Leaders
            of the people

            with shells for eyes

            As she lies, all
            white

II

"Always the land
was of the same beauty,
and the fields
very green"

        The Isles
of the Very Green. Meneptha,
then. The previous Caribbean,
when the sea first
awoke to men's minds. Cyprus.
Or which True Verte?

"Of an infinity of fruits,
as red as scarlet. And everywhere
the perfume
of flowers"

       The Lotus
it was, Cyrenaica, by his time
who projected this other
who says
these things:

"And the singing of birds,
very sweet", he also calling attention
to the breath of pigeons,
that they smelt sweeter
than orange blossoms,
because their crops
were so full

Hear him! the Mediterranean
man

       As another such had it,
       a writer, love was

       Or ought to be,
       like an orange tree!

       (The way they do grow
       in that ex-sea soil,
       in that pumice dust only a fowl
       can scratch a living from.

              Yet when they do come out
              they are sweet

              not at all like what the refrigerator trains
              debouch into our cities, those pictures of

              they taste sweet sweet sweet

As the sun is

(it gave warmth,
he sd, to him
as well as to
others

      And the nerve ends
      stay open on this horst
      of the heat Equator
      as surely as it is evident they did
      —an American sd they did,
      the last one to celebrate
      the old axis—there,

where all the previous celebrating

comes from

      1

Northward,

no pearls as necklaces on the necks of, no value

to be trod on, no slaves

Only the meretricious

And ice, volcanoes, Judas

on his one day holiday

from hell

      Venus

does not arise from

these waters. Fish

do.

> And from these streams,

fur.

> It was the hat-makers of La Rochelle, the fish-eaters of Bristol
> who were the conquistadors of my country, the dreamless
> present

Maximus, to Gloucester

LETTER 14

        on John Hawkins / on the puzzle
        of the nature of desire / the consequences

        in the known world beyond
        the terra incognita / on how men do use

        their lives

    I

"to unite in one lustre,
as stars" it says

And as it might,
"dreams" (?)

        the lard pail of ice cream
        an explosive, the fuse
        an electric plug

        and the silliness of it,
        finally, leaving it there,
        as I did, it sitting there
        in the middle of the afternoon
        in the middle of the street

        (after she had backed a station-wagon
        underneath a porch

The sense of vulgarity as separating me

        after the passage-way of the toilets
        and the whores

           (as that movie-house,
      Boston, you buy your ticket

but you don't enter, you find yrself
in an alley-way

        the whole city
starlight, not even ceiling
as they used to have, glowing
as of stars, by god, pricked out
so that, in the bad grotto of the bad scripts,
you had the firmament
over your head

The fundament
still your own

        2

"to tend to move
as though drawn",
it also says

Or might it read
"compare
the ripe sun-flower"?

        The old charts
        are not so wrong
        which added Adam
        to the world's directions

        which showed any of us
        the center of a circle
        our fingers
        and our toes describe

        (one taught us
        how to stand in crowds
        there we were, three actors,
        in a loft above Tarr's Railway
        in shorts, in front of her,
        doing,

her bidding: "Buttocks
in & under, buttocks"

seeking,
like Euclid,
the ape's line, the stance
fit for crowds, to watch
parades, never
to tire

It was in our minds
what she put there,
to get the posture,
to pass from the neck of,
to get it down,
to get the knees bent

not as he was shown, arms out, legs out, leaping

another Adam, a nether
man

It does stem. And the joker
that the sense is
of a sash-weight,
after the head is clear,
after the burst

a sash-weight does hang
from between the legs

if you are drawn,

if you do unite,

if you do be

pithecanthropus

II

Because of the agora America is, was, from the start, the moral struggle

        it was two things, first: the Banks
        which the Basques, maybe,
        first found, though Pytheus
        had he sounded the sludge
        he took the water and the air and the sky
        all to be one of

                Ultima Thule

        2nd, it was treasure: one fifth
        to the Crown, of all
        And jewels & pearls

Fish stayed
(as so little else)
stay to this day
production, the labor of

But Negroes,
it turned out,
were pearls

            what could be sold
            West, what the Islands
            themselves wanted,

                    And John Hawkins.

            His father
            was old fashion, made friends
            among the natives, Sierra Leone,
            or Brazil

            And had such honor
            in the new places
            he could carry an Indian

back to London, a present
for Henry, and though the fellow die
on the voyage, the people
believe old William's story,
release the hostage to him.
And stock his ship with goods.

He bought ivory
from the negroes.
He used
their labor.
He paid goods
for goods,
he did not grab them,
as his son did, trading
on his father's welcome

It was the son
was knighted, the father
I restore. It was the son
"for a crest:
"a demi-Moor,
   proper,
   in chains". This
was the man broke open
the Spanish main

                    this,
for England,
and for America,

for some of those who built
white houses

            "On board, San Juan de Lua, 57

Negroes, *optimi generis*, each valued at 160£, or a total of 9,120 £

("Schedule of Property Lost, *State Papers*, Dom. Elizabeth, liii")

2

His son in his turn (the family
span America from the finding
to the settling of those fishermen,
Dorchester Company, Cape Ann)

"the name of Hawkyns,
in its French form Haquin,
or in Spanish Achines,
became a sound of terror
in the narrow seas"

Sir Richard is already
what we have been, why it is only
in the harmonic of facts

(the one we all, somehow, get ourselves into ducking)

he gave his intent as:

"to make perfect discovery of all those parts

where we should arrive, known as well as unknown, their longitudes

and latitudes, the lying of their coasts, their head-lands (Cape

Ann, your head-land), their ports and bays (Gloucester!), their cities

(o America), towns and peoplings (o you Americans), their manner

of government (ha!), with the commodities which the countries yield

(your goods, citizen, your polis), and of which they want and are

in necessity" (in necessity, fellow cits? what is your necessity?)

And though his vessel's first name
was "The Repentance"—(o! repent!)—
Elizabeth, mind you,

thought the form of her so graceful
(I do)
she ordered her renamed "The Dainty"

O, rename her

And in the bay of San Mateo,
after three days' fight
with 14 shot under water,
seven to eight feet in the hold,
the pumps smashed, many killed,
more wounded, the rest mad drunk

He was thereafter
five years a prisoner
in Spain's dungeons

                    III

With the gums gone, the teeth

are large. And though the nose is then nothing,

the eye-sockets

And now the shadow

of the radiator on the floor

is wolf-tits, the even row of it

fit to raise

feral children.

        You will count them all in,

        you will stay in the midst of them,

you will know no law, you will hear them

in the narrow seas.

Maximus, to Gloucester

LETTER 15

It goes to show you. It was not the "Eppie Sawyer". It was the ship "Putnam". It wasn't Christmas morning, it was Christmas night, after dark. And the violent north-easter, with snow, which we were all raised to believe did show Bowditch such a navigator, was a gale sprung up from W, hit them outside the Bay, and had blown itself out by the 23rd.

On the 25th it was fog Bowditch had to contend with. The wind was NE allright, but there is no mention of snow. At 4 PM it cleared a little and he was able to see Eastern Point. And at 7 he came to anchor in Salem. In other words it was the beacon at Gloucester, not the light on Baker's Island—there was no light on Eastern Point until 1831—which got him home.

The whole tale, as we have had it, from his son, goes by the board. The son seems to have got it thirty-five years after the event from a sailor who was with the father on that voyage (to Sumatra, and Ile de France, cargo: shoes). This sailor apparently (he was twenty years older than the captain) was the one who said, that night they did get in, "Our old man goes ahead as if it was noonday". He must have been 85 when he added the rest of the tale—how the owners were very much alarmed at Bowditch's sudden appearance "on such a tempestuous night", and how, at first, they could hardly be persuaded he had not been wrecked.

1

He sd, "You go all around the subject." And I sd, "I didn't know it was a subject." He sd, "You twist" and I sd, "I do." He said other things. And I didn't say anything.

Nor do I know

that this is a rail

on which all (or any)

will ride (as, by Pullman

     that sense the ads are right abt, that you are

     taken care of, you do

     not sleep, you are

     jolted

     And if you take a compartment,

     the whole damned family . . .

I sd, "Rhapsodia . . .

II

John Smith's latest book was,
"ADVERTISEMENTS
for the unexperienced Planters
of New-England,

> or anywhere" (dedicated
> to the Archbishops of Canterbury,
> and York, primates,
> it says,
> of England (1630)

The epigraph
is a poem
by sd Smith (refused
as navigator by
the Pilgrims, Standish
chosen instead)

THE SEA MARKE

It reads (Smith died,

that year):

> "Aloofe, aloofe; and come no neare,
>> the dangers doe appeare;
> Which if my ruine had not beene
>> you had not seene:
> I onely lie upon this shelfe
>> to be a marke to all
>> which on the same might fall,
> That none may perish but my selfe.

"If in or outward you be bound,
                do not forget to sound;
Neglect of that was cause of this
                to steere amisse:
The Seas were calme, the wind was faire,
                that made me so secure,
                that now I must indure
All weathers be they foule or faire

                "The Winters cold, the Summers heat
                alternatively beat
Upon my bruised sides, that rue
                because too true
That no releefe can ever come.
                But why should I despaire
                being promised so faire
That there shall be a day of Dome"

III

And for the water-shed, the economics & poetics thereafter?

Three men,

coincide:

        you will find Villon
in Fra Diavolo,
Elberthubbardsville,
N.Y.

        And the prose
is Raymond's, Boston, or

Brer Fox,
Rapallo,
Quattrocento-by-the-Beach, ♯
429

　　　　The American epos, 19–

02 (or when did Barton Barton Barton Barton and Barton?

　　　　To celebrate

　　　　how it can be, it is

　　　　padded or uncomforted, your lost, you

　　　　found, your

　　　　sneakers

　　　　(o Statue,

o Republic, o

Tell–A–Vision, the best

is soap. The true troubadours

are CBS. Melopoeia

　　　　　　　　is for Cokes by Cokes out of

　　　　　　　　Pause

　　　　IV

(o Po–ets, you

should getta

job

LETTER 16

        "not to crowd you. But what do we have
but our wares?

And who to market them to, things being
how they are, but our friends?

It has come to barter, it's got so
primitive—like New England was,
at its start:

        it amused me last night
to learn that Malthus based his notions
on the statistics of abundant births
in the Mass. Bay (Trading) Colony

1

Bowditch (later) ran Harvard,
made enemies by helping to oust Kirkland.
But, it is argued, saved the college
financially (as he also founded insurance companies,
from his knack for figures,
and his years of trading for Mass. merchants
as supercargo on Salem voyages

He represents, then, that movement of NE monies
away from primary production & trade
to the several cankers of profit-making
which have, like Agyasta, made America great.

Meantime, of course, swallowing up
the land and labor. And now,
the world.

It is said, for example, that it is he himself
               (about to start on his fourth voyage,
           he wrote to his future wife,
                fr Boston, 22 July 1799
           "It was with the greatest difficulty

we obtained our complement of men,
& a curious set of them it is:
Tinkers, Tailors, Barbers, Country
schoolmasters, one old Greenwhich
Pensioner, a few negroes, mulattoes
Spaniards &c &c &c but they will do
well enough when properly disciplined"

who was the first "trustee" of others' monies
who treated them as separate from his own accounts.
In other words, he marks that most neglected of all
economic law: how the coming into existence of benevolence
(the 19th century, left and right)
is the worst, leads to the worst, breeds
what we have:

                    that the good drives the goods
after the worst,

what we have a word for
(what he called it, howling,
over another's pay-
cock:

pejorocracy (what you have, my town, what all towns

now have: pee-jaw-rock-

Cressy!

        The thugs,
                    the hypocrites,
        are always more to deal with than

        the Good, the always damn
        Safe

(what they've turned even the 4th of July into, the

        Ones who made this Country

just what it sounds like

just what it sounds like:

Stephen Higginson (1743—

desc. of Francis Higginson

was in Eng 1774, & was examined by a
comm. of House of Commons on the subject
of American fisheries & some other colonial
matters:
    cf. Force's American Archives,
    Fourth Series, I, 1645-1648—*get*

In Cong., was found frequently acting with
Hamilton—& very hostile to Robt Morris

Was chief instrument in suppressing Shay's
Rebellion
Enemy of Hancock

"The high Federalist of the 'Essex Junto'
who sold arms to Va. for a State arsenal
against Fed. encroachment, & if that
doesn't work, suggested their sale to
Toussaint l'Overture, with connivance
of govt., while H is assuring the Sect
of State that he is not doing any
such thing
    Letters 48 on

in Letter 49, to Timothy Pickering, Sect
of War in Adams' cabinet, it turns out
the arms are from Prussia, (1799),
4000 of 'em. And Virginia finds
them worthless

"it will indeed pass off without
notice if well executed. But to attempt
to smuggle the Articles and be detected
would occasion much noise and discussion"

(Toussaint, at this time, was waging
a fierce war in Santo Domingo against
the French General André Rigaud

2

As an example of how wrong you can be and still

run this country,

same Higginson

to Adams, when Adams Vice-President
March 24, 1790

"Those who built Vessels soon after the Peace,
whether for the fishery, or foreign Trade, have suffered more by the reduc-
tion in their value than their earnings will pay; and in the old Towns, the
unusual profits from the fishery the first years after the peace, were consu-
med in expences which They were formerly strangers to. But those who live
upon Cape Cod, and along the south shore, who retained their old habits
of industry and frugality, applied their gains to increase their Business

. . . even in the last year, the cod fishery on the
south Shore was a living business; but in the Old Towns, They took less
fish, expended much more, and had little left to support their families. There
is a strong possibility that this business will, from the causes mentioned, be
in a good degree transferred from the north to the south Shore. This may
be, in a national View, of no great importance; but the Towns of M Head
and Gloucester &c may be much distressed, before they recover those habits
which alone can make them to be flourishing and happy"

the son of a bitch

3

Letter # 27, to Pickering, Aug 16, 1795:

". . . Salem, Newburyport
approve . . .

"At M'Head and Cape Ann
they are all quiet and think
very well of . . .

At Portsmouth "all the best men . . .

No noise.

And no discussion.

On first Looking out through Juan de la Cosa's Eyes

Behaim—and nothing
insula Azores to
Cipangu (Candyn
somewhere also there where spices

and yes, in the Atlantic,
one floating island: de
Sant
        brand
                an

1

St Malo, however.
Or Biscay. Or Bristol.
Fishermen, had,
for how long,
talked:
        Heavy sea,
snow, hail. At 8
AM a tide rip. Sounded.
Had 20 fath. decreased from that to
15, 10. Wore ship.

        (They knew
Cap Raz

(As men, my town, my two towns
talk, talked of Gades, talk
of Cash's

drew, on a table, in spelt,
with a finger, in beer, a
portulans

                But before La Cosa, nobody
                could have
                a mappemunde

2

(What he drew who drew Hercules
going by the Bear off from Calypso

Now, it would be breakers, Sable!
ahead, where, just off,
you could put buckets down

                    (You could go any coast
                    in such a raft as she taught,
                    as she taught him, favoring him

with cedar, & much niceties. It was only because the gods willed
that he could leave her, go away, determined though he had been the whole time
not to eat her food, not to wear gods' clothes,
to stick to what men eat

And wore

                    The Atlantic,
                    just then,
                    was to take kings,
                    & fishermen

                    And Europe,
                    was being drained
                    of gold

II

but cod? The New Land was,
from the start, even by name was
Bacalhaos
            there,
swimming, Norte, out of the mists

                    (out of Pytheus' sludge

out of mermaids & Monsters

                    (out of Judas-land

Tierra,
de bacalaos, out of

waters   Massachusetts,
                         my Newfoundlanders
                         My Portuguese: you

(Or Verrazano has it,
curiously, put down as
a Mud Bank

                         "Sounding
                         on George's
                         25 fath. sand. At the same time spoke
                         the Brig Albion, Packet,
                         John Dogget who told us
                         Cape Ann was 80 leag.
                         dis.

Terra nova sive Limo Lue,
he wrote it who knew it
as only Corte Real   (the first known lost
as Bertomez (as Cabot?

                         Who found you,

                         land,

                         of the hard gale?

1

Respecting the earth, he sd,
it is a pear, or,
like a round ball upon a part of which there is a prominence
like a woman's nipple, this protrusion
is the highest & nearest to
the sky

        Ships
have always represented a large capital investment, and the manning,
the provisioning of same

                    It was the teredo-worm
                    was 1492: riddle a ship's hull
                    in one voyage ("pierced
with worm-holes
like a bee-hive,
the report was

                    Ladies & Gentlemen,
                    he lost his pearl,
                    he lost the Indies
                    to a worm

2

North? Mud. 1480 John Lloyd, the most expert shipmaster of all England,
on behalf of John Jay and other merchants Bristol
set out to
the island of Brasylle, to
traverse the seas

Nine weeks. And storms
threw him back.
                    No worms. Storms,
                    Ladies &

                    to the bottom of the,

                    husbands, & wives,

                    little children lost their

(4,670 fishermen's lives are noticed. In an outgoing tide
of the Annisquam River, each summer, at the August full,
they throw flowers, which, from the current there, at the Cut,
reach the harbor channel, and go

these bouquets (there are few, Gloucester, who can afford florists' prices)
float out
                    you can watch them go out into,
the Atlantic

III

On ne doit aux morts nothing

    else than

la vérité

The Twist

Trolley-cars
are my inland waters
(Tatnuck Sq, and the walk
from the end of the line
to Paxton, for May-flowers

or by the old road to Holden,
after English walnuts

And my wife has a new baby
in a house at the end of
such a line, and the morning after,
is ready to come home, the baby too,
exceptionally well & advanced

Or he and I distinguish
between chanting,
and letting the song lie
in the thing itself.
I plant flowers
(xenia) for him,
in the wet soil, indoors,
in his house

As I had it in my first poem,
the Annisquam
fills itself, at its tides, as she did
the French dress, cut
on the bias,

        my neap,
my spring-tide, my
waters

1

Between Newton and Tatnuck Square the tracks
go up hill, the cars
sway, as they go around the bend
before they take, before they go down to
the outer-land
(where it is Sunday,
    I am small, people go off
    what strikes me as questionable
    directions. They are large,
    going away from my father and me,
    as cows on that landscape

    he and I seeming
    the only ones who know
    what we are doing, where
    we are going

Now I find out it is the Severn
goes from Worcester to Gloucester to
: Bristow, Smith called it,
what sticks in me as the promised land
those couples did go to, at right angles
from us, what does show
between Gloucester and Boston, the landscape
I go up-dilly, elevated, tenement
down

2

It rained,
the day we arrived.
And I have rowed the harbor since,
out the window of Johnny's Candy Kitchen,
through that glass and rain through which I looked
the first time I saw
the sea.

        She was staying,
after she left me,

in an apartment house
was like cake

           When I found her
—the people in it like Macomber
who lived under me on Charles St—next door
a man in a bowler hat scutted away,
the same man had fired a bullet
into her ho-ho

           Or it was Schwartz,
the bookie, whose mother-in-law
I'd have gladly gone to bed with

       Her room (the house
was a *dobostorte*), the door
high up on the wall,
♯ 48,
small,
like an oven-door

The harbor the same,
the night of the St Valentine
storm: the air
sea   ground   the same, tossed
ice   wind   snow   (Pytheus) one

            cakes falling
as quiet as I was
out of the sky as quiet
as the blizzard was

3

When I woke
in the toy house I had headed for, the look
out my window
sent me, the whiteness
in the morning sun, the figures

shoveling

                I went home
as fast as I could,

the whole Cut
was a paper village my Aunt Vandla
had given me, who gave me,
each Christmas,
such toys

As dreams are, when the day
encompasses. They tear down
the Third Ave El. Mine stays,
as Boston does, inches up.
I run my trains
on a monorail, I am seized
—not so many nights ago—
by the sight of the river
exactly there at the Bridge

where it goes out & in

I recognize
the country not discovera,
the marsh behind, the ditch that Blynman made, the dog-rocks
the tide roars over

                some curves off,
when it's the river's turn, shoots
calyx and corolla by the dog
                                        (August,
the flowers break off

                but the anther,
the filament of now, the mass
drives on,

                the whole of it
coming,
to this pin-point
to turn

                in this day's sun,

in this veracity

there, the waters of several of them the roads

here, a blackberry blossom

Maximus, to Gloucester, Letter 19 (A Pastoral
Letter

relating
to the care of souls,
it says)

      He had smiled at us,
      each time we were in town, inquired
      how the baby was, had two cents
      for the weather, wore
      (besides his automobile)
      good clothes.
                   And a pink face.

      It was yesterday
      it all came out. The gambit
      (as he crossed the street,
      after us): "I don't believe
      I know your name." Given.
      How do you do,
      how do you do. And then:
      "Pardon me, but
      what church
      do you belong to,
      may I ask?"

And the whole street, the town, the cities, the nation
blinked, in the afternoon sun, at the gun
was held at them. And I wavered
in the thought.

      I sd, you may, sir.
      He sd, what, sir.
      I sd, none,
      sir.

And the light was back.

For I am no merchant.
Nor so young I need to take a stance
to a loaded
smile.

I have known the face
of God.
And turned away,
turned,
as He did,
his backside

2

And now it is noon
of a cloudy sunday.
And a bird sings
loudly

And my daughter, naked
on the porch, sings
as best she can, and loudly,
back

She wears her own face
as we do not,
until we cease to wear
the clouds
of all confusion,

of all confusers
who wear the false face
He never wore, Whose
is terrible. Is
perfection

LETTER 20: not
a pastoral letter

1

how your own child awakes
how you have slumbered)

how we stayed away from Newman Shea
during the storm, how it is honor
is the measure of, when the squeeze
is on

   as it was a shield
bore charges, and recently,
only gamblers

    until five years ago,
when she lost
her last stitch
of clothes

2

not that any of us
would use such language: the Tree
of Battles: or palette fess nombril
base. Professor stuff,
Red Hanna called Red Rice's
yack-yack

   yet it was between these two
tried trust,
at 20 paces,
M-12's
at a hundred yards

    to stand to it, to see
if though they blanched they'd hold,
they'd chance
the other's
error

3

(Or Stephen Papa,
whom I had to beat
for the rent:

       we carried the books,
clothes, lamp,
all but the mirror

           down
the three flights of stairs

       several trips, each step
over the heads of him and his game
going on
in the basement

           And got away with it.
Yet,
that of all men it should have been he

       4

was such a man
he was embarassed
to ask for the rent

       was only a house-owner
because the punks,
and cops,
had driven him
out of up-town

          he was that straight.
And now,
had only this small game

and Espresso,

to cover
his doings

5

Shea
was the opposite

      had stolen a crew's pay
30 or 40 years before

             The story
you could never get straight,
it was only,
as always

      it is not the substance of a man's fault,
it is the shape of it
is what lives with him, is what shows

in his eyes (in our eyes

the days the water poured down the paul-post,
and no one of us
had any assurance the *Hawes*
wouldn't go over on her beam-ends
the next
sea

      6

 Yet it was Shea
who handled the books, paid off
at the end of the trip, did have,
as the elder of us, the best
bunk

And it was he
I talked most to,
at dawn
on the deck,

after we'd done our duty
and his tobacco
corrected
the air
        (he talked Cun-rudd
to me, and was curious
about books to read

        II

The world of Hannas
(the world of Earp)
went with the blueberries,
the chestnuts

        with the openness the exploiters
had not beat out, was still walking, was going places
in street-cars

Not that the state of it
needs crying over. The real

is always worth the act of
lifting it, treading it

to be clear, to make it

clear (to clothe honor
anew

        1

that just at the moment that the heat's on,
when it's your dice or mine, all
or nothing, that she be there

in all her splendor

Maximus, at Tyre and at Boston

Honor, or color, point

they called it, between the middle chief
and the heart, point

And if the nasturtium
is my shield,

          and my song
a cantus firmus

          1

it is change, no more

and yet no less is
the edge of
the discrimination
wielded: cause

is not the equal of,
the error of,

act

          2

the color of error,
the honor, the point
of error

3

we who throw down hierarchy,
who say the history of weeds
is a history of man,

do not fail to keep
a sort of company: all

is how the splendor is worn. No service

is achieved either from the tight

Or the broad. Helmet

palette breastplate tasses tuille

shall cover our nakedness, our

perfection. Not

His.

II

Hyssop, for him,
was the odor of meat: brought back

a whiff of the wind off Boston Common a day

1681

when he was an apprentice boy, and a Negress

Maria, by name,

was burned alive at a stake

Or Elizabeth Tuttle
was divorced by her husband, was
the grandmother of Jonathan Edwards,

and from whose blood Burr
Grant   Cleveland   scholars
generals and clergymen

for adultery. Whose sister

murdered her child, whose brother

was also a murderer

        III

that we are only
as we find out we are

LETTER 22

(Trouble
with the car. And for a buck
they gave me
what I found myself
eating! A polishing
cloth. And I went right on
eating it, it was that good.
And thick, color
orange & black, with a nap—the billowing dress
the big girl wears
every so often

1

What weeds
as an explanation
leaves out, is
that chaos
is not our condition.

Not that relaxation.

                    All,
has no honor as quantity.

          And the attention,
in each of us,
is that one, not the other
not the perfect one. Beauty,
is too quick
for time

          If man is omnivore,
and he is, he eats anything
every so often, he is also
amorvore
as well

(She lost her finger.
And the problem was,
at the celebration,
where to seat the
stranger:
        Goomeranian,
his name was.
        And he wore
a big smile

2

"Satie, enough"

was what it said

        Satie,

enough

And I wear it,

as my blazon

        moving

among my particulars, among

my foes

3

And what I write
is stopping the battle,

to get down, right in the midst of
the deeds, to tell

what this one did, how,
in the fray, he made this play, did grapple
with that one, how
his eye flashed

                        to celebrate

(beauty will not wait)

men,

and girls

                        (I swung the car to the left, confronted
                        as I was by the whole hill-front
                        a loading platform, the lip of it
                        staring at me, grinning,
                        you might say,
                        five feet off
                        the ground

                        And made it. It was only after
                        that the car gave me
                        trouble.

                        For there is a limit
                        to what a car
                        will do.

Letter 23

The facts are:

1st season	1623/4	one ship, the *Fellowship* 35 tons
		with Edward Cribbe as master (?—cf.
		below, 3rd season)

left 14 men Cape Ann:

> John Tilly to oversee the fishing,
>
> Thomas Gardner the "planting" (meaning,
>
> the establishment, however much a bean row,
>
> and some Indian corn; much more salt,
>
> was the business.) The two of them
>
> "bosses", for a year

But here is the first surprise: all the evidence is, that the Plymouth
people, aboard the *Charitie* (carrying Lyford & some cattle, and Winslow
with the Plymouth Co's patent to Cape Ann) got in from England before
the above Dorchester fishermen made it, and the Pilgrims had their
stage up when these others did arrive, five weeks out of Weymouth.
It was this fishing stage which was fought over the next season,
when the Plymouth men returned to find that Westcountry fishermen
had preempted it; and Miles Standish was sent for, to fight about

it.

What we have here—and literally in my own front yard, as I sd to Merk,

asking him what delving, into "fishermans ffield" recent historians . . .

not telling him it was a poem I was interested in, aware I'd scare him

off, *muthologos* has lost such ground since Pindar

> The odish man sd: "Poesy
>
> steals away men's judgment
>
> by her *muthoi*" (taking this crack
>
> at Homer's sweet-versing)

> "and a blind heart
>
> is most men's portions." Plato

> allowed this divisive
>
> thought to stand, agreeing

> that *muthos*
>
> is false. *Logos*
>
> isn't—was facts. Thus
>
> Thucydides

I would be an historian as Herodotus was, looking

for oneself for the evidence of

what is said: Altham says

Winslow

was at Cape Ann in April,

1624

What we have in this field in these scraps among these fishermen,

and the Plymouth men, is more than the fight of one colony with

another, it is the whole engagement against (1) mercantilism

(cf. the Westcountry men and Sir Edward Coke against the Crown,

in Commons, these same years—against Gorges); and (2) against

nascent capitalism except as it stays the individual adventurer

and the worker on share—against all sliding statism, ownership

getting in to, the community as, Chambers of Commerce, or theocracy;

or City Manager

a Plantation a beginning

I sit here on a Sunday
with grey water, the winter
staring me in the face

"the Snow lyes indeed
about a foot thicke
for ten weekes" John White

warns any prospective
planter

Fourteen spare men the first
year who huddled
above Half Moon beach

or got out of the onshore
breeze by clustering
what sort of what shacks

around the inshore harbor side
of Stage Head where now lovers
have a park and my mother

and my wife were curious
what went on in back seats
and Pat Foley

was furious some guy
on all four legs
crawled

about, to get a better view
when Pat sat spooning (where leisure
occupies shore

where fishing worke
was first set up, and fourteen men
did what with Gloucester's nothing land

and all her harbor?

The ship which brought them
we don't even know
its name, or Master

as they called a Capt
then, except that that
first season, 1623

the fishing, Gloucester
was good: the small ship (the *Fellowship?*) sailed
for Bilbao full

It cost the Company
200 pounds ($10,000)
to try these men

ashore that year,
to plant a land
was thinnest dust

to trade for furs
where smallpox
had made Champlain's

Indians of 1606
as thin as dogs
come in to hover

around what campfires
these fourteen Englishmen
managed

where I as young man berthed
a skiff and scarfed
my legs to get up rocks

this cost is all it's
made of, not soil
not beaver

fish fish fish

Her cargo brought
the Spanish market
exactly the same

the Company spent
Stage Fort: 200
pounds. Thus loss

that season. For the ship's
own charge
was more

for voyage; and her cost,
to buy her when they launched
the adventure

of the new frontier
(not boom, or gold,
the lucky strike,

but work, a fishing
"have set up",
said Smith, "this year

upon the Coast
about 50. English
ships

and by Cape Anne
Dorchester men
a plantation

a beginning") the ship alone
small fiftie tunnes
new sute of sayles amounted

to more than three hundred
pound. And now by Reason
the Voyage

was undertaken
too late, And the whole Provenue
was too little,

the deficit
It cost
$30,000

to get
Gloucester
started

Maximus, to Gloucester

I don't mean, just like that, to put down
the Widow Babson whose progeny and property
is still to be found and felt on Main
and Middle Streets, at Joppa, or
in Wellesley Hills (my Aunt Vandla
had a house on Laurel Avenue before
Babson had his Institute there and once,
when I was older, I swung by,
in a girl's father's Hupmobile
and lawd, how the house had been inflated
in my mem-o-ry

Or Jeffrey Parsons whom the historian Babson
clearly places over the Cut as the man who owned
all the land and boulders, all the hill and hollow
I know best in all the world, how Stage Fort is
what Babson called it, the only hundred acres
on this cape could possibly have fit the foolish hope
of Somerset and Dorset men to do on this rock coast
what England might have thought New England might be

But just there lies the thing, that "fisherman's Field"
(Stage Head, Stage Fort, and now and all my childhood
a down-dilly park for cops and robbers, baseball, firemen's
hose, North End Italian Sunday spreads, night-time Gloucester
monkey-business) stays the first place Englishmen
first felt the light and winds, the turning, from that view,
of what is now the City—the gulls the same but otherwise the sounds
were different for those fourteen men, probably the ocean
ate deeper in the shore, crashed further up at Cressy's (why
they took their shelter either side of softer Stage Head and let
Tablet Rock buff for them the weather side: on the lee,
below the ridge which runs from my house straight to Tablet Rock
these Dorset Somerset men built the Company house which Endicott
thought grand enough to pull it down and haul it all the way
to Salem for his Governor's abode:

                                         an house built at Cape Ann
                                         whc Walter Knight & the rest sd
                                         they built for Dorchester men

The point is not that Beverly
turned out to be their home,
that Conant Norman Allen Knight
Balch Palfrey Woodbury Tilly Gray
are Babsons Parsons there

                          But that as I sit
                          in a rented house
                          on Fort Point,
                          the Cape Ann Fisheries

                          out one window,
                          Stage Head looking me
                          out of the other
                          in my right eye

                          (like backwards
                           of a scene
                           I saw the other way
                           for thirty years)

                          Gloucester can view
                          those men
                          who saw her
                          first

He left him naked,
the man said, and
nakedness
is what one means

that all start up
to the eye and soul
as though it had never
happened before

A year that year
was new to men
the place had bred
in the mind of another

John White had seen it
in his eye
but fourteen men
of whom we know eleven

twenty-two eyes
and the snow flew
where gulls now paper
the skies

where fishing continues
and my heart lies

So Sassafras

Europe just then was being drained swept by the pox so sassafras
was what Ralegh Gosnold Pring only they found fish not cure
for fish so thick the waters you could put no prow'd
go through mines John Smith called these are her silver
streames Spanish north Latitudes to avoid Sable course
W 2 minutes north fetch Cape an or Isle Shoals make $1000 per
man per 7 months than in 20 hiring out for wages Indians
occasionally bloody had trick of cutting off feet and hands poor
John Tilly John Oldham and 69 lusty men Bradford called Weston's it wasn't
pie Wm Bradford John Winthrop were Medici to top the tough
West the Puritan coast was was fur and fish frontier cow-towns
GLOUCESTER Queen of the fishtowns Monhegan Damariscove & 1622:
Cap an all after her Weston Thompson Pilgrimes grabbing
& Richard BUSHROD beating em to the westerly side of sd Harbour
George derby agent and JOHN WHITE old minister John poking out the
green stuff or whatever money looked like don't mistake there wasn't
money Wow sd Pilgrimes ONE HALF MILLION BUCKS in 5 years from
FURS at the same time FISH pulling all of Spain's bullion out of

and where money is,
stronger waters than
sasparilla Our Lady
of bon viaje

under whose foot some necks

                (old man B
who never swore except
housewives could quote
he sd
        jeenie crinie   B

got caught years later
before hardtop was for
driveways/ was for high-
ways his department

Daddy Scolpins was his name
took Dotty the Beauty from
our porch the beauty of the
neiborhood old Daddy Brown-

nose his nose B's nose were
oil Big Train they must have
called the Cod Kings of Eng-

land 1623 who lost money
Stage Head. Not old B he
took it down hill on the

sly off tarvia or what the City
paid and our fireplace made
of pavingstones: o bucks

o city
hall

     2

Nuth Nuth'east o Cally-o Bilbao Bilbow St Kitts
We'll make a buck with Indian truck
or corfish
for the Spicks

We'll hang off Stage Head
nine weeks, & do and do and do
we're for Virgini-ay Fayal & Surinam
to pick up optimis generis
what sauvages the French have left
we'll sell we'll grab
right here what small-pox
(Osquanto dead & wanting
the Englishman's God

Rummage the ship a grab is holt hold on
to what you get
Boston
is where the best fish
go, the bad to cally O

          O specie Fishermen
cost so little. Only grub. And so

But obdurate. Licentious.
Shipbuilders too. To church
& whipping go to keep em in—run bank clerks
for Council and a clown
name Clancy
for his wit to get a
chivery   O people draw

your cent's out

clout

& kench those

who'd keep you

walk 50 miles

nor' nor' West

History is the Memory of Time

1622 to 1626 was the fish rush   (with Pilgrims the Mormons
                                                              on the side like side bets

10 boats New England waters
the year before, then BANG:

37 vessels (mostly Damariscove?) 1622,
45 Piscataqua and Cape Anne, 1623
50, 1624—& WAR, with Spain

1625/6: Gloucester's year,
when she must have been a cowtown from the roar
of men after, fish:

                    how many vessels how many men
                    in the Harbour?

                              @ 40 to 60 per ship?

          200—or 2000?

That year the STAGE FIGHT—and as much a Western as
why not, with Hewes' men backed up on the stage they'd taken
by right of hand from Plymouth poor Johns hadn't yet got to
fishing that season (stayed in bed)
                              Miles Standish,
probably looking just like they tell us coal shuttle
on head silly pistol cocked at Hewes' chest slashed trousers
ballooning over bow legs

          Hewes & men backing back on stage toward water,
pushing hogsheads into place for barricade, meanwhile Standish
small chimney fuming ("lousy Christian" says Rev Hubbard didn't know
enough to turn other fowling piece

          Hewes had reason
          to give way: 3 Plymouth vessels

on station, the *Charity*, 100 tons,
Capt Peirce who quieted
Standish, but the other two
Company ships fr London,
under the crook Allerton:
the *Little James,*
after cor-fish
(and got her fraughtage)
and the big one, the
White Angel, 300 tons
which went loaded
to Bilbao or Sebastians
towing the *Little James*
after her. Only the Turks
took the little one the moment
the Angel let her
loose

Which fight tells
what heat there was
in sd Harbour when
was site of
commerce

    real bucks not
    each man and woman
    and child living off
    things paid on
    33 year schedule

        credit out ahead,
        each generation
        living 33 years
        of shoddy &
        safety—not at all

            living. Not all late
            conantry (for which read

a nation fizzing itself
on city managers,
mutual losing banks,

      how to send yr child
      $100,000 more a
      lifetime than
      poor old
      dad

They should raise a monument
to a fisherman crouched down
behind a hogshead, protecting
his dried fish

The Picture

Exactly what the status
of Thomas Morton was
at Cape Ann, or thereabouts,
and when—

he was the friend
of Ambrose Gibbons
& conceivably was acting
on John Mason's part?

Anyhow John Watts took salt
he said Morton said
was his, or was committed
to his charge

Morton, to New England, is as
Hastings was to California
(misled the Donner Party) a
wide fool but not vicious

as the Pilgrims put him
down. When he was Gloucester
it was after the Rush, after fish
had lost their market. England

plunged into two wars
the same years the first Gloucester
held the stage, in Commons & in mer-
chants' minds: 1624

war with Spain, 1626
war with France, & prices
knocked off the chance
a fishing station here

would pay. John Watts,
and Morton, taking salt
(and shallops) from the store
on Ten Pound Island were

picking over after
a deluge—all gone

THE PICTURE:

1623   voyage of discovery, ship unknown, Bushrod backer
        (John Watts factor?)

1624   1st season Dorchester Company, the *Fellowship*,
        35 tons, 14 men left Stage Head

1625   2nd season 32 men left, two ships the *Fellowship*
        and the *Pilgrime*, 140 tons (which returned to Eng-
        land with little more than a third part of her lading)

1626   last season, the *Fellowship* the *Pilgrime* and the
        Amytie, 30 tons, Capt Isaac Evans bringing
        6 cattle

& 1627 a final voyage, backed by eleven enthusiasts from
        the former Company ship's name unknown but John
        Watts factor, carried 20 more cattle for Roger
        Conant & his faithful; Watts took salt

END, scene shifts to Salem, and then Boston, and there be
11 years until fishing once more, and then a Colony matter,
returns to le Beau Port

Here we have it—the goods—from this Harbour,

1626, to Weymouth (England) consigned to

Richard Bushrod and Company
& Wm Derby and Company

fr Cape An   dry fish[1]

corfish[2]

train oil[3]

quarters of oak

skins: fox
         racons
        martyns
          otter
      muskuatche
        beaver

The *Amytie* arriving Weymouth 1st Aug

and the *Fellowship* followed 11th September

Capts Evans, & Edward Cribbe

1   "so hote this time of yeare except the very fish which is laid out
to be dryed by the sunne be every day turned it cannot possibly
be preserved from burning" Shore fishery

2   Banks fishery, where fish are large and always wet, having no
land heere to drie and were called core or green fish—split
& salted

3   the oil of seal, whale or cod—undoubtedly here cod

14 MEN STAGE HEAD WINTER 1624/5

they required

7 hundredweight biscuit bread @ 15/ per hundred	£ 5.	5.	0
7 hhds of beere or sider 53/4 the tun	20.	0.	0
⅔ hhd beef	3.	7.	2
6 whole sides of bacon	3.	3.	0
6 bush. pease	1.	10.	0
⅔ firkin butter	1.	0.	0
⅔ cwt. cheese		2.	0
1 pecke mustard seed		6.	0
1 barrel vinegar		10.	2
15 lbs candles	1.	0.	0
3 pecks oatmeal		9.	0
⅔ hhd/ aqua vitae	3.	0.	0
2 copper kettles	3.	0.	0
1 brasse crock	1.	0.	0
1 frying pan		2.	0
1 grind stone		5.	0
2 good axes, 4 hand hatchets, 4 short wood hooks, 2 drawing irons, 2 adzes		16.	0
4 arm saws, 4 hand saws, 4 thwart saws			
3 augers, 2 crowes of iron, 2 sledges,			
4 iron shovels, 2 pick axes, 4 mattocks,			
4 cloe hammers	5.	0.	0
heading and splitting knives	1.	5.	0
so much hair cloth as may cost	10.	0.	0
pinnaces sails	2.	10.	0
8 fishing boats iron works	2.	0.	0
10 boats' anchors, ropes	10.	0.	0
canvas to make boats sails and small ropes			
2 saines, a greater and a less	12.	0.	0
10 good nets at 26/ a net	13.	0.	0
fitting for them at 25/ each	10.	0.	0
2000 nails to build houses at 13/4 the thousand	1.	6.	8
4000 nails at 6/8 per 1000	1.	6.	8
2000 nails at 5 d per hundred		8.	0

The above is calculated from Capt Richard
Whitbourne's list of outfit and pro-
visions for a winter station at Newfoundland
as of 1622; it compares to Rev John White's
statement of the cost of maintaining the 14
Dorchester Company men at Cape Ann thus:

     Whitbourne total   £ 113.   12.   8
     White round number   £ 225

The difference may be the measure of a mere
station versus a plantation such as the
Dorchester Company was embarked on—more
permanent stages, possibly more than 2
pinnaces and 8 shallops, and the Big Company
House, later Endecott's, etc.

Some Good News

how small the news was
a permanent change had come
by 14 men setting down
on Cape Ann, on the westerly side
of the harbor

                the same side Bradford,
the fall before, had asked London
to get for him
so that New Plymouth
could prosecute fishing, no place,

in the minds of men, England
or on the ground, equal,
and fitting the future
as this Cape sitting
between the old

North Atlantic (of Biskay,
and Breton, of Cabot's
nosing into, for Bristol)
and the new—Georges
(as the bank was called as early

as 1530: who gave her their
patron saint—England?
Aragon? or Portyngales?)
Or Old Man's Pasture, Tillies
Bank, whichever way

you take what advantage
Cape Ann: Levett
says "too faire a gloss"
is placed on her,
the same year

New Plymouth here,
Dorchester there,

and Levett himself,
at Quack, care
to be right. 1623,

all of them,
suddenly,
pay attention,
to what fishermen
(since when? before
1500) have

been showing: the motion
(the Westward motion)
comes here,
to land. Stations
(going back to sheep,
and goats on Sable

Island, of all sand spits
upon the globe, and terror
of blown or dragged or dropped
earth in the midst of
water—shoals, worse

than rock because
they do blow shift lie,
are changing as you sound—
on this crooked sand
Portuguese (when?)

had a fishing station.
It wasn't new,
what happened,
at Cape Ann. It's where,
and when it

did. Smith
at Monhegan,
1614, and telling
about it, in a book,
1616, is

the demarcation (he,
the Sea-Marke!
as competently Columbus
backwards as Grant
forward, John Smith

the stater of
quantity and
precision, the double
doesn't unravel
so you'd know it

just like that, dragging,
as we do
shifty new
land, sucks
down, into the terrible

inert of
nature (the Divine
Inert, the literary man
of these men
of the West,

who knew private
passivity as these
quartermasters knew
supplies, said
it has to be

if princes
of the husting
are to issue from
the collapse
of the previous

soul: Smith,
too early yet
to be understood
to be the sign
of present

paternities—braggart
fisherman, the
Androgyne who hates
the simulacrum
Time Magazine

takes for male,
the playing coy
with identity)
a man's
struggle

with Caesar's
dream,
that he'd been intimate
with his mother,
and the soothsayer

eased him: it only means
that you shall conquer
the world. Smith,
as Sam Grant after,
was futile

until the place
and time burned
with the same heat as
the man (it isn't
for us to say

what a proper fire
is, it's what,
like Corinth
burning down
produces bronze—

or my Cabbage, we
baked potatoes
Fisher's Hill—or Caesar
dreamed, in Spain—or Smith,
who came to Monhegan

to catch whales,
and found cod, instead.
And furs. And Frenchmen
ahead of him, west
of him. Yet

Smith
changed
everything: he pointed
out
Cape Ann,

named her
so it's stuck,
and Englishmen,
who were the ones
who wanted to,

sat down, planted
fisheries
so they've stayed put,
on this coast, from Pemaquid
to Cape Cod.

One needs
grab hold of,
with purchase
this purpose, that
the Continental Shelf

was Europe's
first West, it wasn't
Spain's
south: fish,
and furs

and timber,
were wealth,
neither plants,
old agricultural
growing, from

Neolithic, sickles
& that kind of
contemplation
of nature, she
the brooder

nor gold, and murder.
We kill
as a fisherman's
knife nicks
abundance.

Which we take
for granted,
we don't even earn
our labor (as patriarchy
and matriarchy)

we do it all
by quantity and
machine. The subjective
hides, or runs riot
("vainglorious",

they put Smith down
as, and hire a Standish
to do corporative
murder: keep things clean,
by campaigns

drop bombs. One cries Mongols
instead. Yet Grant

still is a name
for butcher, for how
he did finally hammer out
a victory over

Clotho Lee, the spinner
the stocking frame
undid: textile

us, South
and North—the world,

tomorrow, and all
without fate
tomorrow,
if we,
who come from a housekeeping

which old mother Smith
started,
don't find out the inert
is as gleaming as,
and as fat as,

fish—so
we move: sd the
literary man, from hidden places
sprang
the killer's
instrument

who is also
the boatsteerer.
The "lily-iron",
they called the swordfish
harpoon when Gloucester

still chased
the blue-backed
thing on Browns (east
of Monhegan, north
of Georges

        West
and south Smith
put down the claim;
and wrote
her paper
and her name

"The which
is riches

will change
the world" not knowing,
as we don't,

he'd hang up,
and be
a mark for all
who on this coast
do fall,

aloof aloof,
and come no near,
we cry. Or we'll over,
and you better
follow us who

from the hustings ("trash",
industrial fish
are called which Gloucester
now catches, all that the bottom
of Georges,

the Channel, Middle Ground,
Browns, Pollock Rip
yields, anything
nature puts in the sea
comes up,

it is cornucopia
to see it
working up a sluggish
treadle,
from a ship's hold

to the truck
which takes it to the De-Hy
to be turned into catfood,
and fertilizer, for nature's
fields

Out of these waters
inland, it went. From then
—from Smith—some good news
better
get after

Stiffening, in the Master Founders' Wills

Descartes, age 34, date Boston's
settling. The pertinence
of yellow sweetings,
among other things which Pur-
itan contingent had

much savor for. As they also
(of which we've heard)
did savor some spiritual
matter—like throwing people
out. Or so fierce the sense

enthusiasm does not lead
to progression they took Quakers
(Mrs. Davis's cookbook's kind)
and sold them,
as slaves, or burned them

Boston Common. Proportion's
not the easiest thing
to bring if character's
(Cartesian monads)
desperate densenesses

be not washed out in natural
or bubble bath. When things
are knots where instance
hides order, and a man
does not run as sheep

(or concubines hid on Jeremiah Dummer's
farm, surprised
in dalliance with him
by a friend, and fled
over each other as,

such leapings, was never
saw! Who stands in

as John Winthrop, sounds
as rattled, questioning
Anne Hutchinson's right

to rouse up women
on Thursdays
at her house
talking grace
versus works, when housekeeping

Dealing with reality's
affairs (as humans are
as apples, said—
or God made right hands
why he didn't make

another right, instead
made lefts), "being exposed,
as I am, so much
to publick view, I shall speak
of the particular"

It matters, and we shall not charge
Winthrop with not knowing
change had come. He walked
one winter night from M'Head
home, through the woods

on a single Algonquin path,
a single man in this wilderness,
a thing surely wasn't
how he'd done it East Anglia
(or another man, when young,

by fields from Shottery home
from her bed (Mistress Hathaway's)
saw William written
in Cassiopeia overhead:
American space

was 1630 still sailors'
apprehension not Boston's

leader's: "A family", he says,
"is a little
common wealth, and a common wealth

is a greate family" Stop
right there, said time, Descartes
's holding up
another hand and your own people
in this wilderness

not savages but thought
has invaded
the proposition. The apple
on Tenhill farm's boughs
("one-third,

my son, you will see come
annually to your mother
and to me though
I give you
the land") was now

already merchandise,
not merely sowing,
reaping, building
houses & out houses,
streams, neat Rother

beasts—Canaan
was Cane's, and
all was faulting,
stiffening in the master
founders wills—

the things
of this world (new
world, Renaissance
mind named
what Moses men tried

to twist back to Covenantal
truth) Continental

loci inside of which they'd
dry, sweet souls to whom
outward was inward
act when inward-outward
was, by being here, being

turned, in Corinth
cooling into mettle—
someness (skeigh
men were coming
along paths we just now

get our feet on, that space,
too, comes in
to compass of
men's hands—and not
hangs out as souls

were kept in, in
Boston: the things
of this world
had moved in in a pre-
paratory

meaning. Conversion,
of another sort than
Christ's—. . . yet
at this further point
of Union,

when the most
have done exactly what
he warned they'd (enthusiasm
is sedition, he flew
in Mrs. Hutchinson's

face, dishonors
parents. Sailors,
come ashore/ tell
the tailor's sewing's

in a different
light. But it's still
sewing. Marshes,

by tidal rivers
flowing far
up into the land
(long grasses
for cattle fattening

as they didn't
on the other shore) boys
and girls grow
long legged and don't want to live

in dead ceremonies
of white bulls, or surplices
of whiteness of the soul's
desire to be blind, in service
or in ecstasy. We pick

a private way
among debris
of common
wealths—Public
fact as sure

as dimensions stay
personal. And one desire,
that the soul
be naked
at the end

of time (the screech
of the tunnel
says
it better be, or
what's all this

for

Capt Christopher Levett (of York)

Levett is a measure
—the writ, that 14 men
had sat down
at Cape Anne, did not run
to him, where Portland

was to be; and didn't get
to London, from the West
country. Levett says only,
1624, I left
some men myself, and Plymouth

people fish . . . Though that
Cape Ann led on
to Commonwealth, and Maine
stayed Maine,
is not the news. The news

which Levett had to tell
(as Conant might have)
was a simpler thing, of such import
an island's named today
"House Island"—and Conant's

house was timbers
in a city's stable
so few years back
I touched them, when a kid,
and didn't know it, the first ones

on an continent which men
have let go so our
eyes which look
to strike
take nothing

of even furthest previous
thought, local
national or new spatial

as tolerable. A man
who speaks as Levett does
of what he's done
("I have obtained a place
of habitation in New-

England, where I have built
a house, and fortified it
in a reasonable good fashion,
strong enough against such enemies
as are those Savage people")

speaks (as he does of each
new thing he saw and did
in these new parts) so we,
who live at this poor end
of goods, & thing, & men,

when materials, of each,
are such a man can't eat
sleep walk move go
apart from his own dwelling,
the dirtiness of goodness

cheapness shit is
upon the world. We'll turn
to keep our house, turn to
houses where our kind,
and hungry after them,

not willing to bear one short walk
more out into even what they've done
to earth itself, find
company. Since these two men
put down two houses

by fish flakes and stages
on rocks near water with trees
against sea—one's forced,
considering America,
to a single truth: the newness

the first men knew was almost
from the start dirtied
by second comers. About seven years
and you can carry cinders
in your hand for what

America was worth. May she be damned
for what she did so soon
to what was such a newing
that we, who out the side
of her come (have cut ourselves

out of her drugstore flattened-hillside gut
like Wash-Ching-Geka cut
the Winnebago nation out
of elephant—"the fish,
sd Levett, which we there saw,

some with wings, others with manes,
ears, heads, who chased
one another with open mouths
like stone Horses in a parcke"—
We have the gain. We know

what Levett Smith or Conant
didn't, that no one
knew better
than to cash in on it. Out,
is the cry of a coat of wonder

February night, or August
on Georges the seas

are short, the room's
small. When the moon's

fullest the tidal currents
set fastest

On the morning of February 14th we started and in twenty-four hours
were over the rocky bottom of the southerly part of the Bank. A hun-
dred sail were crowded in together, half a mile, and some a mile, apart,
handlining, where the cod spawn.

The fishing and the weather were good for days. Although the cold was
intense we were at the rail sometimes a full hour without changing
position, then, if we got a halibut, the cook would bring up a pancake
with plums in it to celebrate. And coffee.

The vessel shifted its berth twice, in the first week, each time drawing
nearer to the body of the fleet. The fish were more plentiful but with
each move our concern grew, for we were all bunched up easterly of
dreaded South Shoal. If the weather stayed fine there was no danger but
if it came on a gale and even one vessel dragged her anchor, or chafed
her cable and went adrift, we might all go.

At sundown on the 24th there was a sudden change. The clouds massed,
and the rising wind roughened the seas. At eight o'clock the skipper was
uneasy, he kept looking up at the sky and at the horizon. The wind had
veered to the northeast, and was increasing. It began to snow, moderately
at first, and then more.

The skipper went forward to examine the cable and gave orders to pay out ten fathom. Our lights, in the rigging, had been lit since sundown, and the rest of the fleet could still be seen, when the skipper, warning that the night would be a watch for all of us, advised those who could, to get some sleep. We went below about half-past eight.

It was now about eleven o'clock. The wind was a gale, the snow came down spitefully, and the seas were so high we could do nothing but look up the sides of them. From the short break of them in these confines of Georges, the way they snapped themselves off, one of them could break aboard us and sweep everything over the rail to leeward, or, worst, coming in too big, set down on us, bury us, smother the vessel under its weight and take it and us down in one crush.

At midnight the tide itself changed, set toward shoalwater, and now the wind, the sea and the tide were in one movement from the northeast, and the gravest strain was put on all the vessels trying to ride out the night. We were on deck to keep what lookout we could for the first vessel which might loose itself and drive on to us. The oldest hand aboard was at the windlass with a hatchet ready to cut the cable if paying it out wasn't fast enough to let a vessel by, and we had to go ourselves.

The darkness had become impenetrable and a more dismal night none of us ever passed. We longed for morning to dawn. Once in a while the storm would lull for a little, and the snow not fall so thickly. Then we would see some of the lights of the fleet nearest us, but this was not often. During the night a large vessel did pass quite near us. We could see her lights, also her spars and sails, as she was driven swiftly along. We trembled at the thought of what she might have done had she struck us, and when we learned of the terrible disaster of the gale, we spoke of this vessel as the cause of some portion of it.

At length the east began to lighten. Morning was coming. Our danger was not over, the gale continued, but there was comfort to the light. The fearful darkness and the terrible uncertainty was relieved. We could now at least see our position.

We had something to eat, in turns, when, about nine o'clock, the skipper sang out, "Vessel adrift, just ahead of us." All eyes were on her. On she came directly for us. A moment more and we'd have had to cut, when she passed with the swiftness of a gull, so near any one of us could have leaped aboard her. We watched her as she went on and a short distance astern she struck one of the fleet and we saw the waters close over both vessels, almost instantly. As we looked they both disappeared.

Our own anchor began to drag, and we yaw. This was dangerous in the extreme, for if the anchors did not take hold again, find new bottom, we too must cut and once adrift go as these others had. Fortunately, the anchors bit up, found holding ground, and we rode again in safety.

All through the day of the 25th we watched. Two more vessels bore down on us, but went clear. We were saved. At sundown the gale moderated and the terror of it, which had swept so fearfully over Georges, was over.

The next day we were back at fishing, we fished through the week, had good fishing, and headed home. Eastern Point Light, when first sighted, looked good to us, but coming in by the Fort, the crowds of people waiting there to see each vessel's name awoke it all again. Several came on board asking if we had seen such and such a vessel since the gale. The town was in commotion. Such anxiety I hope never again to witness. The wharves were full of broken ships and there was hardly a home which didn't have a loss. The gloom was general over the town for many days. One hundred and twenty men had drowned that one night and day, and fifteen vessels gone down, all on Georges

the shoal of Georges
the north, west and south

[*2nd Letter on Georges*]

Frost: 25 miles off the Highlands
Sch. Ella M. Goodwin, Capt. Jimmy Goodwin, January 4, 1905
Boston Post says—"off South Shoals"?
"in South Channel"
Miles: SE edge of Georges

Miles:

McK had a brother
who had a cloth-
ing store in Bev-
erley, & he went
up to see him,
planning to give
up the sea & stay
ashore, but when
he got there &
found that his
brother was out
to New York he de-
cided to make one
more trip before
he'd give up.

Tow you out by
10 lb Island, &
you'd sail out
the harbor from
there

6 AM—Miles:
just at light—
Frost says the

Went out of Gloucester in the winter, around
New Year's. It was the winter before the Chicago
theatre fire. It was the time Johnny McKenzie
was lost. I ran into him up street, and he says
to me, "Come on up to Lynn to see my brother."
So we did, and I said, "I won't go in." But his
brother was gone to Boston, in those days they
used to haul freight by streetcar. And there was
n't anything Johnny could do, and it was the last
time he might have seen him.

So we went out, and were gone a week when the
wind shifts SE, and with it snow. We laid out and
hauled back. About that time the wind began to
haul, and we threw the lead over, and found we
were in 6 fathom of water. So we took the main-
sail in, and put her under riding sail, foresail
and outer jib.

(8 fathom, says Frank)

It breezed up so hard and we were fearful we'd
be driven on the shoals of the Cultivator. We threw
the lead again and found we were in 12 fathom, so
we tacked again. Ed Rose was at the wheel, and the
men below were all iled up on the floor. When I
came on deck for my watch she was in water chuck
to her cabin, with that much sail on here. So I

skipper waited
till morning to
get the light to
put the double
reef in the fore-
sail Also, that
it was the fault
of the man at the
wheel, he let her
off too much.

Boston Post
Sat. Jan 7,
    1905,
     p. 2

Ed Rose mixed up
in the mainsheet
tackle & pulled
in over the taff-
rail — Miles

called down to the cabin, "Jimmy, you better come
up and have a look at her." She was not making any
headway, and he ordered a double reef in her fore-
sail. So we got the foresail down and hoisted. Now
the only thing to do was to jig up the boom. So I
went down to loo'ard.

When the sea struck Ed Rose was roped to the
wheel with the line passing over both his shoul-
ders. Nine men were on deck, including Rose, four
of us to the loo'ard, swaying up the forepeak,
Johnny, Frank Miles, Bob Lee and myself. I took
a turn on the jig and it was lucky I did, for I
see a sea breaking that high she was breaking
through the starboard light, and I sing out,
"Look out," and with that the vessel goes down.
McKenzie had one arm around the rigging and one
arm in the jig. I had the turn in my right hand,
and with the other I caught two fellows by the
oil skins as they went past.

The other men at the peak halyard, McKenzie,
Miles and Lee, taken in the act of overhanding
on the peak halyards, were swept to loo'ard and
over the vessel's sides by the irresistible on-
rush. Another, Leslie Sholds, standing to wind-
ward, also went over. We all came back in with
the back wash of the sea, all but McKenzie.

When we came in again, Ben Frost counted 3
oil hats going along side, and he threw the log
line over to see if there was anybody under
them, cast it, & flip it to turn the oil hats
over.

The sea threw my watch mate, Ed Rose, right over the stern of the vessel. The rope had slipped off one shoulder and was around his neck. And my dory mate went up the lee rigging with the wash, and a gurry kit hit him and a stone ring which hadn't been off his finger in years was gone with that wave.

"stone ring gone, and so was his finger"
    Miles

The skipper sang out, for all of us to come aft to see who was gone. Poor McKenzie was gone, and only 21, and I never heard him use an oath.

"Poor Johnny—
I can see him now, sleeping under the cook and his legs hanging over the edge

Anyhow, we got out of it and got in here. It was 1907, I think.

Johnny McKenzie was born in Bear River, Digby County, but was brought up in Shelburne, where his relatives were, tho I suppose they're all gone now.

The cook in her then was John Nickerson. He went with Jimmy Goodwin all the time he went out of here. She was a poorly built vessel. He went down in the Bay of Islands with all hands.

"to sway"—old English for to hoist

Douglas
Miles clipping
see Ben Frost at Institute

forepeak halyards—peak of the foresail

a whip & a jig the same thing: tied to the fore halyard & came in single to the block & came out double

Frank Miles,   21
Lew Douglas, 23?
Ben Frost,   36

Bill Doucette another & the only other living member

———————————————

McK was up on the rail hauling the others hauling overhand with him on the jig rigged to

the forepeak halyard
The others beneath him…
The others beneath him to looard
So that when the sea struck he was
      thrown out the farthest
We watched him go, & nothing we could do, no way to
lower a dory in the sea, & no line to throw that
far

Ben Frost (in 16 Institute) says he was the 1st to come aft
after it. He was to windward, and a fellow sings out "Look
out" & ducks down the fo'c'sle companionway but I was too
far away, & couldn't get down under the windward rail, so
I grabbed the jumbo stay but she came out at the throat

Frost says the skipper got caught in the mains'l & Miles says his
head was jammed in the crutch of the main boom

John Burke

John Burke did not rise
when Councilman Smith, nor had he signed
the complimentary scroll
handlettered
by Franklin E. Hamilton
of Public Works

Staring into the torsion
of his own face Burke
sat solid in
refusal (as,
in matters of the soul a private man
lives torn
by inspectio
and judicium, the judge
or mischievous woman
who make hob
of us) sweat, Burke
sweat, indubitably,
in his aloneness—or he'd not have said,
"I am no hypocrite"

Against the greased ways
of the city now (of the nation) this politician
himself a twisted animal
swelling of mouth, followed
by squirrels as pilot fish
himself a shark will not
tolerate
the suave / the insolence
of agreement

While he had to listen, Smith,
sticking it at him by that ease of charm
gets everyone to put up sodas
in Sterling Drug, have lunch
of halibut au gratin at
the Tavern, and they all run

with their hands (give up their eyes)
to be pleased by the
please Mr Smith tells fable, Soap
Esop of the present, of beast
a man turned into (Burke)

"Obsessed by fear," sd Piety
with face of fat,
"worried his life away" (I can see Burke,
worrying—who knows a thing or two,
has written on his mouth of a weasel much
munching, a few places Smith
will never get into, who likes
long legs) Burke sat there and heard this parabolist
(the business man is now the minister) go on

"worrying,
something frightful was going to happen
to him" (when surely,
by all the vetos
of his voting record Burke's
attention
on what was happening
to the city, that it was being ribboned,
dolled up like Smith himself) "the fear,"

sd the ponderous Harvard fullback,
"the object of his fear" (Burke's fear)
"never came. The fear itself" (o city's
whore) "like a beast in the jungle,
devoured him" (what a morsel,
Burkey) "and he was unable"
(here we have it—city hall)
"to make any constructive
move"—la

          that you shall sit
          and dwell until the judge
          or goddess of all mischief
          (she holds a city in her hair)
          directs you to your life

————————————

Steele then asked for a rising vote
to pass the resolutions inscribed
upon the councillor's scroll.

Every council member rose
except Burke, who remained in his chair,
staring at the table

A FOOTNOTE TO THE ABOVE,

> To speak in Yana-Hopi about these matters
> with which I, as Maximus, am concerned
> (which is Gloucester, and myself as here-
> a-bouts, in other words in *Maximus* local
> relations are nominalized) one would talk,
> Yana being a North California tongue, &
> Hopi is a language peculiarly adjusted to
> the topological as a prime and libidinal
> character of a man, and therefore of all of his
> proximities: metric then is mapping, and so,
> to speak modern cant, congruent means of
> making a statement), I, as Mr. Foster, went
> to Gloucester, thus:

> > "And past-I-go
> > Gloucester-insides
> > being Fosterwise of
> > Charley-once-boy
> > insides"

Letter, May 2, 1959

125 paces Grove Street
fr E end of Oak Grove cemetery
to major turn NW of
road

this line goes finally straight
fr Wallis property direct
to White (as of 1707/8)

(2) 125 of curve
(3) 200 paces to Centennial

(4)
    47   90   90
                           st
   230 paces

c 300 paces
  Whittemore to the marsh

Kent's property/ Pearce

                          w to marsh
                        (hill falls off

    70   o
  paces   o
  hill falls   o   140
  S to   o
  marsh   o   old stonewall
                   o —between Bruen & Eveleth?
  Babson   Meeting House   (Perkins)
   house   Green   Millet
    Ellery   fence marking

did Eveleth go to present Marsh St?

What did Bruen want? He had already shifted from Piscataqua
to Plymouth, then to Gloucester and now to New London and
would go from New London to found Newark, N.J.

Mellow and enclosed both the local and the past
N.G. not the point not here I am not here to
have to do with Englishmen (in habit, but
canoes dugout as found Indian means of hauling
marsh grass by gundalows possibly old Venetian

                              who came out of their marshes likewise
                              to change the commerce of NW shifting
                              man—it ends, as Stefansson couldn't
                              stomach the dead end of his own prop-
                              osition, in the ice

dogs of the present don't even throw anything back   The sea
it isn't 67 years yet that the First Parish (Unitarian) preach-
er of the anniversary sermon told them we must reckon
with the great sea the influences
of it the salt breath of it
have interfused the sadness of it have interfused
Zebulon

and John Trask Orator dedicated his address my father and mother
born and married in, his text Chapter XX the, Wonder-working Prov-
idence of, Of the planting the one and twentieth church (of Christ)
at a town called Gloster

                              being peopled with
                              Fishermen, this

                              lying out, about
                    fifty known, the access there unto by land becomes

                              uneasy

Which was the cause says the source this early why it was no more
populated

                              Had they men of Estates
                              their fishing trade,

                          Yet
are not without other means of maintenance, have good timber, And
a very sufficient builder (Stevens)

                          But that these times,
                          of combustion, the seas

the Peoples of the Sea Meneptha fell Kadesh they were there Ramses II
Greeks

from the sea Lebanese

to Gloucester these Englishmen what was Bruen doing

Piscataqua Bristol Z. Hill Wm Barnes Gloucester
Gloucestershire William Addes Frampton on Severn
Devon: Avery Parsons Southmead Dutch Dorset Ste-
vens alone London Stepney Middlesex yes Thomas
Millett Southwark: Holgrave, Dorset. Sylvester

                          Eveleth Eveleigh Yeverleigh
                          was selectman 1648 freeman
                          1652 representative 1673 his
                          wall and Perkinses (was Bru-
                          ens) Millett sold to Allen. From

then to now nothing
new, in the meaning
that that wall walked
today, happened a bull-
dozer discloses
Meeting House Hill
was a sanddune under
what was valued for
still the sun makes
a west here as on
each Gloucester hill
why one can say what
one can't say is

when did the sea so
roll over as later
the ice this stuck-out
10 miles Europe-pointing
cape, the lines of force
I said to her as of Rose-
Troup go to as one line
as taught as uroboros ar-
row hooped crazy Zen arch-
er fact that arm of bow Frances
Rose-Troup English maiden
lady told this city what

marchants Weymouth Port Book
No. 873 if East and West the
ship first employed was,
the date everything that
the local get off it Glous-
ter the old railroad joke
from the smell, the lovers
in the back seat the conductor
waking up from a snooze don't
look out the window sniffs
and calls out gloucester glous-
ter All off

       Take the top off
       Meeting House Hill
       is 128 has cut it
       on two sides

       the third
       is now no more than
       more Riverdale
       Park

       and the fourth?
       the west?
       is the rubbish
       of white man

Up River,
under the bridge
the summer people
kid themselves
there's no noise,
the Bridge
's so high.
Like hell. The Diesels
shake the sky

clean the earth
of sentimental
drifty dirty
lazy man:

bulldozer,
lay open
the sand some sea
was all over the
second third fourth
meeting house,

once. I take my air

where Eveleth walked
out the west
on these hills
because the river

it's earth which
now is strange The sea
is east The choice Our backs
turned from the sea but the smell

as the minister said
in our noses
I am interfused
with the rubbish

of creation I hear

the necessity
of the ludicrous reference to Wm Hubbard by the
tercentenary preacher that

the finny tribe come easily
to the hook

        Fishermen
are killers Every
fifty of 'em I pick off
the Records seek
the kame I was raised
on and are startled,
as I am, by each granite
morraine shape   Am in the mud
off Five Pound Island
is the grease-pit
of State Pier

        Go 'way and leave
Rose-Troup and myself   I smell your breath, sea
And unmellowed River under
the roar of A. Piatt Andrew
hung up there like fission
dropping trucks the face
Samuel Hodgkins didn't show
poling pulling I penny
per person 2
for a horse

        step off
onto the nation   The sea
will rush over   The ice
will drag boulders   Commerce
was changed the fathometer
was invented here the present
is worse give nothing now your credence
start all over step off the
Orontes onto land no Typhon
no understanding of a cave
a mystery Cashes? . . . . "but that these times of combustion
the seas throughout have hindered much that work" so sayeth

so early

Mr. Edward Johnson: "yet that there have been vessels built here at the town of late" I haven't noticed any single adult, the children however and up through 17 at least on the Fort or Fort high school men whatever hour of the day I see them even early on the Boulevard and a couple of them in uniform with rifle R.O.T.C. don't look like cowboys and English:

Stefansson's ice, what trade replaced Pytheas's sludge with, man goeth novo siberskie slovo only a Chinese feeling not Canton silk or Surinam Rose-Troup to you, Gloucester, solely gave you place in the genetic world, she said Richard Bushrod George Way etc. she put you back on the launching platform said woman said John White planter Conant said Budleigh she said Cape Ann she said dorchester company she said so much train oil   quarters of oak   skins as well as dryfish corfish   fox racons martyns otter muskuatche beaver   some even entered as 'coats' thus indicating there were Algonquins left after smallpox? It looks as though Miss Rose-Troup connects back to Champlain the number of wigwams show Freshwater Cove above Cressys in Tolmans field near Half Moon or possibly the old Steep Bank where Kent Circle   maybe it's Apple Row or Agamenticus Height

the river and marshes show clearly and no Indians along the Beach   forest on Fort Point   wigwams again at Harbor Cove in fact all up between what 1642 became the harbor and the town in other words "Washington" St to Mill River and on Fore Street to Vinsons Cove otherwise Indians about East Gloucester Square and then it's action: Champlain discovering the Indian attack to Sieur de Pountrin-court in ambush at the head of Rocky Neck, old European business as seven or eight arquebusiers   the depths of the channel more interesting as from Eastern Pt and the compass rose thus:

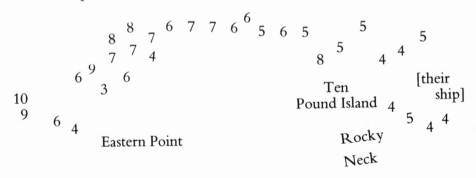

Maximus, to Gloucester, Sunday, July 19

and they stopped before that bad sculpture of a fisherman

—"as if one were to talk to a man's house,
knowing not what gods or heroes are"—

not knowing what a fisherman is
instead of going straight to the Bridge
and doing no more than—saying no more than—
in the Charybdises of the
Cut waters the flowers tear off
the wreathes

the flowers
turn
the character of the sea   The sea jumps
the fate of the flower   The drowned men are undrowned
in the eddies

of the eyes
of the flowers
opening
the sea's eyes

The disaster
is undone
What was received as alien
—the flower
on the water, that a man drowns
that he dies in water as he dies on earth, the impossible
that this gross fact can return to us
in this upset
on a summer day
of a particular tide

that the sensation is true,

that the transformations of fire are, first of all, sea—
  "as gold for wares wares for gold"

  Let them be told who stopped first
  by a bronze idol

  A fisherman is not a successful man
  he is not a famous man he is not a man
  of power, these are the damned by God

                         II

whose surface bubbles
with these gimlets
which screw-in like

potholes, caustic
caked earth of painted
pools, Yellowstone

Park of holes
is death the diseased
presence on us, the spilling lesion

of the brilliance
it is to be alive: to walk onto it,
as Jim Bridger the first into it,

it is more true a scabious
field than it is a pretty
meadow

              When a man's coffin is the sea
              the whole of creation shall come to his funeral,

              it turns out; the globe
              is below, all lapis

              and its blue surface golded
              by what happened

                    this afternoon: there are eyes
                    in this water

the flowers
from the shore,

    awakened
    the sea

                    Men are so sure they know very many things,
                    they don't even know night and day are one

                    A fisherman works without reference to
                    that difference. It is possible he also

                    by lying there when he does lie, jowl
                    to the sea, has another advantage: it is said,

'You rectify what can be rectified,' and when a man's heart
cannot see this, the door of his divine intelligence is shut

                    let you who paraded to the Cut today
                    to hold memorial services to all fishermen
                    who have been lost at sea in a year
                    when for the first time not one life was lost

                                        radar sonar radio telephone good engines
                                        bed–check seaplanes goodness over and under us

            no difference
            when men come back

April Today Main Street

As against now the Gloucester
which came late enough, April, 1642, to stick

April today Main Street the sun
was warm enough I could stay

out of the mean easterly was coming up
each cross street

from the harbor, talked to the cop
at the head of Duncan, discpvered that Joe,

the barber, had inherited the Fredericksons'
shop, that it was Mrs Galler, not the Weiners

"winers" the cigar woman and the greeting card
clerk in Sterling pronounced it

as I said her husband
they said he died

in front of her here
in the store

the street
was rife

of its hills,
and me going

with its
polyconic

character, the slipping
of Main

to Vinson's Cove,
now fill, and parking

with a baker, from Sao Paolo
where the spring

(I was surprised
to learn yesterday, that Eveleth

was a baker in Boston
in 1642, before he came and possessed

so much of Meeting House
Green) The Gloucester which held

was three power points,
three nexuses

and the General Court:
what Endecott

and Downing
divided, April that year

how a town
was created

2 mo 42
There was a stage

on Duncan's Point,
the formulary

for patent or joint
stock company stating

it was Mr Thomson's,
London merchant,

one man mentioned,
the other backers

not named, instead, intend
the Court goes on

to promote
the fishing

trade, trying to turn
Massachusetts into

the staple intended
said Smith, the Indies

lying just
offshore to be drawn up

on silk lines & glowing hooks
fishermen in palanquins, robed women

watching, holding children
on the shore, a daisy world, the silver ore

codfish. "It was ordered"
(the Company

of the Massachusetts
Bay) "that a fishing

be begun, that the said
Mr Thomson, and other necessaries

for that use, shall have sufficient lands allowed,
like railroad companies: how little,

until England
was cut off

by her own trouble (that the Scotch border
had been crossed December

1640 Winthrop
learned from that post office

of the North Atlantic, Smith's
Isles

of Shoals
within weeks) did any of them

know what it would mean
to have these mines

in their waters
to go to

to sell
to Fayal

to go to St Kitts
to take away Newfoundland

to make Spain, and Turks,
to start to make any ocean

a Yankee lake, this fellow here
named Osmund Dutch (or was William

Southmead also) but definitely
Thomas Millward (who went to

Newbury) "Slow",
Smith cried,

upon you
as he died

There is evidence
a frame

of Mr Thomson's
did

exist, Will Southmead's
ux, alia Ash, did sell

to John Jackson, John Jackson
to Peter Duncan, but I write in

the first letter (after Conant's two)
to go

home,
to England: "Me Osmundū Douch

De Capae Annae
in nova Anglia, nautā

Dat' 18. 5. 1639
presented himself and said

take this letter
to my wife

          Grace,

my love

remembered
to you

in the Lord, These
are to lett you understand

that God be praysed I am
in health heere

in this Country
and so I hope

are you together
with our Children. Seeing it hath pleased God

to bless me heere I have cleared
40 £ and shall be able

for to entertaine you
to make good provision

come over
taking such care

as to bring ... Mr. Millward
my partner, of Noddles Island

in the fishing trade
which we now are setting on"   1641: Abraham Robinson

Thomas Ashley Willm
Browne

rent a sloop
of 3 tunes, are to pay

3 £ in good and merchantable
dry fish in 3 months

—a Biskie shallop?
to go with Biskie Island?

to this hour sitting
as the mainland hinge

of the 128 bridge
now brings in

what,
to Main Street?

MAXIMUS
POEMS
IV, V, VI

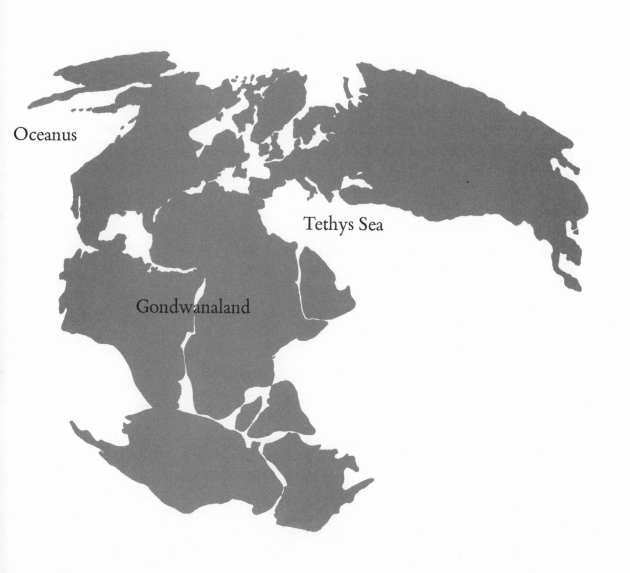

Oceanus

Tethys Sea

Gondwanaland

I owe to Alfred Wegener, and Tuzo Wilson, the basis of the cover—which is of course the Earth (and Ocean) before Earth started to come apart at the seams, some 125 million years awhile back—and India took off from Africa & migrated to Asia.

Olson, September 1968

Bet
for Bet
for
Bet

For Bet

Letter ♯ 41 [broken off]

With a leap (she said it was an arabesque
I made, off the porch, the night of the
St Valentine Day's storm, into the snow.
Nor did she fail of course to make the point
what a sight I was the size I am all over the storm
trying to be graceful Or was it? She hadn't seen me
in 19 years

Like, right off the Orontes? The Jews
are unique because they settled astride
the East African rift. Nobody else will grant
like he said the volcano anyone of us does
sit upon, in quite such a tangible fashion.
Thus surprise, when Yellowstone kicks up
a fuss

Where it says excessively rough moraine,
I count such shapes this evening in the universe
I run back home out of the new moon
makes fun of me in each puddle on the road.
The war of Africa against Eurasia
has just begun again. Gondwana

proem

The sea was born of the earth without sweet union of love Hesiod says

But that then she lay for heaven and she bare the thing which encloses
every thing, Okeanos the one which all things are and by which nothing
is anything but itself, measured so

screwing earth, in whom love lies which unnerves the limbs and by its
heat floods the mind and all gods and men into further nature

                                        Vast earth rejoices,

deep-swirling Okeanos steers all things through all things,
everything issues from the one, the soul is led from drunkenness
to dryness, the sleeper lights up from the dead,
the man awake lights up from the sleeping

        WATERED ROCK
of pasture meadow orchard road where Merry
died in pieces tossed by the bull he raised himself to fight
in front of people, to show off his
                        Handsome Sailor ism

died as torso head & limbs
in a Saturday night's darkness
drunk trying
to get the young bull down
to see if Sunday morning again he might
before the people show off
once more
his prowess – braggart man to die
among Dogtown meadow rocks

                        "under" the dish
                        of the earth
                        Okeanos under
                        Dogtown
                        through which (inside of which) the sun passes
                        at night –
                                she passes the sun back to
                        the east through her body
                        the Geb (of heaven) at night

                Nut is water
                above & below, vault
                above and below
                watered rock on which
                by which Merry
                was so many pieces
                Sunday morning

subterranean and celestial
primordial water holds
Dogtown high

                  And down
the ice holds
Dogtown, scattered
boulders little bull
who killed
Merry
          who sought to manifest
his soul, the stars
manifest their souls

                    my soft sow the roads
of Dogtown trickling like from underground rock
springs under an early cold March moon

                              or hot summer and my son
                              we come around a corner
                              where a rill
                              makes Gee Avenue in a thin
                              ford

                                after we see a black duck
                              walking across a populated
                              corner

                                  life spills out

Soft soft rock
Merry died by
in the black night

fishermen lived
in Dogtown and came
when it was old to whore
on Saturday nights
at three girls' houses

Pisces eternally swimming
inside her overhead
their boots or the horse
clashing the sedimentary
rock tortoise shell
she sits on the maternal beast
of the moon and the earth

Not one mystery
nor man
possibly not even a bird
heard Merry
fight that bull by
(was Jeremiah Millett's house

Drunk
to cover his shame,
blushing Merry
in the bar
walking up

to Dogtown to try
his strength,
the baby bull
now full grown

waiting,
not even knowing
death
was in his power over
this man who lay
in the Sunday morning sun
like smoked fish
in the same field
fly-blown and a colony
of self-hugging grubs – handsome
in the sun, the mass
of the dead and the odor
eaten out of the air
by the grubs sticking
moving by each other
as close as sloths

she is the goddess
of the earth, and night
of the earth and fish
of the little bull
and of Merry

Merry
had a wife

She is the heavenly mother
the stars are the fish swimming
in the heavenly ocean she has
four hundred breasts

Merry could have used
as many could have drunk
the strength he claimed
he had, the bravo

Pulque in Spain
where he saw the fight
octli in Mexico
where he wanted to
show off
dead in Gloucester
where he did

The four hundred gods
of drink alone
sat with him
as he died
in pieces

In 400 pieces
his brain shot
the last time the bull
hit him pegged him
to the rock

        before he tore him
to pieces

        the night sky
looked down

Dogtown is soft
in every season
high up on her granite
horst, light growth
of all trees and bushes
strong like a puddle's ice
the bios
of nature in this
park of eternal
events is a sidewalk
to slide on, this
terminal moraine:

the rocks the glacier tossed
toys
Merry played by
with his bull

        400 sons of her only
        would sit
        by the game

        All else was in the sky
        or in town
        or shrinking solid rock

        We drink
        or break open
        our veins solely
        to know. A drunkard
        showing himself in public
        is punished
        by death

        The deadly power of her
        was there that night
        Merry was born
        under the pulque-sign

The plants of heaven
the animals of the soι
were denied

Joking men
had laughed
at Merry

Drink
had made him
brave

Only the sun
in the morning
covered him
with flies

Then only
after the grubs
had done him
did the earth
let her robe
uncover and her part
take him in

ALL MY LIFE I'VE HEARD ABOUT
MANY

He went to Spain,
the handsome sailor,
he went to Ireland
and died of a bee:
he's buried, at the hill
of KnockMany

He sailed to Cashes
and wrecked on that ledge,
his ship vaulted
the shoal, he landed
in Gloucester: he built a castle
at Norman's Woe

A NOTE ON THE ABOVE

         a Maximus song
         the sirens sang:
         he stopped his
         ears with caulking
         compound he listened
         he travelled
         he went he passed
         he went in and out of wood
         the bugs sang grand
         birds led him on a
         paradise alley (some country roads
         have trees growing and the road
         turns in such a way it is special,
         for a few feet

the Sea – turn yr Back on
the Sea, go inland, to
Dogtown: the Harbor

the shore the City
are now
shitty, as the Nation

is – the World
tomorrow unless
the Princes

of the Husting the sons
who refused to be Denied
the Demon (if Medea

kills herself – Medea
is a Phoenician
wench, also Daughter

of the Terror) as J-son
Johnson Hines
son Hines

sight Charles
John Hines
Ol'
    son

the Atlantic
Mediterranean
Black Sea time

is done in done for gone
Jack Hammond
put a stop to

surface underwater galaxy
time: there is no sky
space or sea left

earth is interesting:
ice is interesting
stone is interesting

flowers are
      Carbon
Carbon is
Carboniferous
Pennsylvania

Age
under
Dogtown
the stone

the watered
rock Carbon
flowers, rills

Aquarian Time
after fish
– fish was

Christ o Christ pick the seeds
out of yr teeth – how handsome
the dead dog lies! (horror X

the Migma is where the
Seeds Christ was supposed to pick out
: Wyngaershoek hoik Grape Vine HOYK the Dutch

& the Norse
and Algonquins:
He-with-the-House-on-his-Head

she-who-Lusted After-the
Snake-in-the-Pond
Dogtown berries smell

as The-Grub-Eaten-Fish-Take-the-Smell-Out-of-The
Air a e r the Ta of
Dogtown   (the Ta metarsia

is the Angel Matter
not to come until (rill!
3000: we will carry water

up the hill the Water the Water to
make the Flower hot – Jack
& Jill will

up Dogtown hill on top one day the
Vertical American Thing will
show from heaven the Ladder

come down to the Earth
of Us All, the Many who
know
      there is One!
      One Mother
      One Son

One Daughter
and Each the Father
of Him-Her-Self:

the Genetic
is Ma the Morphic
is Pa the City is Mother-

Polis, the Child-Made-Man-Woman is

(Mary's Son
Elizabeth's

Man) MONOGENE:
                    in COLLAGEN
the monogene, / in KOLLAgen

                                                       LEAP onto
                                                the LAND, the AQUARIAN
                                                TIME

                  TIME

the greater the water you add
the greater the decomposition
so long as the agent is protein
the carbon of four is the corners

in stately motion to sing in high bitch voice the fables
of wood and stone and man and woman loved

and loving in the snow
and sun
                  the weather

      on Dogtown
        is protogonic but the other side of heaven
        is Ocean

filled in the flower the weather
on Dogtown the other side of heaven
is Ocean

Dogtown the under
vault heaven
is Carbon Ocean
is Annisquam   Dogtown the under
                             vault – the 'mother'
                             rock: the Diamond (Coal) the Pennsylvanian

                                             Age   the soft
                                             (Coal) LOVE

Age   the soft (Coal love
hung-up   burning
under the City: bituminous

Heart to be turned to Black
Stone   the Black Chrysanthemum
is the Throne of Creation   Ocean

                  is the Black Gold Flower

Maximus,
to himself,
as of "Phoenicians":

        the fylfot
        she look like
        who called herself
        luck: *svas-*

        tika BREAK HER up as the lumber
        was broken up in the screw The mess of it astern
        And the ship NOT the vessel NOT fall like dead
        in the water

        NO LONGER
        the dead of winter be
        the birth time.
        THE SKIPPER

        – out. Luck, out. Ling,
        OUT (why was she put up with,
        so long? let in,
        at all? The SWASTIKA

        broken up: the padma
        is what was there BEFORE
        one was. Is there. Will be. Is what ALL
        issues from: The GOLD

        flower All the heavens,
        a few miles up – and even with the sun out –
        is BLACK

                        written on Dogtown,
                        December 22, 1959

For "Moira"

TO HELLWITH, like
– & UP heimarmene the
warmth of Moira
the hand of Isis which
unweavest even the inextricably tangled
web of fate, assuages
any of us ("buried in us to
assuage") & puts the stars
to rights

    (get up off the ass,
    the ever-rutting animal hateful
    to Isis

Maximus further on (December 28th 1959)

ffisherman's FIELD'S rocks with Gen Douglas lying
(having swum from Cressy's out to, with her sister) a kelp
ledge bed split when the rock cooled perhaps water
boiled it the bed of kelp for us to lie on quarter low-tide off
Hammond's

                afternoon Manatee of my mind? Rock picture
of a beast? Lausel woman, holding out a ladle? Actually
sluggish treadle up which nature
climbed Wet white body dried Old picture Andromeda
awash Norn nurse waitress
                          dugong
                          crying
                          on the rock

                    to be delivered
                    of her child
                    restored

the Impossible Rock Perseus the Husband not me

I come back to the geography of it,
the land falling off to the left
where my father shot his scabby golf
and the rest of us played baseball
into the summer darkness until no flies
could be seen and we came home
to our various piazzas where the women
buzzed

To the left the land fell to the city,
to the right, it fell to the sea

I was so young my first memory
is of a tent spread to feed lobsters
to Rexall conventioneers, and my father,
a man for kicks, came out of the tent roaring
with a bread-knife in his teeth to take care of
a druggist they'd told him had made a pass at
my mother, she laughing, so sure, as round
as her face, Hines pink and apple,
under one of those frame hats women then

This, is no bare incoming
of novel abstract form, this

is no welter or the forms
of those events, this,

Greeks, is the stopping
of the battle

        It is the imposing
of all those antecedent predecessions, the precessions

of me, the generation of those facts
which are my words, it is coming

from all that I no longer am, yet am,
the slow westward motion of

more than I am

There is no strict personal order

for my inheritance.

        No Greek will be able

to discriminate my body.

           An American

is a complex of occasions,

themselves a geometry

of spatial nature.

        I have this sense,

that I am one

with my skin

        Plus this – plus this:

that forever the geography

which leans in

on me I compell

backwards I compell Gloucester

to yield, to

change

        Polis

is this

                    Into
In the fiord the diorite man obtrudes Obadiah Bruen's
island on his nose. Into the granite this inlet
of the sea to poke and jam the Cut and fight
the sand off and the yelping rocks, the granite
he rolls as Dogtown throws its pebbles and Merry
lay among them, busted
                              True inclusions
of other rocks are not commonly met with,
in the granitic material, the mass of diorite
is apparently of an irregularly circular form.
On all sides where the rocks outcrop,
it is surrounded by granitite, the two entrances
of the Reach being the only places
where it possibly have cut. These entrances
are narrow, and are bounded on either side
by granitite which is not porphyritic,
which facts almost exclude the hypothesis
that the diorite has cut the granitite.

The River – 2

            the diorite
            with the granite
            of the Poles

             – &
            the
            Basin
            (fiord, the overlapping, both ways:

            up and down and the Closed Wrinkle,

            Open

                    she was the first one
                    to tear off
                    her girdle
                    to expiate
                    –like. The other,
                    who did it to make up for
                    what had been done to
                    Negroes (born
                    in Texas

                    a third for

any man,
no man
to be deprived of, as
she did take it her father was
by her mother a
cold-fucking
speech-making
political kind,
of woman. Her father
an electrical
engineer. An Engine,
her.

The Poimanderes: now I see what was up,
a year ago, chomping around these streets,
measuring off distances, looking into
records, disconsolately
making up things to do – finding myself peeing
under a thin new moon on Dogtown and noticing
rills in the March night

Dogtown   the   dog   town
of the mother city   the C-
city :   METRO –
POLIS

Cashes

I tell you it's cruel. There was the Rattler, pitchpoled
over Cashe's Shoals at midnight some thirteen years ago
in a gale of wind, and came right side up and got into
port safe with every man on board

No ship can live on Cashe's in a storm. Sailing either side
a quarter of a mile and there is sixty or seventy fathom of
room but right on the shoals, which is only a few rod across,
the water isn't much over twenty feet deep. Only smaller
vessels can go over in calm weather. It's so shallow kelp
grows on top of the water and when there's a blow and the
big seas come in, a hundred feet of water chopping down on
the bottom, it's a bad place

The Rattler was headed along down the coast from Newfoundland
loaded with frozen herring. The night was black and the captain
was off his reckoning, leastways the first thing any one knew
a big sea lifted the vessel and pitched her forward. She struck
her nose on the bottom and just then another big one struck her
fair in the stern and lifted the stern clean over the bow. Her
masts struck and snapped off. With that, she went over the shoals
and floated in deep water on the other side, fair and square on
her keel even though both masts were broke off to within fifteen
feet of her deck.

The crew of course was down below. They said it was all over be-
fore they knew what was up. They didn't sense it at all at first.
They said all it was they were sitting there and then they struck
the deck then came down again in a heap on the floor. They got up
on deck, dazed-like, and there she was, a complete wreck.

The man at the wheel was lashed but he said afterwards when he felt
her go over he thought it was all up with him. He held on for dear
life and never lost his grip as he went through the water. But it's
a terrible strain on a man and he was pretty nigh gone. They took
him below and did all they could for him and after they got into
port he was laid up for a long time. He did finally come around
all right.

It was about the narrowest escape ever heard of for a vessel. They
had a fair wind on the lee side of the shoal, the current was in
their favor so they worked their way off and finally fell in with
a vessel which towed them home.

The facts in the case are as described. The man who owned the ves-
sel was Andrew Leighton of Gloucester, and the captain who sailed
her was named Bearse.

like   Mr. Pester acknowledges his sinfulness in being
at the Potter's house, saying: "I was invited
by Prid et ux^r & Jno Stone & his wyfe & was att
Stons hous from whence we weare fetched to y^e
Potters." Benjamin Felton deposed being at Mr.
Pester's. Prid said "he was att Plimoth & it
was after I came fr Plimoth y^t he was invited
by vincen: & he was ther in my absence. Prid
also witnessed it was att diner y^t himself in-
vited by w^m Vincen." Goody Hardy deposed: "I
saw m^r Pester his hos unfastened betweene 8 and
9 in morning & he seemed to me as if he had Laine
all night ther." Goody Felton and Goody Pride
also deposed. Moon rose about eleven or twelve
o'clock at night. Left Goody Vincent there, and
Mr. Pester and nobody else. Wm Vincen and Hary
Weare left the house at eight o'clock. This was
about Nov. 2.

Of old times, there was a very beautiful
woman, and she turned all heads
of men. She married,
and her husband died
soon after. She took another,
and he died. Within a single year,
she had five, and they all died, and they were
the cleverest, and handsomest,
there were. And she married, again. The sixth,
was such a silent man he passed
for a fool, but he was wiser
than people thought and he figured
to find out what was up,
with this woman. He watched her,
all the time, he kept his eye on her,
day and night.

It was summer,
and she proposed that they go into the woods,
and camp there, to pick berries. When they were in,
she had the idea he go ahead
and pick the spot and he allowed
he would, only he doubled back,
and watched her, from there out. As soon as she believed
that he was gone she went rapidly
on. He followed, unseen, until she came
to a pond among rocks in a deep wild place
in the woods. She sat down and sang a song, a great foam
or froth rose to the surface and in it appeared the back and tail
of a great serpent, an immense beast. The woman
who had taken off her clothes, embraced
the creature, which twined around her, winding inside
her arms and legs, until her body was one mass
of his.

The husband,
watched it all, saw that the serpent
let go his venom into her and that this
was what she was passing on to her husbands, to live
by transferring it to others, and he passed swiftly
to the camping ground and built
a place for the night. He laid two beds,
and built a fire. His wife came. She was in earnest
that they sleep together, he bade her sternly
to lie by herself. She laid down,
and went to sleep. Three times,
during the night, he got up
to replenish the fire. Each time
he called her but she did not
answer. In the morning he shook her,
and she was dead. They sunk her in the pond
where the snake lived.

They said she went off fucking every Sunday.
Only she said she walked straight through
the mountain, and who fucked her was the spirit
of that mountain.

A <u>Maximus</u>

As of why thinking of why such questions as security, and the great white
death, what did obtain at said some such point as Bowditch the Practical
Navigator who did use Other People's Monies as different from his Own,
isn't the Actuarial the ReaL Base of Life Since, and is different From
Usury Altogether, is the Thing which made all the Vulgar Socialization
(Socialism CulturiSM LiberalISM jass is gysm) why I Don't Haven't Gotten
it all Further?

Pound, a person of the poem

Ferrini

Hammond

Stevens

(Griffiths)

John Smith

                                                                fish
Conants
                                                            ships
Higginsons

Bowditch   Lew Douglas   fishermen
                  Carl Olsen
Hawkinses   Walter Burke

John Burke   houses

John White   finance
John Winthrop
                                        wood (<u>ekonomikos</u>
                                sculpture

marine
architecture

the plum
the flower
                                        The Renaissance a
                                        box

                                        the economics & poetics
                                        thereafter

        the   God" – Agyasta?
Cosmos "Savage   primitive ("buttocks   the prior
                                        etc

a coast
is not the same
as land
a coast
is not the main
a coast means
travel by horse
along beaches from
Saco south
via Ipswich to,
crossing Annisquam,
Gloucester
or by shallop
(long boat) across
Ipswich Bay
as such the Thatchers,
minister preparing to teach
Marblehead fishermen
got wrecked going
fr the settlement at Ipswich
didn't make it around
north promontory of
Cape Ann. A shore
life. At the time a frontier, woods
and Indians, Pennacooks
from Saco south, Abnaki
from Casco Bay north.
How much shore
so many fishermen
scalped, and schooners
taken, from Cape La Have
and particularly Cape Sable,
westward Fox Island,
massacre Casco, the Wakleys
south of Freeport
Arthur Mackworth
then the Gloucester founders
founding again Portland
driven out twice
and back 'home'
because Cape Ann
no Indians
after the plague:
'safe' (as wasn't
for Champlain, when 200
here, 1606 – under
Quihamenec, brother
of Chief Olmechin
of Saco: able
  Algonquin
  leaders

The same weave
of interlocking

pieces, La Have
to Dogtown in
properties sold
and cross
marriaging:

Nathaniel Wharf
whose mother was
a Mackworth
bought of Josselyn
whose mother was a Cammock
and next door on Washington
at entrance of Gee –
– or Stanwood was cut
through to make Back Road
1717 – had as neighbor William Tucker
whose grandfather was the disposer
with George Cleave of all of Portland land
direct from Gorges

or Capt Andrew Robinson
whose sister Ann
with husband Davis
of Casco Isaac
opened Dogtown
on Gee / is buried
at South Thomaston because
he fought Indians so
successfully Massachusetts
put him up
against Father Lauverjat
and French Atlantic Power
gave way and went
with Cardinal Richlieu
out of future
North American
affair

          one interlocking line
was coast what Eastward
meant Eastward from
Cape Ann

          force down
try out   go down there
to Cape Sable
for fish to Casco
(Falmouth) to
make a new town

                              Ingersolls
                              Rider
                              Wakeleys
                              Coes

Riverdale Dogtown
proprietors
of New Gloucester

these few (1699
40 fishermen says the Frenchman
traveler (like English
on plains 19th
century making drawings
carrying elephant guns
making safari with
mountain men)

and the worst still
to come: war
   with French
   and Indians
   all along sd coast
   until Norridgewock
   1724 wiped out – and Father Rasles
   dead among his notes

in sd period sd schooner
invented and fishing
starts anew 100 years
after Stage Fort
  (what John Winter
  had made do
  at Richmond's
  Island Gloucester
  began to make
  happen, as coast
  fishing
      – Banks
  were first born
  as coast
– fishing,
  to Eastward

with danger
  <u>Indians!</u> imagine
  fishing
  and Indians:
  William Pulsifer
  of John Pulsifer
  who first opened
  land where
  Jones Creek
  turns closest
  to diorite
  edge of meeting
  with granite
escaped home
and whenever heard
by accident someone
say Indian wld bound
off into woods and hide
for days
in shock
because
had watched

5
of rest of crew

of vessel
scalped
on fishing voyage
to the Eastward

all this
what was once
imperial
European
nations
finding
future history
from Portuguese
fishing grounds
under nose
of ice
turned
in century
to domestic
horror: farm boys
going
fishing
and –––––––––
    –––––––––
    –––––––––
    –––––––––

the information of Mr Richard Yorke,
of Gloucester, taken June 22, 1713,
sayeth that on Tuesday being
the 2d day of this instant June
being at Cape Sable in a sloop
on a fishing voyage and in
a harbour called the Owl's
Head, with my sloop, and Mr
John Prince, of said Gloucester, lying
by me with his sloop, there
came down to the water side,
about three of the clock in the
afternoon, two Indian men dressed
in French clothing, with a kind
of white flag on a stick,
and called to us and desired
us to come on shore, and said
they had news to tell us and
showed a paper which they
said they had from Colonel
Vetch, at Port Royal;
and we desired them
to come on board
our vessel, and they said
they had no cause and could
not come, and after
some considerable discourse
with them, one of my men
and one of Mr Prince's
went ashore to them in
a canoe, as namely, James
Davis and Josiah Ingersoll,

who carried a gun with
them in sd canoe, and
when they came to the shore
the sd Indians came to them
and told the Indians that
it was peace; and the Indians
said, so it was, or to that purpose,
and shook hands with the men,
and said "Now Indians
and Englishmen
all own brother" they seeing
the gun in the bottom of
the canoe asked why,
for, said they "we have no
guns" and would have had
the men throw their gun
overboard. The men told them
they would not hurt them with
it. Said Indians desired
them to go on board and fetch
them some rum and tobacco. The said men
asked the Indians to go on board
with them, but they would not,
except that one of them (fisherman)
would stay on shore,
and then one of the Indians
would go on board; but
neither of these two men
were willing to stay
so they came on board
and told us that the
Indians desired to have
some rum and tobacco,
then two other of our men
went into the canoe to
go on shore – namely
Paul Dolliver and John
Sadler, and I gave them
a small pound of tobacco
to carry and give them
and had them carry
a bottle (of rum) with them,
which they did and when
they came to the shore,
one of the English,
as, namely, John Sadler
went out of the canoe
and an Indian came with the other
man on board, and as they
came the Indians kept
singing until he got on
board and when he was
got on board he said
"now all good friends", and asked
who was the skipper,
and when they told him,
said Indian came and showed

me a paper, but it was so much
worn and dusted that we
could not read it so as to make
sense of it, but supposed
it might be a pass, for the said
Indian said he had it from
Governor Vetch, and we found
in it these words, " be kind to
the Indians", and after
same Indian had been on board
a little while the Englishman
that was left on shore,
called on board and bade
us bring the canoe on
shore, and said the other
Indian would come
on board; then two
of our men as namely
Paul Dolliver and James
Davis went into the canoe
to go on shore, and when
they came off the shore
they saw two Indians
with the Englishman
and they asked them
if they would go on
board, and they said
"No", but bade them go
and fetch the Indian
on shore that was
on board, and they
came on board again
and told us that
the Indians would
not come on board,
but would have the Indian
that was on board
to come on shore.
Then James Davis
and one Josiah Lane
went to set said
Indian on shore
and to bring off the
Englishman, and as soon
as they came to the shore,
the Indian went out of
the canoe, and, as the
said Josiah Lane tells
me, they went to set the
canoe off, but the Indians
laid hold of the painter
to stop them, and the other
two Indians came and laid
hold of the painter also, and they hauled
the canoe up on shore; with that
two of the Englishmen, as namely, James Davis
and Josiah Lane, skipt out of the canoe

into the water to swim on board, but one
of the Indians came into the water and caught
said James Davis immediately and brought him
on shore, and the other two Indians went
with the canoe after Josiah Lane, and
when they came up with him one
of the Indians took his hatchet
and seemed as if he was going
to strike at him, but did not
but took hold of him and hauled
him on shore, and when they came
on shore there were several more
Indians that were come out
of the bushes with their guns,
and when they got the said
three Englishmen together they
sett them down, as said
Josiah Lane informed me,
and said they would carry them
to Port Royal

———————————

James Davis, captured

III Josiah Ingersoll,
    prob. Samuel II's
    son, who m. Mary Stevens
      Dec 30, 1712

Paul Dolliver
    m. Mary Wallis
        Feb 11, 1713!
    – Freshwater Cove
    (died c. 1749)
    cf page 87 before:
came from Cornwall direct
      abt 1710

John Sadler, captured

& Josiah Lane: captured
    III:
       m. 1713

            & Dolliver
4 of these men – Ingersoll, Lane & Sadler   just married

the 5th, James Davis, is probably the James IV of Squam (son of
                                       Lieut James III
    (1690-1776) who m. Mary Harraden in 1719

chockablock

Once a man was traveling through the woods, and
he heard some distance off a sound of feet beat-
ing the ground. He went to find the people who
made the sound, and it was a full week before
he came to them. It was a man and his wife danc-
ing around a tree in the top of which was a rac-
coon. By their constant treading they had worn
a trench in the ground, and were in it up to their
waists. When the man asked them why they did it
they said they were hungry and they were trying
to dance the tree down to catch the raccoon.

Now the man told them there was a better way to
fell a tree, a new way, and he showed them how to
cut it down. In return for which he asked the skin
if they had the meat of the raccoon. So they tanned
it and off he went.

Another distance, in the path in the forest, he
met another man who was carrying his house on his
head. He was frightened at first but the man put
his house down and shook hands with him, and while
they had a smoke together, and talked, the man
noticed the raccoon skin and asked where he got
it. He told him, from the dancing man and his wife.

This was enough to get the other started. He offered
him anything for the skin and finally the house. Look-
ing it over our man was delighted to find it had so
many rooms and such good furniture. But he said I
never could carry it as you do. Yes, sd the man who
belonged somewhere else, just try it, and he found he
could, it was as light as a basket.

So he went off carrying his house until night when
he came to a hard-wood ridge near a good spring of
water and put it down. Inside was a wide bed covered
with a white bear-skin, and it was very soft, and he
was tired and he slept very well. In the morning, it
was even better. Hanging from the beams were deer-
meat, hams, duck, baskets of berries and maple sugar,
and as he reached out for them the rug itself melted
and it was white snow, and his arms turned into wings
and he flew up to the food and it was birch-boughs on
which it hung, and he was a partridge and it was spring.

I forced the calm grey waters, I wanted her
to come to the surface I had fought her,
long enough, below. I shaped her out of
the watery mass

and the dragger, cleaning its fish,
idled into
the scene, slipped across the empty water
where I had placed
the serpent, staring as hard as
I could (to make the snow
turn back to snow, the autos
to come to their
actual size, to stop
being smaller,
and far away. The sea does
contain the beauty I had looked at
until the sweat
stood out in my eyes. The wonder is
limitless, of my own term, the compound
to compound until the beast rises from the sea.

Maximus, March 1961 – 1

Maximus, March 1961 – 2

             by the way into the woods

Indian   otter
"Lake"   ponds   orient

   show me   (exhibit
   myself)

The Account Book of B Ellery

vessels
goods
voyages
persons
salaries
conveyances

A Maximus Song

thronged

to the seashore

to see Phryne

walk into

the water

March 6, 1961

from
the Diadem,

"morning"
after

God the Dog,

of the 1st
Angel – who
Adores. Only after
was there a "Soul"
of the World – nafs
the Anima
Mundi, Bred of a Dog's
Admirer. Than which
We Are

        hangs
the 7 Angels of the 3rd Angel's
  Sleep – the 7
Words

       as His Tongue
  Hangs, dropping
Eternal Events
        the Salivarating

Dog

****

March 12. 1961

for Robt Duncan,
who understands
what's going on
– written because of him
      March 17, 1961

to go up & around Gravel Hill the road goes SE to
Jeremiah Millett's (which is my other kame)

and precisely by where his house was shoots NE passing,
on the north side, my personal 'orchard'
where I wrote with a crab-apple branch
                                    at my 'writing' stand-
stump for Michael McClure (after Don Allen
and Charles Peter and David Cummings and I
ran into the pile of rotting fish – fish!
on Dogtown viz. rotting in the rills
and on Jeremiah Millett's field,
on the kame (as my life 'rotted', sd Edward Dahlberg
on my own field, assaulting my mother
because she gave me the pork chops – Edward
glaring out of his one good eye to register
his notice of the preference) "spoiling"
me – la! The which I do here record
for eternity no less, lest it be lost, that
a mother is a hard thing to get away from;
and those who interfere, in the pure sense
–Wordsworth be with me in this line,
whose Preface is a 'walker' for us all
who wld leave art and justice behind,
leave Edward Dahlberg strewn on his own
wires
              The next important spot is Benjamin
Kinnicum's (fr before 1717, then five
very rocky acres, 1717) who married my
other writer of these woods and paths,
another Englishman, non-poet, John
Josselyn via his brother's son's daughter
Margaret: what a crazy early settlement
this road into the woods did have, of such
as Josselyns: John first observed (after
the strawberries all sd early colonists like Higginson
did note) he
              ⟋see below add from Josselyn⟍

BK's a 'hero' of my work (as, on the other – North-
road, the one went to the woodlots, I shall
celebrate Ann Robinson and her husband Samuel
Davis who settled Dogtown first of all, first
before even Kinnicum: Sam'l Davis was at
the muddy place on the N road just where it goes sharply NE towards its
2nd rise, 6¼ acres 1713: that the date
of the origin of my 2nd 'town'.

                    Kinnicum
and Davis lie on a transverse line directly N & S of each other,
and each road beyond their respective homes
is the small areas made the life of the place
for the 50-60 years it was an overlook
of the Gulf of Maine
                         and the Province
of Massachusetts way down to
La Have (between La Have and Lunenberg,
Nova Scotia falls into tidal rivers
and meadows on which we saw fish
being cured 1960 as Gloucester's Meeting House
Green & estuary of Annisquam was
when fishing was to Gloucester as fishing
was to Europe, then: green fields
to dry the silver wealth in steady
sweetening sun
                    So small the areas are
the distances are 2500 feet from Kinnicum's
to Wm Smallmans, and 1000 feet from Widow
Davis's (1741) to James Marsh   /in 1727
the North road is characterized by Joshua
Elwell's house, between the Davis house and
– what the record says – the way leading by
Joshua Elwell's to, the wood-lots, divided
1721. My problem is how to make you believe
these persons, who lived here then, and from these roads
went off to fish or bought their goods 1 mile and a half
further north, at George Dennison's store, or were
mariners – sailors – and a few farmers (though farming
was pasturing, and actually the older generation's
use of Dogtown before these younger persons chose
to live there) so far some of them went one, John Adams
was the name he took – actually born Alexander Smith
on the Backroad, was with Christian mate when sd crew
busted Bligh and sd Smith of Dogtown's people
now breed in New Hebrides –
                         but this is romantic
stuff I promised never to leave life riding on,
as Pegasus poetry was when Hector was not yet seen
to be cut from under muthos, lovely lying muthos
we breed again right out of our cunt-loving cock-sucking mouths,
who breed now when species has replaced man
and nature's gone away to furnaces men shoot
bodies into, and our love is for ourselves alone
I walk you paths of lives I'd share with
you simply to make evident the world
is an eternal event and this epoch solely
the decline of fishes, such a decline Bayliss,
my son calls her his first teacher, suggested
to her husband Gorton's have an aquarium
to show what fish look like – or it was already said
it won't be long, with fish sticks, pictures

will be necessary on the covers of the TV dinners
to let children know that mackerel is a different
looking thing than herrings

o John Josselyn you

"on the coast of Maine
 shop-keepers there are none,
 being supplied by the Massachusetts
 merchants, with all things
 they stand in need of;
 keeping here and there
 fair magazines stored with
 English goods; but they set
 excessive prices on them:
 if they do not gain cent
 per cent they cry out
 they are losers. The fishermen
 take yearly upon the coasts
 many hundred quintals
 of cod hake polluck,
 which they split, salt and
 dry at the stages, making
 three voyages in a year"

o Josselyn you noticer

"When they share their fish
(which is at the end of every voyage)
they separate the best from
the worst, the first they call

209

[II.39]

merchantable fish, being sound
full grown fish and well made
up; which is known when it is
clear like a Lanthorn horn
and without spots, the second sort
they call refuse fish, that is such as
is salt burnt, spotted, rotten and
carelessly ordered; these they put off
to the Massachusetts merchants:
    the merchantable for thirty
and two reals a quintal;
the merchants sends the merchantable
fish to Lisbourne, Bilbo, Burdeaux,
Marsiles, Toulon, Rochel, Roan
and other cities of France, to the
Canaries with clav-board and pipe-
staves which is there and at the Charibs
a prime commodity; the refuse fish
they put off at the Charib-islands,
Barbadoes, Jamaica etc, who feed
their negroes with it. To every shallop
belong four fishermen, a master
(or steersman), a midshipman,
a foremastman, and a shore
man who washes it out of the salt
and dries it upon hurdles pitcht
upon stakes breast high and tends
their cookery; they often get
in one voyage 8 or 9 £ a man for
their shares; but it doth some of them
little good, for the merchant, to
increase his gains by putting off
his commodity in the midst of their
voyages and at the end thereof,
comes in with a walking tavern,
a bark laden with the legitimate
blood of the rich grape which they bring
from Fayal, Madera, Canaries, with
brandy, rhum, the Barbadoes strong water
and tobacco; coming ashore he gives them
a taste or two, which so charms them that
for no persuasions that their employers can
use will they go out to sea, although fair
and seasonable weather for two or three
days, nay sometimes a whole week, till
they are wearied with drinking, taking ashore
two or three hogheads of wine and rum
to drink off when the merchant is gone. . . .
When the day of payment comes
they may justly complain of this
costly sin of drunkenness for their shares

will do no more than pay the reckoning;
if they save a quintal or two to buy
shooes and stockins, shirts and wastcoats
with, tis well, other-wages they must
enter into the merchants books for
such things as they stand in need off,
becoming thereby the merchants slaves
and when it riseth to a big
sum are constrained to mortgage
their plantation if they have any"

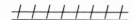

Further Completion of Plat

Lt James Davis 14 acres 1717 and to share 4
more 1728/9 with his son-in-law James
Stanwood – all on the east side of the lower
road, defining therefore that stretch: the first
10 acres, May 23, 1717, are "of land and Rocks
between Joseph Ingarsons and Bryants."
Ingarson Ingersoll, and Bryant tied, as
Smallman, and James Stanwood is to be,
to Falmouth (Portland's) rearising

                                        James Demerit,
the other later surviving one, with Ingersoll,
on the E side altogether – to Smallmans –
married Mary Briant and seems therefore
(as James Stanwood) to have come on,
as the fishermen and mariners did, to take over
earlier pasture uses of this higher land
up above Mill River. For, besides James Davis
his brother Ebenezer, and James' own son Elias,
also had acres, intermingled with John Day's
and Ezekiel Days',

                    and as the Days, but
as ship-owners, at the head of Mill River the Davises
were, like Captain Andrew Robinson, evidence how
quickly fishing came up in the 1st quarter of
the 18th century. And flushed their children
into Dogtown. Ebenezer died in 1732 leaving £ 3047
and Elias, coming on so fast the guess is he
was to be the strongest man in Gloucester, died
at 40 and already at sd age was worth

        £4500

with a wharf at Canso (a fishing room);
and 6 schooners,

John, Mary, Molly, Flying Horse
& 3/4s of Greyhound and Elizabeth

            [More on Joseph Ingersoll
to follow; and on the other side of the lower road,
Deacon Joseph Winslow, who bought from his father-in-law
Day, in 1724

A Prayer, to the Lord, cast down like a good old Catholic,
on the floor of San Vitale, next to Dante's tomb, in the
midst of the mast/bast of the construction

                                    so I can get on with it,
my great White Cadillac driving through Dogtown

                              March 28, 1961

fr Cape Sable into the stream in
Gloucester Harbor in 14 hours
& 25 minutes – the Nannie
C. Bohlin September 30, 1893,
225 sea-miles   or average of
15½ knots per hour. Under
both topsails, & each sail rove
flat as a yacht's

Bohlin 1

Bohlin 2

Bohlin
hove to, once
loaded down
with pickled herring,
in barrels – & with more
lashed on deck:

  all having breakfast
  with their boots on
  from the boards
  being sprung: Mr Bohlin

    did not believe in a vessel
    until her 3 inches of oak planking
    is loosened up

imagine if Bohlin had sailed
the Lady of Good Voyage
or his own Bohlin instead
of Dr Stimson's in
the ocean race

   he'd a rolled down a hill
   in a snow storm
   to arrive at the bottom
   where his vessel was moored

Gee, what I call the upper road was the way
leading by Joshua Elwell's to the wood-lots
1727

and Cherry or the lower road was, 1725, the way that
leads from the town to Smallmans now Dwelling house

B. Ellery   Cinvat Bridge   aer

what did Stevens do if he didn't make ships? as late
as 1667, when signing the oath asked of all Americans then
to pledge allegiance to a new English king, Stevens
is listed as ship carpenter

                                  no 'wharf' as such
is known to have been his

                                      tho his descendents
all come to play a leading part in the
life of the Harbor – especially his great-
granddaughter Susanna who became the mother
of David and William Pearce – Stevens,
tho the leading citizen, is all over the
Cut: was, then, the "Beach" his
private graving yard? or did he
build at all? The question has
that power in it, that previously to coming
to Gloucester this man had built the largest
ship then known in England – and had been
so desirable Spain's spies had sought to
buy him, as they had earlier tried to John Hawkins

           he would have lived a life as large as
John Winthrop Jr also refused

                             but even colonially
Stevens dwindled, on the face of the record
I'm not sure he did   He lived here on the front
of the city 40 years, until the day
he ran away, age 70, to wherever he
did go

          The question stays: what did he
do? did he contract vessels for out of
Gloucester? what was ship-building, if
Stevens did build, to bind his coming to the later act
of Andrew Robinson – or Ingersolls and
Sanders? It stays, that not after so much
of a break in time, the type of vessel
which changed fishing from that point on
was built or invented in Gloucester

          One wld say, not out of thin air.
1713, a schooner. 1693 Stevens dies,
a ship builder. In those 20 years the
Ingersolls the Sanders and Robinson are
continuing ship building. Was Stevens not the
head of something – the winning thing –
got hidden all the years?

Bailyn shows sharp rise
shipbuilding Gloucester: in 1706
its production amounted to 17.3
per cent of the registered vessels
and 12.8 per cent of the tonnage
produced in that year by towns in the
Bay Colony whose names were specified

But these are not her fishermen: average
tonnage is 46.4: the schooner

             or then still
called 'sloop' or ketch (William Baker,
1962, is of the opinion
what Robinson did do, 1713 was
to fit the long known two-masted fore-
and-aft rig – the Dutch fore and
main mast combination – to
a typical ketch hull (though Gloucester records

1702 show Nathaniel Sanders buying twelve trees,
and they to be oak of the town, for the sloop he is building,
and the same year, December, his brother Thomas building
likewise a Sloop for the Parsonses.

23 School and 16 Columbia:
myrtle and violets. and wood.

————————

the bottom
            backward
(of
    the sea (grounds

fish eat on   cod bred in winter in

Massachusetts bay, went off shore

with spring   then Georges with winter

again

            ice had dropped

Banks in the water, kame of the bottom, fish orchards and gardens,

                                                    tenements

messuages of the billions of generations of halibut paralleled

settlers' lives

            where fish go, **after**

and Danish cylinders now descend to measure

paleontological times when figureheads from East India brigantines

sat in formal gardens so that old maids held their stomachers

running as girls on Pearce Street

            the Atlantic is a bottomed

Pacific

            I stand on Main Street like the Diorite

stone

Jl 17 1961

         as John Burke
read the comics
   at the City Council

   table saying

when you guys have played

long enough there's no use

of my wasting my

time: brains

are not to be

   wasted

'okloloidoros

of love & hand–holding sweet flowers & drinking
waters) Hilton's & Davis', Davis' the

garden of Ann

get back to   & Elizabeth & Eden

Nasir Tusi   & where I fall

man is the fallen angel

and after Davis' swamp – Joshua Elwell

sitting high in heaven

Bennett placed himself

above 75′

Hilton above the trough between

(on the edge of 75′ too)

– & Sam'l Davis on the height of

the next rise, inside 125′

(100′ lying almost exactly the middle

of the 600 foot distance between his

& Hilton's houses); and Joshua Elwell

the other rise on the Commons Road,

or "to the wood–lots" (1727),

on the other

side of the 2nd trough, at

125′ Thus

three 'hills' or hogbacks

& two brooks

characterize the upper

road (as against the lower

or dog Town road proper,

where moraine, and the more

evident presence of rock-tumble

gives the road, & center, its

moor character – moonscape

and hell) the Commons is

garden, and manor, ground rose

                              & candle

shapes of spruce & bayberry garden

The View – July 29, 1961

        the arms
        of Half Moon Beach,
        the legs
        of the Cut

                    Descartes soldier
                    in a time of religious
                    wars

a map of Dogtown: St   cod via
Sophia, Fishermans   /   racks
Field, Fishermans   /   in a field
2 acres on which to dry   like snow
                                            fences or tables
                                            at a lawn
                                            party

            & ladies
            in boots
            who wear
            coifs to keep
            the sun from burning
            their necks

                            The Shoreman, Sunday Sept 10
                                                    1961

1646, August   1.   The great pears ripe.

3.   The long apples ripe.

12.   Blackston's apples gathered.

15.   Tankerd apples gathered

18.   Kreton pippins,
Long red apples,   } gathered

1647, July   5.   We began to cut the peas in the field.

14.   We began to shear rye.

Aug.   2.   We mowed barley

The same week we shear summer wheat.

7.   The great pears gathered.

Sept.   15.   The Russetins gathered and Pearmaines.

1648, May   26.   Sown 1 peck of peas, the moon in the

full. Observe how they prove.

July   28.   Summer apples gathered.

1646, July   20.   Apricocks ripe.

(as in footnote in
Winthrop's Journal

ta meteura

    meteor things

 after the weather the
 meteors

parsonses
field

Elicksander
Baker,
on the River Bank Above
Done Fudging 16-
THIRTY-FIVE
and to:
FORTY-FIVE, his age
28 to 38, and having
by wife Elizabeth in those years
5 children – certainly the earliest
known births Gloucester (except for
Conant children, Woodbury? Balch?
Stage Fort 1623/4 to 1626/7 –
Alexander, born Done Fudging Jan 15, 1635/6
(the father and mother had arr. Boston
    in mid-summer, aboard the Elizabeth
    & Ann, Capt. Roger Cooper, with
    two first children, Eliz age 3 and
    Christian age 1) thus Alexander Baker
II possibly 1st child Gloucester
among the persons of the incorporation
of the Town;   Sam'l,
born January 16, 1637/8;
John, June 4, 1640;
Joshua /from whose blood Ethan
Allen/ born Gloucester April
30th, 1642 – just about
day Endecott & Downing divided
Gloucester up – and Hannah
September 29, 1644: sometime
after her birth and before
October 4th, 1645 (date the
mother & father are admitted
Boston Church) the Bakers
sold out, at Done Fudging, to
George Ingersoll, from Salem
(Ingersoll was still in Salem date
    his father's will, 1644)

———————

One has then
a placement:
a man, & family,
was on the River,
just above the Cut,
by 1635. And for
10 years. Also probably
his neighbor Stephen
Streeter may have
been there that
early? In any case

as goodmen
Baker & Streeter
the two get referred
to in jointure the
moment the Town is
found; and, curiously,
their adjoining
property is
picked up from
them by another
pair equally
holding together
Gloucester
for similar
10 years, Ingersoll
and Kenie, though
each leave
Done Fudging quickly
for the Harbor:
each is possessed
of a front
on Fore
street,
& the water, by
1647 (Dec.

————

Baker thus fixes
occupation of Cape
during least known
years between
1st settlement and
incorporation
as Osmund Dutch
does the 'fishermen'
of the Harbor front:
his letter to wife Grace
is – from Cape Anne as
nauta or sailor --
July 18th, 1639

and Abraham Robinson
Thomas Ashley (whose
property Widow
Babson bought up
at his bankruptcy
1642) and Willm
Browne show
– via shallop –
as down there
on the Harbor
before June
1641 – and "fishermen"

specifically
*[*Thomas Lechford,
Notebook, page
406*]*

Add Wm
Southmeade
or Southmate
as possessing
Thompson fishery
stage Duncan's
Point and
therefore probably
here as early
as Dutch (and
Thomas Millward AND
you have a handfull
who are the hidden
handfull from which fell
the later life as though
they were . . .
yes:

       Elicksander
       Baker
       goodman
       Streeter
       Osmund
       Dutch
       William
       Southmate
       Thomas
       Millward
       Abraham
       Robinson
       Thomas
       Ashley
       William
       Browne

& definitely the ministerial student Thomas
Rashleigh, traveling
from the Divinity School which
Harvard college was 1639
to hold service on
Curtis Square
(where
 R R
 cuts between
 Burial Ground and
 hill) so
more persons by
Baker and
Streeter?

– and other fishermen
at head of Harbor
Cove

FILL
Harbor
and
River
FILL

quiet
few originally
experiencing
what we have each
differently
known – like the mocking bird
drove me hard (mocking
me? if he mocks 28
different sorts of
song does a mocking bird not also mock
the living person? such curiosity
must
extend
to looking in on
the secrets of
my cabinet as well
as the songs of
his companion
birds) like the mocking bird
last night
in the slow coming in
of the fog – a hot
night such the creature a
mocking bird is – loves
heat, and night – no mocking bird
was here
1635 1639 1907 was
accidental visitor
from the south
Mimus polyglottos

But by 1920
had increased so
was becoming almost
authority Dr Townshend
a resident – and at all times
of the year F B Currier
found them nesting (at Newburyport)
in 1914. Four young
grew to full size. A
second
pair nested
the same year. In 1915
two pairs also
nested;
one
in 1916;
and two
in 1917

    I pick out
the Garden, the Spring the well
of George Henry's division with
his brother the
flat stone by a cherry tree

the Garden Nathaniel's, deceased
when Samuel fisherman alias coaster
sold it to Ebenezer tanner abt
19 rods of land called the
Garden

1732

SWly to
a Plumb-Tree. The well

exactly opposite the Morse
house, on the westerly side across
from the middle of it, 1 acre of
rocky ground where said Solomon
Parsons house stands, and is bounded. . . Excepting
Mr John Parsons' land where his well is & there
to bound by sd land as it is and no way to infrindge
on sd well privileges, Eliezer & wife Mary, May
1736/7

Mr John Parsons orchard Gravenstein
russets Greenings and Northern
spies in the complex westerly
of the Morse house with the well
and the spring – the "Spring House"
the Leach's now winter home was summer camp
I went through today with Stewart
and Mrs Leach, when Walter Cressy
was selling water after he'd blown up
the rock vein and dried the Parsons
spring, to get his own a Cressy-
Strong strongway Walter and Neal,
and Bertha, living it up with a pony
a goat a sheep a Labrador retriever while acquiring
more & more of the old Parsons
woods and ledge fronting over the
Cut like Frontenac bearing
down:

     greensward
is a light of the fall of ground
may not be the like of light
coming off water but land's
fall causes feeling to run as
spirit does from sea & sky, she
said at 10 in the morning she
felt she was her mother meaning my

body was hers I went to
the mirror to look if it was
me and called her, on the phone,
she joshed me and it was that night
when she went with Josie Boone
to see the Chocolate Soldier she
was struck by a taxi getting off
the street car and Josie was so
scared she didn't find out what
hospital they took her to – 12
hours of premonition had not known
before & never knew again

Spring lane leads from the S end
of the Morse house (across the street)
in, 8 rods W'ly it says from
the house there a line to begin
fr the rock to a great rock by
the Spring which is abt 10 poles,
leaving the Spring common, thence
NWly etc

THE BEGINNINGS (facts

> Dutche mariner New England coast & transport England to
> Bay 1632 – along with John Gallop who
> ran his pinnace back & forth to
> Ipswich

> Babson guesses Robinson might have come across from
> Plymouth 1631

> 1633 anyway Rev Eli Forbes says (1792) on authority
> "Vide ancient Mss" persons here and met to carry on the worship
> of God among themselves – and sung psalms

THE BEGINNINGS

>   old Englonde   new England
> 1636 old John (White) to new John (Winthrop) urgeng
> "to sent on for fishing
>   which is the first means that will bring
>   any income into your lande

> halfe a dosen good boates masters
> & three or foure good splitters talks John
>   who hath known fishing since early Dorchester
>   Company days – now getting on 13 years agone

>   1637: the longer you defer fishing &
>   use other means that may bring you in some
>   supplys the more
>   you weaken
>   your body & will ere longe
>   etc

Hugh Peter pushing 1639 – sd year Gl.
gets going: stages builded nautas turning
            fishermen (Dutch example
                Millward another – young Gallop maybe

>   March 1640 Craddock
shoving at Winthrop

>   & then with war
>   England civil war & West Indies open
>   further to Yankee
>   Trade come Gloucester
>   into
>   Being : April   SIXTEEN
>   Forty-two

On Bemo Ledge he fell
one dark night – and didn't
crawl up out of that one
in his red Jacks, the pet child
of the lucky sea

THE CUT

March 13, 1638/9

    to view, whether it may not be
    cut through

December 10, 1641

    that they that cut the beach between
    Cape Ann & Annisquam
    shall have the liberty to take sufficient
    toll, for 21 years

Scheria – ?
                                        island
                                (near Miletus, &
                                    below Scamander?
                                on the River –
                                            Hercules
                                or Athena, balled
                                    headed clerks etc hauled
                                    hair via hair rope
                                the statue into
                                place

                                        Oct 18, 1961

My Carpenter's Son's Son's Will, Lt
William Stevens, 1701, Inventory 1712/13

. . . .

a certain previledged place
call the Cutt where   34 – 10 – 00
vessels pass through for money

                                       comparison (for value)
                                       house sawmill barn
                                       74 £

Maximus, at the Harbor

Okeanos rages, tears rocks back in his path.
Encircling Okeanos tears upon the earth to get love loose,

that women fall into the clefts
of women, that men tear at their legs
and rape until love sifts
through all things and nothing is except love as stud
upon the earth

love to sit in the ring
of Okeanos love to lie in the spit
of a woman a man to sit in her legs

(her hemispheres
loomed above me,
I went to work
like the horns of a snail

Paradise is a person. Come into this world.
The soul is a magnificent Angel.
And the thought of its thought is the rage
of Ocean   :   apophainesthai

roared the great bone on to Norman's
Woe; apophainesthai, as it blew
up a pool on Round Rock shoal;
apophainesthai it cracked as it broke
on Pavilion Beach; apophainesthai

it tore at Watch House Point

        II

              apophainesthai
              got hidden all the years
              apophainesthai: the soul,
              in its progressive rise

              apophainesthai
              passes in & out
              of more difficult things
              and by so passing
              apophainesthai

              the act which actuates the soul itself –
              she loomed before me and he stood
              in this room – it sends out
              on the path ahead the Angel
              it will meet

                        apophainesthai

          its ascent is its own mirage

        III

The great Ocean is angry. It wants the Perfect Child

                    October 23rd and 4th
                       1961

brang that thing out,
the Monogene

the original unit
survives in the salt

Going Right out of the Century

I, John Watts, via
Thomas Morton, claimant
to possessing disposal
of lands & islands of
sd coast including
Gloucester Harbor, did take
salt stored on
10 Lb Island by
ship Zouche Phoenix, London

& did not disturb
shallops thereon lying
as well as other
fishing gear – sd salt
in tunnes for use in
drying fish was
all I took, the
provenance of same being
sd Morton declared

in his hands & skipped
I wld suppose with
value received
I herein testify

Nov 19, 1961

V

A Later Note on
Letter # 15

In English the poetics became meubles – furniture –
thereafter (after 1630

& Descartes was the value

until Whitehead, who cleared out the gunk
by getting the universe in (as against man alone

& that concept of history (not Herodotus's,
which was a verb, to find out for yourself:
'istorin, which makes any one's acts a finding out for him or her
self, in other words restores the traum: that we act somewhere

at least by seizure, that the objective (example Thucidides, or
the latest finest tape-recorder, or any form of record on the spot

– live television or what – is a lie

as against what we know went on, the dream: the dream being
self-action with Whitehead's important corollary: that no event

is not penetrated, in intersection or collision with, an eternal
event

      The poetics of such a situation
are yet to be found out

January 15, 1962

128 a mole
to get at Tyre

"View": fr the Orontes
          fr where Typhon

                    the 1st to navigate
                    those waters
                    thus to define
                    the limits
                    of the land: Helen,
                    said Herodotus,
                    was only the last
                    of the European girls
                    to be absconded with
                    by the Asiatics

                    for which read
                    Phoenicians,
                    Semite sailors

Along those extending lines (rhumbs)
there was Manes first (Minos
maybe) there had been
Gades there was Pytheas
out into the Atlantic

                    far enough up into the North
                    for the Atlantic to be known

                              Portuguese
                    are part Phoenician (?
                    Canary Islanders
                    Cro-Magnon

Islands,
to islands,
headlands
and shores

                    Megalithic
                    stones

Stations
on shores
And Sable

                    Then England
                    an Augustine
                    land

                                        January 15, 1962

The Young Ladies
Independent Society
of East Gloucester
has arisen
from the flames:

the Sodality
of the Female Rule
has been
declared: We will Love
with Kisses

Each Other; and Serve Man
as Our Child

I

patriotism
is the preserved park
of ▮▮▮▮▮▮
Magnolia pirate,
and Oliver Viera
his First Mate

II

Ralph Harland Smith at least
thinks that his intelligence
was given him by nature
or his mother or father for
some use which he at least
has tried
to use it for

      ▮▮▮▮ ▮▮▮
borrows it it is clear from
some one else

      ▮▮▮▮ ▮▮
      it is clear
      thinks nature
is an ambulance

III

the wild life
CREW
of the Nancy Gloucester Elspeth ▮▮▮▮▮
and the former head of the Harvard Business School
and the Brookline
lawyer
the NANCY GLOUCESTER'S ahoy

boys – at least Mr Brown
of Old Magnolia
made a pass

Bk ii chapter 37

1. Beginning at the hill of Middle Street the city
which consists mostly of wharves & houses
reaches down to the sea. It is bounded
on the one side by the river Annisquam,
and on the other by the stream or entrance
to the inner harbor. In the Fort at this entrance

are the images of stone and there is another
place near the river where there is a seated
wooden image of Demeter. The city's own
wooden image of the goddess is on a hill
along the next ridge above Middle Street
between the two towers of a church called
the Lady of Good Voyage. There is also a stone image
of Aphrodite beside the sea. 2. But the
spot where the river comes into the
sea is reserved for the special
Hydra called the Lernean monster,
the particular worship of the city,
though it is proven to be recent
and the particular tablets of Poseidon
written on copper in the shape of a heart
prove to be likewise new.

the rocks in Settlement Cove
like dromlechs, menhirs
standing in the low tide
out of the back of the lights from Stacy Boulevard
at night

out of the back of the light,
from Stacy Boulevard on the water
at night

my memory is
the history of time

Peloria   the dog's upper lip kept curling
in his sleep as I was drawn to the leftward to
watch his long shark jaw and sick brown color
gums the teeth flashing even as he dreamed.
Maximus is a whelping mother, giving birth
with the crunch of his own pelvis.
He sent flowers on the waves from the mole
of Tyre. He went to Malta. From Malta
to Marseilles. From Marseilles to Iceland.
From Iceland to Promontorium Vinlandiae.
Flowers go out on the sea. On the left
of the Promontorium. On the left of the
Promontorium, Settlement Cove

I am making a mappemunde. It is to include my being.
It is called here, at this point and point of time
Peloria.

November 12, 1961

on what grounds shall we criticize the City Manager?

or the D P W ?   as easily as we do

the Superintendent of Schools for the texts

he buys?   for the snow left on the streets

so a car slews and a boy has a broken

pair of eyes?   for the insufficient time the City Clerk

spends on the earlier records of the City

even if like dog-licenses, and births and marriages,

he is up-to-date on the latest

of the suit-clubs and the bowling alleys? Business is obviously

cant and social life almost entirely

liberal but public office, as forever,

remains distinct – and moral – or

the life of the individual dwindles into

stink – a man in his own kitchen boiling

paregoric is he then and there on an open line to

the vein of the police, and invadable as such, by what

term ? Cant mores praise accomplishment

obvious competence clear management of

$5,000,000 a year's receipts for ex-

penditures leaves open what judgement

if the color of the lights on the Main

Street turn the lips of women blue

and all days are cheery too

with the smiles of windows washing clothes?

                                        The few,

and the masses, as though they constituted

possible public life – while those who lead them

are as cherry-red after golf or shoveling

their sidewalks clean as Santy Clauses hung from silver wires

fat or lean dirty or clean, the differences

of Santy Clauses not by any tally measure for what is what

the single probity public figure better be

what had he better be?

January 5, 1962

while on
Obadiah Bruen's Island, the Algonquins
steeped fly agaric in whortleberry juice,
to drink to see

Shag Rock,
bull's eye

& gulls
making such a pother
on the water in the sun
I thought it was Round Rock Shoal
in a south easter

Τὰ Περι Τοῦ Ὠκεανοῦ

A 'learned man' sd Strabo (meaning Pytheus:

the Greeks

were the 'English'

of the Mediterranean,

as the Germans

were the Romans

had rushed up into theWhite

Sea – & "travelled all over by foot"–

And did it all with limited means and in a private

capacity ⌈*Tanais!* itself

Cyprus
the strangled
Aphrodite – Rhodes

Crete
– the Mother Goddess
fr Anatolia
Phrygian Attis

Malta : Fat Lady

Spain

Jan 17 1962

after the storm was over
out from his cave at Mt Casius
came the blue monster

covered with scales
and sores about his mouth
flashing not too surely

his tail but with his eyes
showing some glare
rowing out gently

into the stream, to go
for Malta, to pass by
Rhodes and Crete

to arrive at Ireland
anyway to get into the Atlantic
to make up a boil

in northeastern waters
to land in a
grapevine corner

to shake off his cave-life
and open an opening
big enough for himself

Jan 17 1962

to travel Typhon
from the old holdings

from taking the Old Man's
sinews out and hiding them under

the bear rug, from Sister
Delphyne

who listens too easily
to music, from Ma

who is always there
and get that building up

at the corner of
Grapevine Road & Hawthorne Lane

with Simp Lyle
for manager

up the steps, along the porch

turning the corner

of the L,

to go in the door

and face the ladies

sitting in the comfortable

chairs,

and greet Simp

with the morning's mail

January 18, 1962

            people want delivery

When I used to stop to talk to the Parenti Sisters

or Susumu Hirota, the McLeod sisters

who ran the Harbor View

would call up the post office

and ask what my truck was doing

at the corner of Rocky Neck Avenue

the coast goes from Hurrian Hazzi to Tyre
the wife of god was Athirat of the Sea
borne on a current flowed that strongly
was taken straight through the Mediterranean
north north west to Judas waters
home to the shore

Jan 19 (Friday) 1962

tesserae
        commissure

                          Jan 19th 1962

Lane's eye-view of Gloucester
Phoenician eye-view

1833   14 october 443 Vessels at anchor in the harbor besides what Lay at wharfs

Older than Byblos
earlier than Palestine
and possessed of an alphabet
before the Greeks

round about the pawl-post
the heavy lines are wound
which hold by the chocks
the windlass when wound

from running back

CHRONICLES

1

As Zeus sent Hermes
to draw Agenor's cattle
down to the seashore
at Tyre, date

1540 BC, and thereby
caused the pursuit
of him by Agenor's
sons – one to

Carthage, one to the edge
of the Black Sea, one
to found Thebes,
another

to establish the rich
gold mines of Thasos –
meanwhile Zeus
as an immaculate

white bull with one
black stripe down him
has caught Europe
up on to his back,

his softness
fooling her,
she placing flowers
in his mouth,

he sails off
to Crete, near
Ida, and there
also Phoenician

persons are
born, Europe's
sons Minos,
Rhadamanthys,
Sarpedon

2

Taurus,
King of Crete,
caught Tyre
when Agenor

and his sons
were rallying

from a sea-
battle,

and plastered
it – the Evil Night
of Tyre John Malalas
calls it,

when Cretans
took everything
and blasted her
back in to the sea

from which
she came, when
Ousoos the
hunter

was the first man
to carve out
the trunk
of a tree

and go out
on the waters
from the shore

These
are the chronicles
of an imaginary
town

placed as an island
close to the shore

Sanuncthion lived
before the Trojan War
a self-conscious historian,
then, existed in,
and as of Phoenicia,
before 1220 BC
(or 1183). The details
of the Parian Chronicle
and such matters as
two Hercules, a
Phoenician Melkart-
Hercules more than
5 generations previous
to the Greek Hercules
(born 1340 BC,
by the Parian Chronicle)
make sense

which loan-words
& other epigraphical
matters now available
enforce: that the Libyans
and the Phoenicians (Agenor
was said to come from Egypt
& to be the son of Poseidon
by Libya – who herself
was the daughter of
the king of Egypt) one
sees a hub-bub
of peoples – Indo –
Europeans,
Libyans (the least known
of all sources of
serious inroads on
Egypt & collaboration
by the Libyans with
the still unknown Raiders
of the Sea) – and Uganda:

is there anything
to the possibility
that some of the non-Euclidean
roughnesses are here
involved – Hittite, or Hurrian
may not be the only evidences,
there may be East African
– and again what about Libyan?
movements to the center
of the 2nd Millenium:
Semite Sailors? They may be
Gondwannan creatures
who swung off,
for market
from the Eastern Edge

(where did the Sumerians
come from, into the Persian
Gulf – sea-peoples
who raided and imposed themselves
on a black-haired previous people
dwelling among reed-houses
on flooded marshes?

John Watts took
salt – and shal-
lops, from
the Zouche Phoenix
London's supplies
10 Lb Island

3rd letter on Georges, unwritten

[In this place is a poem which I have not been able
to write – or a story to be called the Eastern End of
Georges, about a captain I knew about, as of the days
when it was important to race to market – to the Boston
market, or directly in to Gloucester, when she had fresh
fish, and how this man had such careful charts of his
own of these very shallow waters along the way
to market if you were coming in from the Winter Cod
Grounds on the Eastern End – the point was to cut the
corner, if you were that good or that crazy, though he
was as good as they come, he even had the charts marked
in different colored pencils and could go over those
rips and shoals dug out in a storm, driving a full-
loaded vessel and down to her deck edge, across them
as a wagon might salt licks or unship her wheels and
ferry across – it is a vision or at least an experience
I make off as though I have had, to ride with a man
like that – even have the picture of him sitting on
his cabin floor following those charts like a race-
sheet while taking the calls down the stern passage-
way and if it sounds more like Henry Ware & Paul Cot-
ter in the Eyes of the Woods, it could be so, for I've
looked & looked for the verification, and the details
of sail at a time when there were no engines – and I
went to James Connolly expecting to be able to depend
upon him, but somehow he hasn't come across, or it's
all too prettied up, and it was either Bohlin or Syl-
vanus Smith or it may have been someone as late as
Marty Callaghan but the roar of this guy going through
the snow and bent to a north easter and not taking any
round about way off the shoals to the north but going
as he was up & down dale like a horseman out of some
English novel makes it with me, and I want that sense
here, of this fellow going home]

Altham says
they were in a pinnace
off Monhegan
season
1623, having left
Cape Anne

and trove
mightily
until in
Damariscove Harbor they
split up
in a storm

the sides
of the vessel
with the current running North North East
were ground
in turn
by the same rock wall the vessel

switching about
like a bob and his wife
and Captain Bridge's, in London
reached by mail via
Plymouth's agent

address
High Court Row and St by Chancery Light
could not have imagined
had they known,
that night,
their husbands

were on such a shore
and bandied
as they were: 4 men
alone, of all of them,

dragged themselves up
in the early morn
out of the wash
of that dreadful storm
so many chips among ground timbers

of what was left
of the pinnace. Such was the coast
when sturdy oak–built 17th-century
little boats out of London and Plymouth
cast their nets, King James said We do approve

of the Pilgrimes going
to the sand shore of
Virginiay
if fishing is
the holy calling

they go there
about, dear James for corfish
did they go Madame Altham
Madame Bridge
called on James Shirley

one bright City morning
for pounds and sterling
sturdy pence
in recompense
of their dear husbands

so. The night
was growley
the waves
were high the high built pinnas
tossed the winds down
pressed

the Little James
until she was far spent
& fore went head down
into the sea below the
waves her sticky masts

with thick crows nests
were up above the
waves and broken–stumped
wild balls of fire
played over

where their heads
below the water
filled and shoes
and coats pulled down
the crew

and Captain Bridge
& Mr Altham swam
like underbodies going by
in an outrageous park

or film until
their knees
were smashed
on small rocks
as their poor pinnace likewise poorly lay

chawn mostly but some parts of her bruised sides
now resting on the sands where we shall
dig them up and set them upright as posts
at just the signal place for tourists
to come by and not give one idea

why such odd culls
stand along a fishing
shore
though not used much at the present time
and mostly well-dressed persons
frequent it

existed
3000
BC?
from
Red Sea, via
Bahrein? /

Poseidon
(Samothrace?
——————
Taurus
the beetle
stuck in his
leg

Minos
Megiddo
Jericho
Sarpedon /

Rhadamanthys
Europa
Dardanus?
(Electra?
Atlas /

and Zeus?
name-wise
derivation
——————
Cabiri the 7
great planets
(things? the
'great gods'
meaning?

Additional "Phoenician" notes

                    phalaropes
            piled up on Thatchers

        (struck in the night
          of September 2nd, 1899

        and 800

        to 1000 of them

        killed themselves

        against the lights between

        12:30

        and 4 A.M.

Aristotle & Augustine

clearly misunderstood Anaximander

And in doing so beta'd

themselves

off-upland

   only Ubaid

      gets "in"

         to riverine

           (Squam

Old Norse/ Algonquin

Sunday June 17, 1962

VI

The earth with a city in her hair
entangled of trees

And now let all the ships come in

pity and love the Return the Flower

the Gift and the Alligator catches

– and the mind go forth to the end of the world

HEPIT·NAGA·ATOSIS

entwined
throughout
the system,

they saw a Serpent that lay quoiled like a cable
and a boat passing with English aboard, and two Indian
they would have shot the Serpent but the Indians

dissuaded them, saying

that if He was killed outright they would all be in danger
of their lives (upon a rock at Cape Ann, Josselyn, Rarities
Discovered in Birds, Fishes, Serpents and Plants, London

1672

Barbara Ellis, ramp

the diadem of the Dog

which is morning

rattles again

They brawled in the streets, trapped the night watchman

with his own stick, made such an uproar

the Bay itself was notified and Endecott

had to apologize that he hadn't yet brought them

under his control

DEEREST SIR, I heard nothing further of Glocester
business till the 3d day of this week at even, when
I received a letter from Mr. Blinman, together
with a complaint of the towne against Griffens
companie for severall misdemeanours, And
at the foot of the complaint a reference
from your selfe and 3 other Magistrates to
mee for the redress of them. I therefore despatched
away a messenger betimes the next morninge with
a letter to Mr. Griffen, that hee would sende me

such of his crew whose names I had under written
his letter, to answer to the misdemeanors of Sabbath breaking
swearing and drunkenness If they did resist
or refuse, not to strive with them nor to use
any provoking termes, but to take witness of
their cariadge and to returne mee an answere;
which here I have sent you inclosed. I
would have proceeded against them according to your
former directions (to wit) with force: but I had
rather if you see good try first an other way,
which is to send a prohibition, under your and divers
of the Magistrates hands besides forbidding Mr. Stephens
and the rest of the ship carpenters there, or any
other within this Jurisdiction upon some penaltie,
not to worke a stroke of work more upon Mr. Griffens
shippe till they had further order from the governour,
etc. I desire therefore to heare from you what you would have
done

Mr. Griffin presented for swearing by the name of God
Mr. Philip Thorne, mate to Mr. Griffin, presented for
swearing and drinking to excess.
John Hodges, Stephen White, Edw. Bullock and Anselm
Whit presented for swearing, and fined 10s. each.
Richard Hedges presented for swearing and abusing
the watch, and fined 15s.
John Bruer presented for swearing and drunkenness,
and fined 1 li. 10s.
Mr. Philip Thorne gave bond for all.

out over the land skope view as from Alexander Baker's still

stonewall orchard pasture land-bench over the River looking

to Apple Row and the Sargents other side the scoop out of

the surface of the earth a lone woman sat there in young

skirt the gulls use it in early morning to drop mussels

on the low-tide rocks

                          Dogtown to the right the ocean

to the left

                 opens out the light   the river flowing

at my feet

                Gloucester to my back

        the light hangs
        from the wheel of heaven

                      the great Ocean
                      in balance

                                        the air is as wide as the light

Hesiod said the outer man was the bond with which Zeus bound Prometheus

                  the illusory
                  is real enough

        the suffering
        is not suffered

                the foreknowledge
                is absolute

                            Okeanos
                          hangs in the father

                          the father
                          is before the beginning of bodily things

Part of the Flower of Gloucester

    from the sunsets

    to the rubbish on the Harbor bottom

    fermenting so bubbles

    of the gas formed from the putrefaction

    keep coming up and you watch them break

    on the surface and imagine the odor

    which is true

    at low-tide that you can't stand the smell

    if you live with Harbor Cove or the Inner

    Harbor to your side

Veda upanishad edda than

Wrote my first poems
and an essay on myth
at Kent Circle
at Kunt Circle

there was a Dance Hall there
like literally ye Olde
West on the spot whar he
looked out and saw the sun gleaming
on the snow after
the St Valentine Day's
             Storm spring
                1940

                     exactly
                       300
                     years
                       writing
                   at the stile
                      before
                   the town
                      age
                       29

where Cunt Circle
was to be where the inverted triangle
of the road
went around
Steep Bank Hill

              eating packages of peanut butter
              sandwiches
              bought from
              Peter Anastas's Boulevard Sweet Shop the Bridge
              as far as I chose to go in the February air

Went off to New York
by the Boston boat
as soon as the work
was over wearing
going through the Canal
an Arctic cold weather
completely smothering
upholstery fabric
hair mattress
headgear with eyes only
protruding

until I couldn't stand
the god damn thing and went out
on deck
with my head
itself

the 1st lot from the Cutt

lying next to the stile

the sea added

I am the Gold Machine and now I have trenched out, smeared, occupied
with my elongated length the ugliest passage of all the V
running from the Rest House down the hill to the
Tennis Court, the uncontaminated land which of all Stage Fort
does not bend or warp into new expressions
of itself as De Sitter imagined the Universe a
rubber face or elastic bands falling
into emergent lines from which string the crab-apple
tree is a dollyop on the lawn of the Morse house over
Western Avenue

Through the grate in a door of a cell
inside which about where the Rest House is another man
and I were I had then in my hand a wooden page or block
with tissue covering its face in which two jewels one
of which a long red drop and I wished
so strongly to show right away to Robert Duncan
and another who were walking away down the V and shot it
into the space of the door which it exactly fitted
and they turned, and saw it, and went on and taking
the block out of the window stuck my fingers vertically
through the same hole or grating and waved by moving
my fingers at them where they were towards the Tennis Court

The land was relieved. I had drawn my length all this way
and had covered this place too

In the harbor

    Can 9 Nun 8

    Nun 10 Can 11

                  Charles Olson

             Friday November 23rd

                         #1

Kent Circle Song

at My Aunt Vandla's

village a carbuncular

(goiter) gambrel

and Federal

all frilled with lace

and a gold brooch

at their throat

a silvered handle

in the door

and the walls

all made of cake

and into the oven with her

I swung out, at 8 or 10

waking to the bedroom wall

and the sweet smell of toilet soap

in the house at Wellesley Hills

in the 3rd floor bedroom

of the

JW (from the Danelaw) says:

They don't know they spoil – and from the beginning.

and as those words go down they set free, he

is non-referential in that moment this John Winthrop

had as a leader Vedic

senses he was a magistrate

in the mixed rule   the people

were the liberty   the ministry

were the purity – Hebraic

and the civil, which Winthrop was, was

authority. 1593 Arisleus'

Vision was published Basel

to make sure that what was known was

passed on to posterity viz that the planting

shall be

        on the widest possible

                        ground

Fri Nov 23rd

<u>proem</u>

the Algonquins had cleared the land there, Champlain
shows Stage Fort as containing five wigwams with
crops, it was the first place the English as fishermen
Westcountry men used to settle on, importing
the large company house in which the original
14 men lived, the first stage was built
there, it was divided among 17 men
in 1642 as – what they were – fisherman's
field, and the Parsonses made it their
village or homestead from shortly thereafter
until my father's time – and mine
when it was 'Barrett's' so far as we
were originally concerned
he building his first summer camps
about the time he was Mayor of Gloucester (1914)
on the model of his sister Lizzie Corliss's
henhouse – in fact the first one was
a hen house the one the bed broke down under
my mother & father the first night we came to Gloucester
slept in, and with the rain
which I had seen
out Johnny Morgan's Candy Kitchen window
the afternoon previous,
continuing through the night my mother
had had a lot of Gloucester already
and never ceased
remembering

We shifted around thereafter
were up on Bond Street
with Bill Collins the letter carrier
another summer
and at the Morse's the next
and for some summers had the gambrel,
the old schoolhouse of the Cut
which Ed Millet has had now for years
But my father was always planning
to get back up on the front
and when the big camp
was maybe first built
we had it from then on forever
fronting out on the Park
exactly at the stonewall line
of what was probably always
a certain division of fisherman's field,
that the edge of the cultivatible,
or usable sun and air edge
for salting and drying fish,
was that line which goes in angles with some strictness
from the Cupboard to the low spot of Western Avenue
opposite the marsh
– the old stream

which now backs down the new houses
on the marsh side and is a mess where the Strongs
have kept horses since they were Cressys
and tar trucks and broken–down road
equipment were since Homer was also
(later) superintendent of streets, for years
and Roland had the oil & hop-top contract and
                                        the two brothers
who owned the American Oil Company courted
the two beauties of the camps
– & one walked away with the darker

the brook, coming out of the forest,
at just about Bond Street
at 1 mile from the City
flowed then by John Parsons
orchard, and well, made James
Parsons house a dell (see
Bertha Cressy's mother's painting
of the old Cressy homestead, just there)
and Jeffrey the original wampum
of the tribe, the buck and founder
his house which George Ingersoll
had owned and before him George Norton another
ship's carpenter had built, the first
house settler after the Algonquins
(and the Dorchester Company house, which was probably
up in the field over Settlement Cove like a fortress
or Christopher Leavitt's at Portland on an island
to have room around it and sight in an enemy
country on shore
                    – this is a precis
of land I am shod in,
my father's shoes

not the intaglio method or skating

on the luxurious indoor rink

but Saint Sophia herself our

lady of bon voyage

(Friday

November 23rd

♯ 6)

mother-spirit to fuck at noumenon, Vierge

ouvrante

(A Prayer to Our Lady of Good Voyage

Sunday November 25th

1962

Monday, November 26th, 1962

and his nibs crawled up

and sitting on Piper's Rocks

with a crown on his head

and looking at me with a silly grin

on his face: I had left him out

of my monuments around the town

I

he who walks with his house on

his head is heaven he

who walks with his house

on his head is heaven he who walks

with his house on his head

II

she who met the serpent in the pond the adulteress

who met the serpent in the pond

and was kissed

by him was wrapped in his

coils

she had to die if she could not pass, by fucking,

the poison

on if her husband would not fuck with her

and die if by fucking she could not get rid of the

poison after

she had fucked with the king of the pool

III

the woman who said she went out every Sunday
and walked right through the rock of the mountain

and on the other side she said she was fucked
by the Mountain

all that, was her joy
every day of the week, and she was the happiest
of the tribe,

and that was her explanation, given by her, of why

and that was how it was she was
so happy

November 1962

into the Stream or Entrance to the Inner Harbor, Gloucester

the Inner Harbor also known as the River, Gloucester

on the other side of the River, Gloucester

the Head of the Harbor, Gloucester

at the place where   Dutches Sloo drained in

THE FRONTLET

into the light
of Portuguese
hill Dogtown

Dogtown's
secret
head
& shoulder

   bull's shoulder

lifting Portuguese hill into the light

the body
of Dogtown
holding up Portuguese hill into the light

Our Lady of Good Voyage sitting down on the front of the
unnoticed head and body of Dogtown secretly come to overlook the City

the Lady of Good Voyage held out there
to keep looking out toward the sea
by Dogtown

               the Virgin
held up
on the Bull's horns

                      THE CITY
               (OF GLOUCESTER

                   December 9, 1962

Homo Anthropos

– and Our Lady: Potnia,

and Poseidon (Potidan

[Theroun]

Thursday January 10th 1963

to enter into their bodies
which also
had grown out of
Earth

                Mother Dogtown
of whom the Goddess
was the front

         Father Sea
who comes to the skirt
            of the City

My father
came to the shore
the polyphony
came to the shore

he was as dust
in the water
the Monogene
was in the water, he was floating
away

        oh I wouldn't let my Father
get away

           I cried out
to my Mother
"Turn your head
and quick"

            & he came
to the shore
he came to the
City

      oh
and I welcomed
him

& was very glad

The Cow
of Dogtown

Shaler says
On Dogtown Commons
several of these areas (he is speaking of the
stratified elements of glacial accumulations
which, he has just said, generally do not rise
more than sixty feet above the sea level
[that is, now; he has already of course
made it clear that at the time the glacier
was over the land the land mass itself
was depressed from its present level by
at least double the 65 feet; which
makes it necessary to add, that, at
that same time the sea itself was 'out'
– drawn up as vapor which had else-
where formed the ice – to a depth by which the Banks,
for example, off-shore, were themselves – like
these Dogtown Commons – deposits of good
top-soil carried from other places in the feet
of the ice and only finally left – as
Dogtown and the off-shore Banks – when
the wall of the last ice began to give way)

He continues:

            These elements (of glacial
accumulations) are hardly traceable in
any continuity above the level of 40
feet; but at a few points they extend
in an obscure form nearly to
the summit of the great moraines
[an example the 'top' of Dogtown,
via the Upper Road, where one comes out
(missing the Whale-Jaw) on an upland
or moor which must be about like
the barrow Bob Lowrie thinks is
a covered Viking ship
and burial. The top of Dogtown
puts one up into the sky as free-
ly as it is possible, the extent of
clear space and air, and the bowl
of the light equalling, without at all
that other, false experience of mountain
climbed, heaven. One would sit here
and eat off checker berries, and blue-
berries in season – they are around
the place, at this height,
like cups and saucers, and one moves around to
eat them, out of one's hands,

not by getting up but going from
place to place on one's own behind. Burning
balsam, or the numerous bushes of bayberry
one could stay here with the sky
it feels like as long as one chose; and
there is enough wildness, or profiles in
the rocks, the inhabitation of their shapes,
to supply plenty of company – none of the
irritation and over-presence of nothing-
nesses which makes woods, or any
place else than the kame meadows of
Dogtown and this bold height of
it, not as interesting. Shaler says: "On Dogtown Commons
several of these areas of kame deposits
were during the period in which this
district was inhabited brought into
the state of tilled fields, and now
appear as small pasture lands destitute
of boulders."

         *[This is of course identical
with Stage Fort Park, of which the
highest point is exactly Shaler's statement
of the highest of such deposits – 65']*

"These high-lying benches of stratified drift
material," he continues, "probably
indicate points where small subglacial
streams emerged during the process
of the retreat of the ice, bringing forth
a quantity of detrital matter and
depositing it upon the surface of the
shoved moraine at a time when the
mass lay below the level of the
sea."

On to this kame
on to this shoved moraine
when the ice moved off
or was melted

And the land came up
and the sea rose
to the beach levels it now assumes,

and the sky
was as near, as,
at the top of the long slow rise
of either of the Dogtown roads

*[or Hough avenue – or the path
from the Barrett's more steeply up to the
crown, now that Ray Morrison has cleared
away Lizzie Corliss' hen house the Barrett's
backhouse Lizzie's sad pear trees

Viola's true rubbish heap flower garden]
the far sky is as near as you stand,

Nut is over you
Ptah has replaced the Earth
the Primeval Hill
has gone directly
from the waters
and the mud
to the Cow of Heaven
the Hill stands
free

She leans
from toe to tip of hands
over the earth,
making the Cow–sign
with the earth

(she is the goddess
of earth and heaven and sea)

one could live in the night
because she has to do with it,
encompasses it
in the day on Dogtown the day
is as close as the sky

her air
is as her light
as close
one is not removed even in passing through

the air, moving around, moving from one place
to another, going even across the same field

                    Nut is in the world

                              (Monday February 11th,
                                        1963

Stage Fort Park

an ice-plug a wherry where I hid my car a nights a fucking

and they tell me this was a gore under ice where the rocks made a whirlpool

when the land was then depressed below the level

of where the sea now is but the sea was out and here

in the hole of Stage Fort Park forty feet further down and then let up was the bed

of a Merry mac as wide as Massachusetts

                          the earth was down from the weight of the ice upon it

and great beds of water flowing under carried detritus

was my kame and those hollows and the rise

of choke-cherry trees I have eaten my father

piece by piece I loved my cannibalism

of the cake and flesh I now have windings of as steep and left-ward twisting

as those ice-rock grindings were

the giant river ran over and caught

where ground itself is a fucking hole

Further Completion of Plat (before they drown

Dogtown with a reservoir, and beautify it)

Lower Road, Kinnicum, before 1717, Joseph Ingersoll and Bryant houses above him
by 1717, and Smallmans up at the end before 1725: eight
or possibly ten years to 'settle' that

Upper Road, earlier: Samuel Davis (where reservoir probably won't reach),
1713, William Hilton where reservoir will be (in swamp directly sheared
off him) before 1719, Elwell next above (on Hilton's side) 1719
– the upper end – and all of it for sure by Jabez Hunter, 1725

So, on the outside, Dogtown established 1713-1725, twelve
                                        years

          The division of wood-lots was 1725-6 – and the
statements, which lock both roads up, are these:

1725 (Lower Road) "by the way that leads from the town to
Smallmans now Dwelling house";

and – 1727 (Upper) "the way leading by Joshua
Elwell's to the wood-lots"

          In the expanding period of Gloucester (and the nation)
directly after 1703 (3rd generation of settlers
 –Malthus' evidence on population)

     – 'set' by 1725, & living up through 1775
(when B. Ellery

       etc

                              Saturday February 16 1963

<u>Sequentior</u>

Smallmans definitely there 1721 *[* action of committee on
wood–lots at first report, Dec 19 1721 *]*

Thus spread, of time, on Lower Road
probably 4 years all told, for it to be occupied to the end.

These were the 'marrying years' of most of these men. Thus
in their twenties.

And the Reverend John White, who had been their Pastor,
is on the record (letter to the General Court,
on their behalf, 1740) that
                        "the Petitioners are most of them
Seafaring Men

                     February 22nd, 1963

Licked man (as such) out of the ice,
the cow ——— did who
herself came into being
so that Ymir would have some source
of food (her milk one supposes

Odin was born of either this man directly
or one generation further on, Odin's mother
was the giant ——— .

Gylfaginning VI

a cow Audumla,
which had come into being to provide food
for Ymir, licked a <u>man</u> /not a
iotunn/ out of ice <u>whose</u> name was
Buri, whose son (or maybe it was <u>Burr</u> himself)
Burr (or Borr) is the <u>father</u> of Odin

Heaven as sky is made of stone (Diorite – ex-
granitite) Tartaros's threshold at least
is made of a metal <u>native to itself</u>
And Earth
   – is made of grout

All night long
I was a Eumolpidae
as I slept
putting things together
which had not previously
fit

the Vault
of Heaven,
from which the rains
spring

      all the horns of the cattle
particularly the deformed horns
come upward to carry the impression to
Ptah

        Ptah,
the man of the earth. Over the earth
is the Dome
of the sky "deformed"
by the sea, terminated
by the exercise
of holes.

turn out your
ever-loving arms, Vir-
gin And
Mother

        Vulgar
swamp And cow
or sow. Wetlands.
Juice. And in the triple-force
dripping

<u>Orge</u>

"at the boundary of the mighty world" H. (T) 620 foll.

Now Called Gravel Hill – dogs eat
gravel

Gravelly hill was 'the source and end (or boundary' of
D'town on the way that leads from the town to Smallmans
now Dwelling house, the Lower
Road gravelly, how the hill was, not the modern usableness
of any thing but leaving it as an adverb as though the Earth herself
was active, she had her own characteristics, she could
stick her head up out of the earth at a spot
and say, to Athena I'm stuck here, all I can show
is my head but please, do something about
this person I am putting up out of the ground into your hands

Gravelly hill 'father' Pelops otherwise known as
Mud Face founder of
Dogtown. That sort of 'reason': leave things alone.
As it is there isn't a single thing isn't an opportunity
for some 'alert' person, including practically everybody
by the 'greed', that, they are 'alive', therefore. Etc.
That, in fact, there are 'conditions'. Gravelly Hill
or any sort of situation for improvement, when
the Earth was properly regarded as a 'garden
tenement messuage orchard and if this is nostalgia
let you take a breath of April showers
let's us reason how is the dampness in your
nasal passage – but I have had lunch
in this 'pasture' (B. Ellery to
George Girdler Smith
'gentleman'
1799, for
£150)

overlooking
'the town'
sitting there like
the Memphite lord of
all Creation

with my back – with Dogtown
over the Crown of
gravelly
hill

It is not bad

to be pissed off

where there is *any*
condition imposed, by whomever, no matter how close

any
quid pro quo
get out. Gravelly Hill says
leave me be, I am contingent, the end of the world
is the borders
of my being

I can even tell you
where I run out; and you can find
out. I lie here
so many feet up
from the end of an old creek
which used to run off
the Otter ponds. There is a bridge
of old heavy slab stones
still crossing the creek on
the 'Back Road' about three rods
from where I do end northerly, and from my Crown
you may observe, in fact Jeremiah Millett's
generous pasture
which, in fact, is the first 'house'
(of Dogtown) is a part of the slide of
my back, to the East: it isn't so decisive
how one thing does end
and another begin to be very obviously dull about it
I should like to take the time to be dull
there is obviously very much to be done and the fire depart-
      ment
rushed up here one day – they called it
Bull Field, in the newspaper – when just that
side of me I am talking about,
which belonged to Jeremiah Millett
and rises up rather sharply
– it became Mr Pulsifer's and then,
1799, the property of the town
of Gloucester – was burned off.
My point is, the end of myself,
happens, on the east side (Erechthonios)
to be the beginning of another set
of circumstance. The road,
which has gone around me, swings
just beyond where Jeremiah Millett had his house
and there's a big rock about ends my being,
properly, swings
to the northeast, and makes its way
generally staying northeast in direction
to Dogtown Square or the rear of
William Smallman's
house where rocks pile up
darkness,
in a cleft in the earth

331

[II.161]

made of a perfect pavement
                    Dogtown Square
of rocks alone March, the holy month
                    (the holy month,
                    LXIII
of nothing but black granite turned
every piece,
downward,
to darkness,
to chill
and darkness. From which the height above it even
in such a fearful congery
with a dominant rock like a small mountain
above the Hellmouth the back of Smallmans is
that this source and end of the way from the town into
the woods is only – as I am the beginning, and Gaia's
child – *katavóthra*. Here you enter
darkness. Far away from me, to the northeast,
and higher than I, you enter
the Mount,
which looks merry,
and you go up into it
feels the very same as the corner
where the rocks all are
even smoking a cigarette on the mount
nothing around you, not even the sky
relieves the pressure of this declivity
which is so rich and packed.
It is Hell's mouth
where Dogtown ends
(on the lower
of the two roads into
the woods.
I am the beginning
on this side
nearest the town
and it – this paved hole in the earth
is the end (boundary
Disappear.

a century or so before 2000

BC|

    the year rebegan in

March|

      festival days

of wild untamed undomesticated hence wild

savage feral (Father's

Days our father who is also in

Tartaros chained in being

kept watch on by Aegean-

O'Briareos whose exceeding

manhood (excellent manhood

comeliness

and power – 100 or possibly

to use the term of change (with

the reciprocal $1/137$ one of the two

pure numbers out of which the world

is constructed

             (the other one is

'Earth' mass mother milk cow body

demonstrably, suddenly, <u>more</u>

primitive and universal (? Hardly

The problem here is a non–statistical

proof: Earth 'came into being'

extraordinarily early, ♯2

in fact directly following on

appetite. Or

as it reads in Norse

hunger, as though in the mouth

(which is an occurrence, is 'there',

<u>stlocus)</u>

   that the Earth

was the condition, and that she

there and then was the land, country

our dear fatherland the Earth,

thrown up to form a cairn, as spouse

of Uranos: a i a

    the original name

of Colchis (cld be a 'local'

reference, that the Great Name

the Earth shall have been

Kuban where those

inventors of the Vision – the

Civilizers – were

'local'? some sure time prior to

2000

BC

  the statistical

 (stands)

outside

the Stream, Tartaros

is beyond

the gods beyond hunger outside

the ends and sources of Earth

  Heaven Ocean's

Stream: O'Briareos

helped out by Poseidon by being given

Cymopolea, P's daughter, for

wife sort of only superintends

the other two jailers of those

tied up in

Tartarós – and those two,

ʃin other words below below – below

is a factor of being, <u>underneath</u>

is a matter this is like the vault

      you aren't all train

of Heaven it counts

if you leave out those roots of Earth

which run down through Ocean to

the ends of Ocean as well

the foundations of Ocean

    – by Earth's prompting

and the advice of Heaven, his grandparents, this person

Zeus put the iotunns those who

      strain

       reach out are

       hunger

put em outside (including the last

the youngest child of Earth

her last one, by love of Tartarós,

by the aid of Love as Aphrodite made

strength in his hands and untiring

feet – and made of all the virtues

of Ocean's

children – snakes a hundred heads

(a 'fearful "dragon"') dark flickering tongues

the eyes in his marvelous heads 'flashed

"fire", and fire burned from his heads

when he looked (at the enemy or

as Shakti was shooting

beams of love directly

into the woman he wanted to be

full of love) and there are 'voices'

inside all his dreadful heads

uttering every kind of sound (imaginable?

unspeakable HughWhite says Hesiod

says (not to be voiced?

    for at one time they made sounds

      such as solely the gods

      caught on to

but at another Typhon

was a bull

when letting

out his

nature, at another

      the relentless lion's

heart's sound

and at another sounds

like whelps, wonderful to hear

and again, at another, he would hiss

so the sky would burn

          they threw him

into his father's

place it would take you one year

from the tossing in this direction and that before you got

to its pavement, Tartarós lies

so thoroughly out 'below' but 'outside'

(having nothing whatsoever to do with

gods or Earth's . . . but suddenly

a 'loss' has been suffered: Tartaros

was once 'ahead' of

Heaven was prior to

(in coming into being) this 'child'

of Earth: Tartaros

was next after Earth (as Earth

was next after hunger

itself – Typhon

was her child, by Tartarós, even if last

as Heaven was her child, first

The step back, to the seam

of the statistical Nebel

and "End of the World" out of the union of which

by what occurrence was <u>before</u>

hunger – it is like Ocean

which is 9 times around

earth and sea (Heaven is 9 times

around earth and sea folding and folding

earth and sea in its backward it

wraps and wraps the consistency

of mass in until the stupid story

of earth and nature is lent

what in its obviousness and effort it

can't take time for, and makes its stories

up, temporality sifts

out of Ocean out of Ocean was born

                            3000

(when his wife was Tethys)

daughters —— Tartarós the 'prison'

beyond the gods and men beyond hunger

and the foundations of Ocean

are a seam: Cottus and Gyes,

with whom Briareos is the third 'guard'

have their dwelling

                    ep' 'Okeanoio 'Themethlois

the lowest part the bottom tithemi

Θe

        Ocean deems

himself

On that edge or place

inverted from Ocean starts

another place

Tartaros̀ in which all

who have been by the statutory

thrown down or overthrown, are

kept watch on Night and Day

(Night's house is right over

their heads, in which one door

Day goes out when her mother

comes in and neither

are ever together at the same time

'at home' – Hell is just over

their heads

and so is the 'way-up', Bifrost

(Styx's house and Iris the messenger are

bungled prettinesses of this way

        this marvelous ladder the

color of all colors

back where the gods, and appetite,

and so is the way out for them,

for these imprisoned original

created – all of the first creations

of Earth and Heaven (or of Ocean and Tethys

all these instances forward of except

the official story

Heaven himself the 2nd, Kronos

who acted for his mother in de-maleing

his father

        is in Tartaroś

      away from all the gods

while the glorious allies of loud-crashing Zeus

Cottus and Gyes, and o'Briareos

guard them

       Typhon

is in Tartaroś,

threatening as he did (as they had,

the last to give the gods a scare

who would have come to reign over mortals

and immortals

      the heat took hold on the dark-blue sea

      when Typhon and Zeus engaged

      Hell trembled, where he rules

      over those who have come to him

and the iotunns before Typhon

locked up in Tartaroś swung

from the clangor and the Earth

shaking

      he burned all the marvellous heads of the monster

and conquered him and lashed him

and threw him down in his mother,

who groaned

and a great part of her melted
as tin does from the heat of him blasted
   where Zeus had tossed him

and then in the bitterness of his anger Zeus
tossed him into Tartaros

     The life-giving earth
had crashed around in burning
the previous time when all the land had seethed
and Ocean's streams and the sea
had boiled – and it was this 'lava'-
like which had undone the earlier
Giants because they were Earth-born
Earth's own meltedness had burned
their underpinnings and
defeated them, against Zeus's
stance
       Cottus and Briareos and Gyes
had done that day, of the Civilized War,
their turn – for the Boss

   with their missiles added to his
'bolts' they did their co-evals in, and
were the ones who chained them

(as the Theogonia poet says,
for all their great spirit, their

metathumos

There it was, Tartarós

which had been there as early as hunger

or at least directly after hunger & Earth

and before Love

       Yet Love

in the figure of the goddess born

of the frith from her father's Heaven's

parts accompanied Tartarós

– as Night had Heaven the night

his son had hurled off his parts

Love accompanied Tartarós

when with Earth in love he made

Typhon

         ♯

                  Thus

                  March

I looked up and saw
its form
through everything
– it is sewn
in all parts, under
and over

One of the Bronze Plaques Which Decorate These

Shores

   John Hays Hammond Jr
   Yale University graduate
    Sheffield Scientific 1907
   first user of the super heterodyne
   for directing surface craft
   & later underwater missile
   control

aren't you at least equal to Russia Cement

and Gorton Pew's, Mighty Mac Hammond?

A Letter, on FISHING GROUNDS [of, THE GULF OF MAINE] by
Walter H. Rich

      If the marine features
        of this region are radically different from
those of other coastal bodies of the eastern United States,

so, too, the shore land, battered as it has been by sea and
storm or worn by glacial action or by Arctic currents,

is no less remarkable. No other section of the eastern United
States has a similar coast, so serrated, indented, and ragged,

as has this shore line of the Gulf of Maine. Here the battering
by the forces of nature has resulted in making

thousands of safe harbors and havens
for the navigator. All along shore are strewn

hundreds of islands, a characteristic feature of the region
and one noted with wonder by every early explorer. These

islands, if near the land, are beautiful and smiling; if
in the open sea, of such grandeur; and mainland and island alike

are inhabited by a numerous and hardy race of fisher folk.

      The tides within
        the Gulf of Maine
have a very great rise and fall as compared with other waters

in this region. At the south
of Cape Cod

tides are seldom over 4 feet in their range, but beginning at
once at the north of Cape Cod with a rise of from 7 to 10
feet these increase quite constantly as they go eastward,
reaching about 28 feet in the neighborhood of the original
Micmacs, and touch their highest point in Fundy Bay, where
in many places is a rise and fall of 50 feet,

and in some few places tides
of 70 feet are reported. These Indian tides are probably

the greatest in the world. This great ebb and flow of water
serves to aid shipbuilding and the launching of vessels as
well as to carry the deep water far up into the inlets of
the coast and into the mouths of the rivers, making these
navigable for crafts of considerable size well into the
land or up to the lowest falls of the streams.

      The climate here
        is one of extremes,

and, lying as it does between 42° and 45° north latitude,

the region may be said to be

cold. Apparently the waters of the Gulf of Maine are not affected
by any stray current from the Gulf Stream, which passes at a con-
siderable distance from its mouth – from the mouth of the Gulf of
Maine, and Brown's Bank – thus doing little to temper the cold
of this area either on land or at sea. Whether these waters are
cooled further by any flow from the Labrador Current may be
questioned. The winters are long,

   usually bringing heavy snowfalls, but not now any
longer since the Horse Latitudes have shifted north. Strong gales
used to be frequent during much of the fall and winter time. Perhaps

the most dangerous
of these "blows"

come out of the mountains to the north and northwest of the gulf.
Thus, in addition to the uncertainty of an opportunity to set gear
when once upon the fishing grounds, the winter fishing here is not
without its element of serious danger. While the ice crop in
northern New England never fails, yet,

perhaps because of the strong tidal currents of these glorious waters,
the principal harbors rarely

are closed by ice, or, if closed,
for but a few days only. While the summers

used to be mild and in certain parts of them
extremely hot, fogs are heavy and virtually continuous
during the "dog days" (July 20 to September 1), when southerly
and southwesterly breezes bring the warm moist air from the Gulf
Stream into the cooler currents from the land. The fogs of Fundy

the mists of the Indians
on the land, the flow,
from the ice, of the hidden
speech, the tales they tell
of the m'teoulin, of the masques performed
in the waves, of the Indian watchers making on
to these other men who have come to the shore

the fogs the fogs are especially noted you can walk at night
and read your shadow slanted upward by your side, the tales
the tales to tell in the continuous speech. During the summer seasons

winds from the east and north

bring the only clear weather experienced in the outer chain of
fishing grounds.

      'Bahia fonda' – and with my thanks to
      R. H. Marchant for letting me keep his
      copy of Walter H. Rich, to do this.

        an old Indian chief as hant
        sat on the rock between
        Tarantino's and Mr
        Randazza's and scared the piss out of
        Mr Randazza so he ran back into
        his house

The house I live in, and exactly on the back stairs,
is the sight

of the story
told me by

Mr Misuraca, that,
his mother, reports

that, the whole Fort Section, is
a breeding ground of the ghosts of,

dogs, and that, on those very steps, she saw,
as a girl, a fierce, blue, dog, come at her,

as she was going out, the door

        The Tarentines
        were the pests

        of the coast, a bunch of shore Indians
        who raided as far south

        as Gloucester, and were themselves conceivably
        parts among the Algonquin people

        of them there 1000 AD Wikings:
        as these Sicilians

        talk an Italian
        which is Punic. For the Tarantinos

        were Micmacs, first spotted off La Have,
        and had been dealing,

        before they got down here,
        as traders with fishermen

        since the beginning
        of the occupation of the coast

from whom they got
knives and kettles

and coats and then sold them
stolen corn, from peaceful

Indians or shamefully cowardly
Indians who put up with these

Tarentines, huddling in their
shabby huts begging the new-come white man to

help them up against this raiding bunch
of old tough remnants of the older

coast. Or they were dogs, the Tarentinos,
come in to feed on the after coast,

after the white man disease
– the yellowing disease,

the Indians themselves called
what no man yet has diagnosed,

except that Indians,
who had been hauled,

to London,
seem somewhere,

to have brought it
back. These Tarentines

were intrusions
on all the coast, east

of Penobscot Bay

why light, and flowers? Paul Oakley,
directly, from Main Street down Water
                              over the water
at the other side of the inner harbor

                on the other side of

                              over and above
the masts, looking down on the Older Scene

gardens ran
to the water's
edge (on East-facing appropriated
quarter-plots

                  I'm looking
at how the Virgin
does dominate
her Hill and place
between the Two Towns

from the East to North fall
of Main, at Water, right angle
Paul Oakley, directly down Main she
in the same direction & picking up the same light

as 90 Middle, the gambrel
which is sliced off,

                        the shape of light

the lay,
        of flowers

Fort Point section

                you drew the space in
reticule
                        now spread the iron net,
Enyalion

Civic Disaster   for Ed Bloomberg

There's a peach tree growing at least
on the Fort though Dutchie
the two dark last old country drest
Sicilian ladies, who sat under it
and under the grape vine, cut their
cherry tree down before Dutchie his
and his apple finally because
some idea of threat that children's
parents would sue – I said have they?
                          He paid $30, and one morning
the dirty whine of an automatic saw
(I thought I was back in the mountains)
woke me the house was in a flap out the window the apple tree
was gone
              So I console myself
in the last spring discovering
that down on the other side of the hill
where Sam Novello who now owns the Federal Fort property proper
throws his rubbish up over the fence by the barking dogs
who yell each time the city Fire Alarm goes off
there is these days this peach tree bravely blooming

                          best spring yet, 19-
                          63 (it was Levasseur's
                          nursery he works for and
                          drives their truck cut
                          Dutchie's tree – Bartlett's
                          Tree Nurses or something like
                          that, 30 dollars; and Ed
                          Bloomberg told me weeks later
                          he wanted me to explain to him
                          the poem and I said what do
                          you think and he sd I guess
                          it means never give up (hope?

                           Well, his blue eys shown (one
                          other man I met in Nelson's
                          pharmacy (haveing an ice cream
                          cone, has one every afternoon
                          2:30 two years since his re-
                          tirement) had em too; and they
                          are not the fireing aquamarine
                          eyes of the Devil of half-
                          lust which burst like four-
                          footed movement of Nebuchad-
                          nezzar's tile of the lion
                          and the bull was it he is
                          flanking???)

June 6th, 1963

the Head and Chariot
of the Maiden laid
out in gold fillet

With Horsemen
and Senior Citizens
half the size
of the Single Wise Female Body
holding the Saucer up, over their Heads
in the center of the Crowd of them
mounted on the Platform of the 4-Wheeled
Vehicle

Among the 8
24 pounders
on the rampart or bulwark
of the Fort raised on the granite
of the island, or head of the Neck,
sticking out into the Harbour of
Glowceastre

the Head was Chariot
for the Maiden drawn
on the 4-Wheeled Vehicle,
or Cart

By the rock
behind the tenement
beside the Orlandos
the road or entrance – gorge –
to the Fort, by which soldiers
supplies food ammunition guard
whatever was the necessities to
maintain the bastion (properly speaking)

the Exterior Slope
made nearly vertical (already

deviation from grammar of
fortification) was more properly
character of
glacis

the Head of the Maiden layed
in the Fort or Castle

                    in honor of JOHN WHITE,
                    of Dorchester, founder
                    of
                    the Dorchester Company
                    (on grounds of
                    Hanseatic League – Bel-
                    gae) and directly as of
                    appeal Conant, Stage
                                        Fort,
                    by letter received,
                            "receptacle
                    for those of religious
                    purpose to found in
                                        this
                    new country a permanent
                    settlement", 6 of the
                                        90
                    of the Dorchester Co.
                            survived into
                    the New England Company,
                    also of Mr. White's
                    urging and creating

into the hill went into
the hill every Sunday
went through
    the face of the
      mountain

and on the other side
was fucked by
the mountain

the distances

up and down

that the sea

may not rush in   an abatis

to be put around the work   a palisading

be carried across the gorge

Col J G Tottin's

report 1833

Tantrist
sat saw
on the Lingam
of the City
Hall 4 Wheels
Taken off
at each Corner
of the Base of
the City Hall
Tower

I stand up on you, Fort Place

rotundum   the dome
                            of the City
                            Fort
                            defiance
                            Hill

Or Lindsay

roared upon the town

firing barges,

cutters,

schooners landing parties marines

boarders and those to set fire

to the flake-yards on Pavilion Beach

to let them then ignite the town,

the whole thing to go in flame

and satisfy his whim

because a prize

had driven into Gloucester and ground

on the flats between Pearce's Wharf

and 5 Lb Island

ho-ho sd Captain Englishman

I'll burn the whole town down

meanwhile some musket men

had gathered at the wharf

and killed the 1st 3 Englishmen

who reached the prize's deck,

then Captain Lindsay in his rage

threw balls and balls into the Unitarian

Church, and the other schooner

which he had seized as prize

came in & was equally

retaken as well as 28 marines & assorted

actual English sailors plus

several impressed Americans

in the engagement off Vincent's Cove.

while on Fort Point, or the neck connecting it

to the main, among the fish flakes

where the fellows

from the Falcon

were trying to fire

the flake-yards,

other men of the town

with no trouble at all

gathered up those fellows,

and one of them

had such a short horn

or he was taking such time

trying to set the town on fire,

the combustibles

he had to do it with,

which he had already lit,

curiously enough back right up

very quickly

to his own powder horn

& did blow his hand off

'Tis true two Gloucestermen

did lose their lives

the August day,

and there was fear,

the morning after,

the English sloop-of-war

would surely murder

the defenceless town

but in the morning dawn

lo there the Falcon battleship

in the middle of the harbor

was being warped away

to get a wind and go

out of here

13 vessels, and David Pearce's
Corporal Trim
among them, value of that
cargo 19,000 £ (dollars

and so far as I believe is known
no legislation as of this date yet,
1963, from that period 1794 to 1798,
of a Federal settlement,
      it was a President's Private War

treated as such anyway
any indemnity Gloucester
possibly the sole place
which did suffer damages
from the French
who had supported
the youthful U. States
of America with her Navy
in the previous engagement
of Thomas Jefferson and the
George Washingtons
of the Declaration and the First
War for Independence?

I should imagine
that Federalism
has every right still,
as an objection,
undoing its Stars
and Bars of banking and
collaboration with a South
which does not include Thomas Pinckney
and did Pickering of Salem,
to sit as I did yesterday
in front of the same Library
out of which I regarded City Hall
three days ago and be sure
that a vow one year's long
is now as just a commitment
to a life of the love of God and to do work for others
as it was when the Society of Mercy
was new
            David Pearce
they do say
went broke
      for the last, of four times,
that time due also
to the contemporary loss
of one more cargo
by the maritime law of
port of proposed sale
deviated from
by his captain
unable in storm
to make the entrance mouth

of a tricky river
on the Portuguese shore
of India, or Madagascar,
and was lost trying
to be a Yankee and sell
at another depot

        These portions
of a country
        which is Northern
and were supported
until Universalism occurred
in Gloucester (the
Tyrian Lodge possibly
was identical with
the Sons of Liberty
        the Committee of Correspondence,
for example, was on board Mr. Lindsay's ship
as hostages when the townsmen
of Gloucester did take & retake
the prizes August 8th, 1775
and drove the boarders off Fort Beach,

it is the question of value
        which opens again
as though we well were
back in Al 'Arabi's
        circumvallum
again right now with
David Pearce's indemnity
not yet paid

        I want to open
Mr Oppen
        the full inherited file
of history –

        that extension
is not satisfactorily
organized

        and that order
is for sure art

the heavens above
do declare
the handiwork
of the orbits,

        and the axis
of the earth's day,
and the sun's year on earth,
are more important
than the parietal

        the societal
is a undeclared war
which, if there are damages,

no matter that the Congress
will not support the President,
the problem then is whether
          a Federal organization
or organization at all except as it comes
directly in the form of
the War of the World
is anything:

          I seize once more
Timothy Pickering as
much which is
what is always wrong

and now say it without any argument
that we are placed
solely on what anyone of us does bring to bear

Written Fort Point
     1st Federally
and effectively fortified
1794-1798,

June 1963

     The total price
lost by the city
in those years was
presented in a bill to the Federal Government of
$200,000

The lap
of the one of the two women who were told
by me, at the water side, to turn around, and be of some help
to get my Father up out of the river,
and Nepthys the queen
of the underground house
wealth (money) is buried
in the hole in the earth
and all I had to do
was scratch with my fingers
and the little people come out
& passed me $1.37¢ worth of change
whenever I wanted it

┼┼┼┼┼┼┼┼

Directly in front of my own house
(by the choke-cherry tree) at
Stage Fort Avenue. A depression,
in the ground, up hill from the tree
is still there. Or was, the last time
(recently, 1964)
I took my son and daughter
so that they might know
if they wanted to
where to dig

a Contract Entered Into By
the Aforesaid Ship or Vessel Owners of
the Port of Gloucester to
Divide Their Losses By
Agreement to Share Insurance On
Sd Vessels or Ships of Their
Ownership How I Know That
The Dolphin and the Britannia Were
Definitely B. Ellery's Own Owned

Vessels Which the Daily Entries On
His Business of Supplies And
Services Were or Included Obviously

Trips Including A Southern Voyage
Each Year From What Sounded Like
His Back Door at the Green

signed himself B. Ellery Dog Town

<u>The River Map</u> and we're done

by Master Saville who, conceivably, from the accuracy of his drawing of the Fort,
was the Keeper as well as the Drawer
of both the Harbor and the Canal?

wreck here flats Old Bass Rock channel Annisquam
Harbor toll up river Obadiah Bruen's
        Island   granitite
          base   river   flowing

in both directions   ledge only
at one point Rocky Hill and Castle Rock
           a few yards further
           than Cut Bridge enabling sand
           to gather

           off mouth
           a Table
           Rock
           like Tablet

   a Canal Corporation
   to be formed
   drawn for the record
   of the incorporation

           Between Heaven and Earth
kun   and   on any side   Four

directions   the banks

and between them the River Flowing

        in North and South out

        when the tide re-

        fluxes

carrying a crest
at the mixing point
filling Mill
Stream

     at flood immersing
     all the distance over

from
Alexander Baker's
goldenrod
field

      and dry lavender
field flower guillemot sat and fattened
and the herring gull wasn't even here
mullein aster mustard specularia
knotweed now in the front yard

With the water high no distance
to Sargents houses Apple Row
the river a salt Oceana or lake
from Baker's field to Bonds Hill

nothing all the way
of the hollow of the Diorite
from glacial time to this soft summer night
with the river in this respite solely
an interruption of itself

the firmness of the Two Hills
the firmness of the Two Directions
the bottom of the vase the rise
of the power of the Sea's plant

right through the middle of the River
neap or flood tide

inspissate River
times repeated

    old hulk   Rocky Marsh

I set out now
in a box upon the sea

THE MAXIMUS POEMS

VOLUME THREE

having descried the nation
to write a Republic
in gloom on Watch-House Point

Said Mrs Tarantino,
occupying the yellow house
on fort constructed like
a blockhouse house said
You have a long nose, meaning
you stick it into every other person's
business, do you not? And I couldn't
say anything
but that I
do

The Big False Humanism
     Now on   ←————→

Bona Dea (Athena
Polais) the polity
is necessarily as stretched
I am a ward
and precinct
man myself and hate
universalization, believe
it only feeds into a class of deteriorated
personal lives anyway, giving them
what they can buy, a cheap
belief.   The corner magazine store
(O'Connell's, at Prospect and Washington)
has more essential room in it than
      programs.   The goddess
      of the good doesn't
      follow any faster
      than how a person may
      find it possible to go out,
      and get what it is they do want
      wherever they do go

The last man except conceivably
the Soviets—or Mao when he was
living in the Yenan cave community

                    and our need anyway
is that in the <u>West</u>
some men have their bed in their head Richlieu

            if he spent some time making love
he was as busy at the same time
on what it was he was supposed
to be doing—in fact specifically
(if he had a mistress) he was
routing three attack-lines
of French and Indians down
            Lake Champlain and the West Branch
            of White River (then solid ice)
            to strike at once three exposed
            English settlements just along the frontier
of which Cape Ann was then one of the salients
(the nearest of the three hits to this one was
Salmon River and involved, in reflex action,
the Main St Gloucestermen who were then
the chief military officer (Ingersoll)
and part of the fighting force at Casco—or where Portland
later was

I believe in God
as fully physical
thus the Outer Předmost
of the World on which we 'hang'
as though it were wood and our own bodies are
hanging on it

I told the woman
about the spring
on the other side of Freshwater
Cove which lies
right on the edge of the
marsh and is flooded
each high tide by
the Ocean which it then
expells it runs so fast itself
from its sources and to drink it
the moment the tide has pulled off even one little bit
is a water untasteable elsewhere.

I showed her the trees
under which it sits
from where we were standing
on the Dolliver Neck side
with the tide all out

Main Street
is deserted, the hills
are bull-dozed
away.   The River alone,
and Stage Fort Park
where the Merrimac
once emptied under the ice
to the Banks survive

And on the Polls
at the edge

where the rocks are soft
from the scales

and in the heat-edges
grass and thorny

bushes
are   I idle

overlooking
              creation

more versant
on the western side

than on the eastern

and several of these areas
on Dogtown Commons

than on the minds
of men, during the period

in which this district
was inhabited, brought into the state

of tilled fields and now appear
as small pasture lands devoid

of boulders. Humps
        of Devil's glens
on Great Hill, and just
at Dogtown Square
to strip the soul
into its wild
admissions

and one sit
in the starkness
as though this
were anything
and go away
left with one's own
resort, wishing
for grass and the air
of heaven.   Finding out
there is no doorstep
equal to the heart
of God   sitting by
the cellar
of Widow Day's
kame   These high-lying benches
of drift material
where subglacial streams emerged
lay down there fields when Dogtown lay
below the level of the sea, Fled

the softness
for the west

or the top of the hill, fled
the deserted streets   a December
            stayed at home

until human beings came back,
until human beings

were the streets of the soul
love was in their wrinkles

they filled the earth, the positiveness
was in their being, they listened

to the sententious,
with ears of the coil of the sea

they were the paths of water green and rich
under the ice, carrying the stratified drift kame

dropping their self-hooded anger
into the dialogue of their beloveds
taking their own way to the throne of creation

                                        the diorite
                                        is included in the granitite

                                        the granitite has burst up around
                                        the diorite,
                                        leaving it as an undivided mass

the power in the air
is prana

it is not seen
In the ice,

on top of the Poles,
on the throne

of the diorite, the air alone
 is what I sit in

among the edges
of the plagioclase

Imbued
with the light

the flower
grows down

the air
of heaven

I looked up
and saw
I was faced
to the left

Okeanos,
the wobbling
ring

The shape of Weymouth   for there Gloucester
was first hustled   New England and so
Massachusetts   making sure that those words

sound like Alfred and Algonquin and over
the water bobbed
those boats   The Grace

of Waymouth   The Diligence a
Honfleur   The Mary gould to
Thaon   pipes a

Rouen   ballots
very much William
Blatchfords and bro.

or son—and Henry
Waltham the port
of   Into the Out of

Excise/ Im-
post the said
John Larsen said (is

Arabic?
          unk unk
nescio   ballotes

June (29th ?) 1963

[III.20]

it says the Amitie sailed
for New England with etc

30 tons [as against 35
tons   the Fellowship February

1625]

& returned from Virginia
on another hand–what does it

mean, 1626, Vir-ginia?

The Return to the Mail-Bag, or,

The Postal Union

of the Son with the Father

A View, in the Mirror, of Myself,

Age 52

followed his sow to apples
lying in the snow

blossoming apple trees
in the Paradise of Dogtown
in the spring   crabbed apples

dried out apples   apples as dry
as thorns   boughs of apple trees
to write with as a swatch grabbed off
at the writing table in the whole outdoors   the air

scented of the struggle of the three century sap
finding no outlet like semen in the trunk arising
to barren bark   scarfed grey block walls of the color
of tree trunks to be inside the window to look out of
on the original actual tree trunks—Glastonbury

thorn of Joseph from his staff put into the soil there
or was the apple tree the sow of Glaston came there to
the thorn of Joseph's tree on the eve of Christmas
leafs in the Westcountry air,   Arthur is there
                                 his sister
                                 Osier the Dane whom she
                                 is determined shall be her lover
                                 Oberon their brother
                                 and, so few miles from the sea
                                 Mallabron
on the road up Dogtown in the area of the Lower Road

the authority of Cape Ann
the arbitrariness
of the children buried the lovekin
the source of the turning of the streets
the line of demarkation of the Abnaki
the extent
of the old Norse tales
all the way from beyond the Micmacs (from John Neptune
and other Indian shamans—that all this should have arisen
from the Earth, that Bristowe in fact was a land to be discovered
that Bridge Street on this side is exactly
where dogma does begin again

Ships for the West Indies, or southern voyage
the 4th or last trip of the year after the fishing
was over and October December went off
to southern waters   Virginia or Charleston or
further to sell the fish or as often? picked up
loads of grain in Walker's Creek? the West Gloucester
farmers by and about 1690 were wealthiest
persons in Gloucester and seemed to have loaded
their bumpy fishing boats back from Cape Sable
to send them off to the south, same crews
and master, to trade food stuffs for gold?
or sugar or tobacco? and come home in January
to go fishing again—summer resort
in winter from Haskell Street: the mill
perhaps where tide water still gave berthing
for the bobs of boats the small fishermen
were or one imagines they came further
up the Creek turning in and along the crookedness
until the banks themselves like Freshwater Cove
or the Panama Canal would squeeze their sides
or tie them up in mud right in the back yard
of Richard Window's kitchen slope drawing down
from Haskell homes right by the road to
Gloucester, corn going off to the southward
with fish from the Creek just to Bayward
of the spring there: Haskells are the
palm in the hand of the open Harbor Cove of the 17th
Century and Henry Walker who married Abraham Robinson's
widow (also by the time he married her William Brown's
widow as well) raised Abraham Robinson II
and married off his step-daughter
(Mary Brown, who had taken his name) to the Haskells

these were the farmer giants—of 40 fisherman houses
Cape Ann—1690, men who poked
into the Caribbean or up Virginia creeks themselves
in a period of minutiae when greater European boats
and Yankees not yet born or invented
must have swallowed them wherever they did appear
as I have watched young fish rush down
to water out beyond the sluice at Mill River

Watch-house
Point: to descry
anew: <u>attendeo</u>
& broadcast
the world (over the
<u>marshes</u> to the outer limits even when minutiae
hold & swim in the electro-magnetic
strain—and there are only seasons
to be there [at the outer places
                    Ut gard   Out-Yard   when
those particular seasons (<u>days</u> actually hours
make it possible
(impossible: modes
not the same as
necessary
or contingent fate
    & grief   love
            & knowledge

one house—
one father one mother one city

West Gloucester

          Condylura
          cristata
          on Atlantic
          Street West
          Gloucester
          spinning on its
          star-wheel
          nose,
          in the middle of the
          tarvia,

      probably because it had been
      knocked in the head (was
      actually fighting all the time,
      with its fore-paws at
      the lovely mushroom growth
      of its nose, snow-ball flake pink flesh
      of a gentian, until I
      took an oar out of the back seat of the station wagon
      and removed it
      like a pea on a knife to
      the side of the road

      stopped its dance dizzy dance
      on its own nose out of its head
      working as though it would get rid of
      its own pink appendage

      like a flower dizzy
      with its own self

      like the prettiest thing in the world drilling
      itself into the

      pavement

          and I gave it, I hope, all the marshes of Walker's Creek
      to get it off what might also seem
      what was wrong with it, that the highway
      had magnetized the poor thing

the loveliest animal I believe I ever did see
In such a quandary

and off the marshes
of Walker's Creek fall
graduatedly so softly to
the Creek and the Creek to
Ipswich Bay an arm
of the Atlantic Ocean

send the Star Nosed Mole
all into the grass
all away from the dizzying
highway if that was what was wrong

with the little thing, spinning
in the middle of the
highway

William Stevens,
first to venture
on to the sea,
primary Selectman
of Gloucester Massachusetts
1642, had been builder
Salem Neck,
Marble head,
Boston harbor [the Sea
Fort, Massachusetts Colony Records, 1633
24′ by 70′ to be built at cost
2400 £ as complete protection of
infant shipping, and the young town
patrons the following, & the amounts
they pledge:

sd Stevens
Sat down
on the Harbor front
at the Beach or what is now
the Boulevard
by the River
Annisquam
with creek
flowing down
Washington Street,
to crook
at turn
opposite
old A&P and run,
in a jog,
down the 4% grade, perhaps,
to and into the
sea there about where
the Stage Fort Apartments
built by a blind man
now do sit (in fact just some few further
up the Boulevard (about where Billie Wynn's
been working in the Greek's Boulevard Grocery
all the years he has been also taking care
of the roads, and paths, of Ravenswood
Park

there on the City's Front
the Chief Selectman of the 1st city proper
sat down just to the east
of Stage Fort Park, and holding
the rights of the River's
passage, for timber cut
for the apartments
of Boston (the River trade
of 1713)

he went to sea so early in Deptford
as Hawkins (& Pepys contemporary with him)
and built as Hawkins had never dreamed
(Pepys commanded so he sent
to sea as David had Uriah & possessed
his sick little lay in Deptford
he couldn't ever resist not screwing
covering his face with camphor and handkerchief
to go through the plague to her rich soft bed
                              (Mrs ————, in Deptford

came to the Bay
fr St Swithins
(his household
birth record)

as early as almost any

and if I say he ventured
on to the sea in the trunk of a tree
                    the Bark Royal was the ship he built
                    had Spain on fire to get him then & there
                    to give them a Navy to whack England down
he founded Troy
on this side of history

Stevens song

            out of the fire out of the mouth
            of his Father
            eating him

Stevens ran off,

        having called Charles the Second

a king he could not give allegiance to

Stevens was then

63 years old and did he ever

return?   when was the chief shipbuilder

of England and

the maritime world of the day (1683?)
in Gloucester, first doing
running off, where?
So that his wife had to petition
the General Court for relief
from his punishment for refusing
to sign the Oath of Allegiance

and his remarks
to officers of the Crown

which were considered
seditious (as my own Father's

remarks to Paddy Hehir
and to Blocky Sheehan

were considered
insubordinate

            that hemp you promised
            for caulking the pinnace

Stevens ran off
My father

stayed
& was ground down

to death, taking night collections
joining Swedish fraternal

organizations, seeking to fight back
with usual American political

means, Senator David I. Walsh, Congressman
Hobbs, Pehr Holmes Mayor and so forth

On the side
of the King the Father

there sits a wolf
which is not his own will

which comes from outside
it is not true

that the demon
is a poison in the blood

only, he is also
a principle

in creation, and enters unknown
to the being, he is different

it is true,
from the angel   but only

because he travels even further
to get inside, and is not bearing

light or color, or fruits, not one garden
ever a garden ever a walled place

not anything resembling Paradise

nor Sneferus's
intended ship

imported forty shiploads of cedar logs
from Byblos

and in 1954 AD,
when the funerary boat

of Kheops,
Sneferu's successor

happened to turn up
as previously undiscovered

in a shaft of the burial base
of the sd Kheops' pyramid

the boat,
which was intact,

gave off
the original odor

of its cedar wood fittings.   This also
is a possibility of the other

of the three matters here
under concern, of three kinds of way

by which the prince
is instructed

to have in his mouth
the ability to lend

aid
to the bewildered

mob.   the
creature, from outer space

who comes in unknown
and lives unknown

in the son, craving
to be able

to be himself, not the question
of youth not the matter

is he a male
is he a daughter even

or the daughter's
original question

either of them,
and not even in face of

the father or the mother, not any of that
the dirty filthy whining ultimate thing

entered,
when none present knew

entered as the dog,
slept in the night

tore the bloody cloak then
literally tore the flesh

of the conjoined
love I was

a dog who had
bitten into

her body
as it was joined

to mine,
naturally,

in normal bedstead
fashion, no excessive

facts here, no special
or sought meaning

no more than
that

the demon
the canine

head piercing
right through the letter carrier

trousers and into the
bone, the teeth of Fenris

craves and locks
directly

into
the flesh, there isn't

any room
except for

pieces, holes
are left

when
I was

a dog   when Tyr
put his hand

in Fenris
mouth

—it was not a test,
it was to end

that matter, Fenris
simply bit it

off Thereby
there awaits

a Reason: the Quest
is a Reason

                Stevens
went away across Cut Bridge

my father
lost his

life the son
of the King of the Sea walked

away from the filthy wolf
eating the dropped body, the

scavenger

Astride
the Cabot
fault,

one leg upon the Ocean one leg
upon the Westward drifting continent,
to build out of sound the wall
of a city,

the earth
rushing westward 2'
each 100
years, 300 years past
500 years
since Cabot, stretching
the Ocean, the earth

going NNW, course due
W from north of the
Azores, St Martin's
Land,

the division
increasing yet the waters
of the Atlantic
lap the shore, the history
of the nation rushing to melt
in the Mongolian ice, to arrive
at Frances Rose-Troup Land, novoye
Sibersky
slovo,

the Wall
to arise from the River, the Diorite Stone
to be lopped off the Left Shoulder

                    rages
                    strain
                Dog of Tartarus
                Guards of Tartarus
            Finks of the Bosses. War Makers

                            not Enyalion. Enyalion
has lost his Hand, Enyalion
is beautiful, Enyalion
has shown himself, the High King
a War Chief, he has Equites
to do that

                Enyalion
is possibility, all men
are the glories of Hera by possibility, Enyalion
goes to war differently
than his equites, different
than they do, he goes to war with a picture

        far far out into Eternity   Enyalion,
the law of possibility, Enyalion

the beautiful one, Enyalion

who takes off his clothes

wherever he is found,

on a hill,

in front of his own troops,

in the face of the men of the other side, at the command

of any woman who goes by,

and sees him there, and sends her maid, to ask,

if he will show himself,

to see for herself

if the beauty, of which he is reported to have,

is true

he goes to war with a picture

                                              she goes off

in the direction of her business

       over the city   over the earth—the earth

is the mundus   brown-red is the color

                          of the brilliance

                             of earth

he goes to war with a picture in his mind
that the shining of his body

           and of the chariot
           and of his horses
           and of his own equites
         everyone in the nation of which he is the High King

he turns back

into the battle

              Enyalion

is the god of war   the color

of the god of war   is beauty

                    Enyalion

is in the service of the law of the proportions

of his own body   Enyalion

             but the city

is only the beginning of the earth   the earth

is the world   brown-red is the color of mud,

                 the earth

shines

        but beyond the earth

          far off Stage Fort Park

     far away from the rules of sea-faring   far far from Gloucester

far by the rule of Ousoos   far where you carry

the color, Bulgar

        far where Enyalion

      quietly re-enters his Chariot   far

    by the rule of its parts by the law of the proportion

              of its parts

over the World   over the City   over man

                    7 years & you cld carry cinders in yr hand
                    for what the country was worth broken
                    on the body
                                    on the wheel of a new
                    body
                            a new social body

                                        he was broken
                    on the wheel   his measure

                            was broken   Winthrop's

                    vision was broken he was broken the country

                    had walked away

                                        and the language
                    has belonged to trade or the English
                    ever since   until now once more J W

            can be said to be able

            to be listened to: wanax

            the High Governor

            of Massachusetts   John

            wanax who imagined

    that men

    cared

    for what kind of world

    they chose to

    live in

and came here seeking

the possibility: Good News

can come

from Canaan

                wonis kvam
HARBOR the back
of the Cape bump
Lobster Cove   bump
Goose Cove run   bump
Mill River—right there Alewife

            or Wine
            Brook

                    in Winter
Time   GRAPE   VINE

HOEK   wyngaer's

HOEK   Dutch

bottom   Svenska

bottom   ladder

of the Cut water

ran up hill from bump

        on earth's

                tit

The Condition of the Light from the Sun

—for John A. Wells (Oxon.
1934) and for Alan Cranston

on ground level
up on top of the world
the Bulgar and his sons
in the eye of ice
over the left shoulder
North North East
on a line extending
directly half way distance
between the left neck
and the ridge above
the road which passes over
the top of the world
constituted of color
divided among them
the Throne the Kingdom the Power

Signature to Petition
on Ten Pound Island asked of me by Mr. Vincent Ferrini

John Watts took salt
stored in shallops on
Ten Pound Island
1622 or a year
thereafter

[Admiralty Bundle,
of Court Papers 78639,
John White, of the Dorchester   Reign of Charles I, Suit
Company—the salt spoiled   of Owners of Zouche
anyway the spotted   Phoenix, London, against
fish   John Watts   Watts and other Members,
in that Court   including the Reverend

declared.   Thereafter
the Court fined
Watts, and White
and 17 others
to the full value of
the 10 shallops and
the 100 tunnes of
the salt: an evidence
of how Virgin
a country Cape Ann
was at date
after Quahamenec,   these silver waters would be
and early Dutch   the Golden Bay
and John Smith's   of northern peoples:
earlier prognostication that   that she wasn't
                                       wasn't
                                       all, only
                                       a Renaissance
                                       dream (Cicely,
                                       over the,
                                       Sea: she was also
                                       Pan Cake
                                        Ground where Armored Cruiser
                                       Boston can comfortably
                                       sit down
                                       These are memorial
                                       words, having to do

with,
in what sense
Utopia is
all dream: here on the top of all tit the waters
                            do run down in bumped
                            courses to rush
                            the tiny Columbia ship
                            behind the will of its Commander
                            up the shining course
                            who says, in so many words
                            and by the sign of his name
                            as Christ-bearer and
                            the Dove, the river
                            of Agyasta does not
                            fall   it washes all

away

February, 1964

Space and Time the saliva
in the mouth

your own living hand amputated living on
in the mouth

of the Dog

the Alligator,
clapping at my balls

the Soul
rushing before

Sun
upside down

buried in a grotto under-
water   sister of the goddess who removes from sight hobbled

tin and copper   Corycian
cave: where he set up his first

forge   who shines
by day

connection to
the Dogs

Wyoming New York
March 9th XIX-LXIV

"home", to the shore

bu-te   pu-bu   bu-nu-šu

bayt.   "house,"

to the

shore

pa-ba   pa-'i-to   "Phaistos"

    pa, as in a for

       Apple

    tu   tuppûh

and bird or ku is "town":

kr-ku   (Her headland, over

the sea-shore

Saturday March 14th 1964

    Her Headland
over
the sea-shore
krk, or "town", in
the language now
bitten off bird or of beast of
prey hooked beak rest of
migrating birds N
a headland for migrating birds
North kr-ku her headland up above the
        seashore
a bird or town kr-ku

To have the bright body of sex and love
back in the world—the moon
has her legs up,
in the sky of Egypt

Maximus to himself June
1964

            no more,
            where the tidal river rushes

            no more
            the golden cloak (beloved
            World)

            no more dogs
            to tear anything
            apart—the fabric

            nothing like
            the boat (no more Vessel
            in the Virgin's
            arms

            no more dog-rocks
            for the tide
            to rush over not any time again
            for wonder

            the ownership
            solely
            mine

Publish my own soul August my father's month
I was conceived in the ions of March my Mother and Father
were married in winter used an umbrella in the snow

August 1st XLIV

I believe in religion not magic or science I believe in society

as religious both man and society as religious

fire it back into the continent
the free association of Gloucester persons

the sky,

of Gloucester

perfect bowl

of land and sea

August 6th

The-Man-With-The-House-On-His-Head carrying
the OVEN
on His Head, the Otter Pond the
grant to Benjamin Kinnicum
(Cunningham, married
one of the Josselyns—a small body of water in
Dog'town on the road to
William Smallmans
now dwelling house

—Dogtown under
    City Dogtown granite
    -tite Dogtown under
    sky under the city to the shore under the
    sea under the banks as far as
    (Oceanographers Canyon)

I am the
Child, Jupiter
furens—Ocean's
Child; I am
Round Rock Shoal

I am the one from whom the Kouretes
bang their platters

August 7th, LXIV

The Feathered Bird of the Harbor of Gloucester

He was here, 1817 August 23rd

and seen by all involved including

scientists from the Linnaean Society,

Cambridge

—drawings exist

of his appearance August 14th

as well (by Captain John Beach

a dark brown snake

sailing around Ten Pound Island

not like a common snake

but a caterpillar

and when he chose he settled directly

like a rock

How fast did it move?

Faster than any whale

—a mile or more

in three minutes

What were its color, length

and thickness?

Most say brown; two and a half feet

thick size of a man's

body

        Once 200

were watching at one time

And it went, very rapidly northeast

on August 28th

        Several feet of tongue,

resembling a fisherman's harpoon

it threw out several times,

perpendicularly,

and let it fall again.

The head?

Rounded like a dog's

August 8, 1964

Coiled,

throughout the system

the jewel

in his eye

Right at the Cut,

on the Dog rocks,

there indeedy

    he Sat

The Wolf
slinks off,

Fenrir's
mouth

salivarating.
And my arm

on my own body,
my own hand

mine

There was a salt-works at Stage Fort

There was a salt-works at Stage Fort, in 1656,
and, in the nature of the settlement probably
for at least the 14 previous years: Elias Parkman
was the name of the salt-maker in that year, and,
if the 2 acres he had then, of the allotments of
Fishermans Field, were habitually the salt-makers'
I may list the following as the possessors, and,
if this was the use of that part of Stage Fort
they are, then, salt-makers all:

> Edmund Brodway
> Giles Barge
> and Christopher Avery.

(The 2 acres are described in such a fashion it is
difficult to say whether they butted on Half Moon or
on Cressy Beach, but they were either in one or the
other access to the water.)

What emphasizes this more, is that the land appears
initially to have been Thomas Millward's, and as he
was here by, or immediately after the Thompson fish-
ery of 1638/9—was in fact with Osmund Dutch the ini-
tiator of the action of the London merchant on this side (he is still
put at Noddle's Island in Dutch's letter to his wife
from Cape Ann, earlier in that year)—it makes sense that these
two enterprisers of that fishery might, as several of
the earlier stations had, try salt on this new coast.
Poor salt, it always seems to have been, and Trapiano
barks were dominating sights in Gloucester Harbor with-
in living persons memories.

The "station" as such, on this coast, never was the home
of the fishing industry. The Bay, once cod were shown
to be its silvermine, jammed fishing on, at Marblehead,
and vessels too were built (at Salem Neck), until all
trade of the Atlantic world was swung on fish—and Bay
had pine-tree monies of its own, as well as many children,
as Malthus found, to make his point.

To make mine, "second" Gloucester (the one after the orig-
inal Dorchester Company station) more resembled the Maine
coast since—and Rockport still, and just such coves and
inlets—than the vision the place here from the start

supports and then requires: Champlain's original center
of French power (instead of Castine, as it did work out);
John White's clear shot to make Northern America breed
here first; and the Bay's alertness, 1642—which took
another 60 years—to place this eastward pointed Cape
against the French, and get Cape Sable in the end, from
Indians and from French.

And halibut, in 1936, when the waters of the Atlantic had
still not warmed up swordfish too were on the Peak of Browns—and
a French barque, with lanterns like the Novy fishermen and full rig
sailing vessel still, would sit at night at no great distance from
the Gloucester fleet, jogging, until the morning light and twelve
hours of double-tide would place all where they had been to fish
again today where they had stopped at evening the night before.

The 2nd Gloucester was a fastening, of around 40 men and families,
to hold the future until the future made back to the spot,
course almost due West from Biscay, where fishing Europe found her
floating, an island floating in the Western Sea

Wednesday August 19th
1964

The NEW Empire

There was Homey, over the Cut, Homer Barrett,
former Mayor, of Gloucester, and as I came up,
Superintendent, of Streets, a play-maker of the
Old Renaissance, and not I his Poliziano, there was
a Gloucester of that as much as there is still, here,
at least, on the Fort, Neolithic family life: Rank sayeth,
in great error, there is mother (family), father (heir)—
& (self). Self, he says (hero, poet, psychoanalyst, in that
order (!): boo, Rank. As though sociology wasn't as chewed
as Homer's (Barrett's, that is) cigar, nervous little Homey,
with fingers as fine as a woman's, and after he was through
using the public till for the public's spill-out, evenings,
to the Park—only when the Two Brothers of the American Oil
Co. led Homer over, was there dirty money, out of Gloucester

: money was, small, and a percent given back, in forms of
favor. But with Homer, in City Hall, and prior, when Alderman,
after the Prohibition of the 19th Century, when America was,
for the first time, Renaissance (before Arizona came)—when
there was money enough, for the first time, Homer spent it,
took his take, from the West End of Main Street, and put it
back, in entertainment, over the Park

                                        his fingers, finally,
delicately jabbing the fertilized top-soil, of his flower
garden, in the spring, to transfer plants he had grown earlier,
from glass-covered boxes, to earth. Homey was a form

of power as child (collective guilt as collective soul) more
to the tone of Politian than post-2nd WorldWar American ad-
ult, the gross individual of presumed progress (collective bitch
for Army life, the get-mine honesty of this? the modest, straight
advance, to World Wide News? the self, all self-selves having
that's his, or hers, problem? a term, of possibility, of the soul,
that any one of us proves something by showing these evidences
of any one of us's ability to, separately, make evident that
we can do the things that we are responsible for? Responsible
(said Rank) for being fathers, for achieving our immortality in
our said children? Procreation?

                                a secondary function of man:
if man does not spill out his being so, if he hath not the axis,
unwearingly revolving in the act of initial creation—not the
reproduction of nature alone, this getting-it because they got
you—what child is it (born male) to be an heir? to be a mother,

to be a self? When I was a Blue Deer Viola Barrett was my mother, and when I was a child Homer Barrett brought us in the world, at Stage Fort—children, and grown-ups, of the City of Gloucester, not at all to speak of what he supported, and took his take from, when Mayor, so that 1923, 300 years after, if I wasn't an Italian poet, it wasn't also Florence

But it was indeed a New
Empire

Thurs Aug 20th

The Cormorant
and the Spindle
which marks Black Rock

COLE'S ISLAND

I met Death—he was a sportsman—on Cole's
Island. He was a property-owner. Or maybe
Cole's Island, was his. I don't know. The
point was I was there, walking, and—as it
often is, in the woods—a stranger, suddenly
showing up, makes the very thing you were do-
ing no longer the same. That is suddenly
what you thought, when you were alone, and
doing what you were doing, changes because someone else
shows up. He didn't bother me, or say anything. Which is
not surprising, a person might not, in the circumstances;
or at most a nod or something. Or they would. But they wouldn't,
or you wouldn't think to either, if it was Death. And
He certainly was, the moment I saw him. There wasn't any question
about that even though he may have looked like a sort of country
gentleman, going about his own land. Not quite. Not it being He.

A fowler, maybe—as though he was used to
hunting birds, and was out, this morning, keeping
his hand in, so to speak, moving around, noticing
what game were about. And how they seemed. And how the woods
were. As a matter of fact just before he had shown up,
so naturally, and as another person might walk
up on a scene of your own, I had noticed
a cock and hen pheasant cross easily the
road I was on and had tried, in fact,
to catch my son's attention quick enough for him
to see before they did walk off into the bayberry
or arbor vitae along the road.

        My impression is we did—
that is, Death and myself, regard each other. And
there wasn't anything more than that, only that he had appeared,
and we did recognize each other—or I did, him, and he seemed
to have no question
about my presence there, even though I was uncomfortable.
  That is,
Cole's Island
is a queer isolated and gated place, and I was only there by will
to know more of the topography of it lying as it does out
over the Essex River. And as it now is, with no tenants that one can speak of,
it's more private than almost any place one might imagine.
And down in that part of it where I did meet him (about half way between the
two houses over the river and the carriage house
at the entrance) it was as quiet and as much a piece

of the earth as any place can be. But my difficulty,
when he did show up, was immediately at least that I was
an intruder, by being there at all
and yet, even if he seemed altogether
used to Cole's Island, and, like I say, as though he owned it,
even if I was sure he didn't, I noticed him, and he me, and he
went on without anything extraordinary at all.

Maybe he had gaiters on, or almost
a walking stick, in other words much more
habited than I,
who was in chinos actually and
only doing what I had set myself to do here
& in other places on Cape Ann.

It was his eye perhaps which makes me
render him as Death? It isn't true, there wasn't anything
that different about his eye,
it was not one thing more than that he was Death instantly
that he came into sight. Or that I was aware there was a person
here as well as myself. And son.

We did exchange some glance. That is the fullest possible
account I can give, of the encounter.

Wednesday, September 9th, 1964

My shore, my sounds, my earth,

afterwards, in between, and since

my place

Hector-body,

my Cow to the left my Cow to the right:

                              Goddess-

shield Ajax

    or the Knossian

who is compared to Enyalios

        crossed in Helladic to

Troy
            now moves on east from

west of Albany

            got home again,

        Wednesday

    January 20th

    1965

Sweet Salmon
from the coldest clearest
waters.   Cut the finest
on the bone.
                    Rose
directly from the stream straight into my greedy
throat.   And breast.   A home
for life.   Wise goddess

of the straightest
sapling

                    Saturday March 20th
        1965

Poem 143. The Festival Aspect.

The World
has become divided
from the Universe. Put the three Towns
together

The Individual
has become divided
from the Absolute, it is the times promised
by the poets. They shall drop delta
and lingam, all forms
of symbol
and mystery. As well as all
naturalism. And literalness. The truth

is fingers holding it all up
underneath, the Lotus
is a cusp, and its stalk
holds up it all.
It isn't even a burning point, it is a bow
of fingers shooting
a single arrow. The three Towns
are to be destroyed, as well as
that they are to be made known,
that they are to be known,
that there is no three Towns
now, that without three Towns
there is no Society, there is no
known
Absolute: we shall stand on our heads and hands
truly, kicking
all false form off
the surface
of the still, or active,
water-surface. There is no image
which is a reflection. Or a condition. There is solely
the Lotus
upside down. When the World is one again
with the Universal the Flower
will grow down, the Sun
will be stamped
on the leather
like a growing
Coin, the earth
will be the light, the air and the dust
of the air will be the perfume

of sense, the *gloire*
will have returned
of the body seen
against the window. The flesh
will glow.
                    The three Towns
will have become populated
again. In the first Town
somebody will have addressed
themselves
to someone else. There will be no need
of the explicit. In the second Town
the earth
will have replaced
the sun. In the third Town the man
shall have arisen, he shall have concluded
any use of reason, the Dialogue
will have re-begun. The earth
shall have preceded love. The sun
shall have given back its deadly
rays, there shall be no longer any
need to be so careful. The third Town
shall have revealed
itself.

The third Town
is the least known. The third Town
is the one which is the most interesting—and is overpopulated—
behind the Western
sun. It shall only come forth
from underneath. The foot of the Lotus
is not its face, but the roots
of its stalk. The Elephant
moves easily
through any trees. He is Ganesh
with the big Hands. His hands alone
offer all. Through the mountain
through the bole
of any tree through the adamantine
he passes
as though it were nothing. Only the God Himself
of whom he is the frazzled stalk
in each of the coolness, and ease, of his power
is more than water. Water is not equal
                    to the
                    Flower. The three Towns
                    are the fairest
                    which the Flower
                    is. Only when the Flower—only when the uproar
                    has driven the Soul

out of me, only then shall the God
strike
the three Towns. The three Towns
shall first
be born again. The Flower shall
grow down. The mud of the bottom
is the floor
of the Upside Down. The present
is an uproar, the present
is the times of the re-birth of
the Lotus. Ganesh
is walking
through anything. There is no obs-
tacle. There will be no more
anger. There is only one
anyway. It is too early
for anger. The third Town
has only just
begun.

Thus March, LXV.
                    The New Year
            is One Week
            Old.

            March 29th
            1965.   (The feet of Maximus
            in the air.

George Decker   ; A fisherman
                        told him, George Decker, over at
Lancey Meadow   l'Anse aux Meadow   l'Anse aux Meadow

                                    And George Decker (when he got there) sd
                                    Anything goes on
                                    at Lancey Meadow
                                    I know—there is
                                    evidence down at
                                    Black Duck Beach.
                                    There was. Norse
                                    persons,
                                    by carbon date
                                    1006 had
                                    come ashore
                                    here Had built
                                    houses, had set up
                                    a peat bog iron
                                        forge. Were
                                        living
                                    Lancey Meadow
                                    1006
                                    AD
                        Los Americans
                        Number One (after
                        Skraelings)
                        Skraelings
                        —are Indians. Iron
                        against
                    Indians, on Lancey
                        firm
                            natural
                                place
                    for Norse—Norse are
                                    Anglo-
                            Saxons. Norse are
                            early Greeks. Norse are
                            Kelts. Norse are
                            Gauls. Norse are
                                Rus (Russia)

                                    Norse are
                                    all but
                                    Constantinople

Strzegowski only
removes the division
of Mesopotamian and
European. Mesopotamian
and Europeans is only due
to
Mediterranean
mindedness. MINDEDNESS

Norse are
able to
travel
to America
to Russia
to all but China
in the 2nd half
of the Christian
Era they travelled
as Greeks Vedic Indians Irish travelled likewise
in the 2nd
BC.

ramp:

to eat God's food
raw

April 1,
1965

He came
accompanied by
the night. His son
hung
in the bushes. When Heaven was again
on top,
he swung
And altered
him

Down came
his parts
upon the sea. Out of the foam the form
of love
arose. Was ferried over
by the waves
to the shore. To the nearest edge
of the furthest
near.

   The end of love
is on either
side.
Enyalios.

Each Night is No Loss, It is a daily eclipse,
by the Earth, of the Sun

      the universe unfolded in sound, light
      is only the drum—the hourglass—of the earth's atmosphere
      not the sun which is an orange lozenge
      nailed on blackness above our air, sound first
      even before color of the darkness and the blue
      or green or red, of eyes, night itself
      only an eclipse by the earth of the sun, so air
      or night conducts as dreams: we are
      wrapped in the elephant's
      skin, all the outside of
      all above deadly
      destruction which the species now craves
      wrapping itself in impenetrable garments
      & chasing in little cars motion
      of a receding
      universe, rushing
      to return, helplessly in time, out of time, outside
      the lucky
      sky, dancing
      Ganesh, all cock
      and axe, Him in
      skin, right foot stamp on
      Sloth, fear-not
      any thing, left foot lifted—gaja
      —delight

Maximus, in Gloucester Sunday, LXV

Osmund Dutch, and John Gallop, mariners, their wages

asked that they be paid to the Dorchester

Co., July, 1632.   Thus Reverend John White writing

to John Winthrop at Boston locates

Dutch and Gallop as on this coast or ferrying

others across the Atlantic at a probable date earlier

than 1630.   With Abraham Robinson the two

then constitute the probable earliest

new coast types to follow

the original Stage Fort few, who were already

by the date 1630 or before

well hidden now by Beverley

marshes, and the farming creeks

of Bass River, exception

John Tilley who, like Gallop

shows on the life of the coast years

1628 thereafter coastal 'captains'

or Masters—'mariners so useful

valuable or innovators Banks

Coves —Slews   are named still

after them

Now date August 1965 returning

Gloucester from as far out in the world as my own

wages draw me, and bitter

police cars turn my corner, no one in the world

close to me, alone in my home where a plantation

had been a Sunday earlier than this been

proposed, it is Osman (or Osmund) Dutch's

name, and Gallop whom I am closest to,

it turns out, once more drawn into the

plague of my own unsatisfying possible identity as

denominable Charles Olson add here as 4's

on a weather shingle our

names

       Charles Olson

       Osmund Dutch

       John Gallop

       Abraham Robinson, our

       names (written 28

     Stage Fort Avenue Gloucester

     August 22nd 1965

O Quadriga,
here in the Eastern sky,
there, in winter, directly above my head
so I had to strain my neck to see you
(happy, on my hill, in the clear cold
of the best of my life) salute you,
tonight, life no longer what then I
did not know how to identify why
you, in particular, of all the night's forms
had come to be important to me, replacing the known or more stylish
exhibits, a lessoning I did not understand
yet stood certain under you, you were a window-light
of my own skull.
Now in summer in Gloucester, driven as a Christian out onto
the highways, suckered into the present as a soul
forced out of fortune, with no lead but myself,
with no love, with life solely to be lived,
with nothing, therefore, of any of it interesting, see you
ahead of me, and it is one of the seven sacred wonders
you are my instructor at last, there are no landings
you also were Pluto, you did take my girl, you are
triumph (trump before the Trump herself) I hail you, Driver,
in your place upon the sky

Swimming through the air, in schools upon the highways,
                                                    their minds
swimming in schools, the lower atmosphere
gelatinizing from their traffic, cities like cigarettes,
                                                    country side
sacrificed to their eating time & space up like fish
Fish-people   their own UFOs   the end of Pisces
could be the end of species   Nature herself
left to each flying object passing in a mucus
surrounding the earth

The Savages, or Voyages of
Samuel de Champlain of Brouage

look at this! 1529   Ribiero

(or 1537 anyway)

Cape Ann is Cape

<u>MAR</u>Y!

   Portuguese or

Spanish Cape

MARY   Cabo de Sta

Maria

land discovered by the pilot Estevan

   Gomez — 15

     25

        And as early as 1506

           fishermen

of Portugal on their return from Newfoundland to

Portugal should pay, the King's demand said, one tenth

          of their profits to

          his custom house

Gomez, land

of the hard

teeth

Music the night

I fell down from the skies upon Cape Ann in

Nineteen

65   and of the Norse so well
                                        Land of the
                              Bacall
[the scene of Cabot's landfall]   a   o

son
1498 Sebastian
Cabot

John Cabot, Discoverer

of North America

Fourteen

Ninety-Seven, there northwest out of the

slime

I'm very happy I should worry

about you in my eerie

up over the plunging

sea with the sudden storm from eastward

       throwing rain

on my windows as I sail

in toward this unknown shore like Gomez

        pushing

his nose into everything westward

and northward of Florida

and south of Cape Race to see

if he might find entry

for the King of Spain forward

through the new-found country

which lay across the King's ambition

and his path

Physically, I am home.　　Polish it

The Earth—and sea level.　　Now,
Heaven:　　be the Moon reflecting,
from the Earth the Light
(of the Sun.　　Be Charles the
Product
(of the Process) as Gloucester is the Necco

　　　　　　　　necessary woman　　　　　　not go away

　　　　　renders service
　　　　　of an essential
　　　　and intimate
　　　　　kind

　　　of the
Pragmatism (secular
cosmology, not　　　materials
theology of most (or highest—hypsissimus

　　　Tower
　of Ziggurat Mount hypsistos
Purgatory "Heaven"
　in that 7, or Colored
　such

　　but
　saecula
saeculorum
　　　　　conditioned—limited
　　　Necessity is essential to an end (boundary　　Time 82,000,000,000
　　　　or condition (conditio　　　　　　　　　　　years
　　　　　　　　　founded—Creation
　　indispensable

of this age　　saeculum　　a race, age, the world——and I,
Charles @ the
Vision (Video to　　　　　　　　"look"　View Point
see (C @ ⊙ ◎　　　　　　　　　　　　　　skope

　　　　　　　　"Height"

                                      [to
             sea level——masts, of Winthrop Fleet in Western
                                            Harbor seen
           from Salem faster than telegraph than radar than
                              computer is

                    sight   [faster than
                          flight

              sea-level perfect
           'ground' (perfect
         'Earth') Wm Saville's
         drawing, of Gloucester Harbor
         better than
         Champlain's—Champlain
         a European with a home, American
         no place
         to go in landlessness alone
         resides, the Earth a skid
         for the American the
         Skater all over the
         surface of (the
         skin
                    Breughels
         Didimus

              As far as the earth,
         in any direction,
         goes

              Not what is on it, qualitatively. Simply,
         skin. One big
         balloon. Prometheus.
         One big Ape. Man,
           Erectus (Americanus). Precise. Winthrop's
         First Map here re-produced:

         is shore Cape Ann to
         Boston [Boston unknown as such
         at this date—June 1630

         map probably drawn by
         whom? what form
         imaginable a
                          logarithm
         parataxis (logo rhythm
         previously?

Mental. Heaven is,
mental. No Viewpoint,
from within. No "height" (no Face
of God, no clogging
in the light. Night
is solely
an elipse
by the Earth
of the Sun. Night is solely
not day.
        Heaven
is a condition,
likewise. Heaven is
                Mind (drawn to
Gloucester
            From the surrounding water
[on four sides] the light
of the sun—or from the air
[from the sea, on three sides, freshened
or wettened lightened from shadows—by
fog]   the night
has big stars—it is like Champlain, water
lends even a night sky no such infinity
as space-search, no such distance.
Night sky
is an air
of Heaven, de bout
of growth, love and desire
[not their products] are
Meaning. Night is Heaven
as growth, Night is
[not stlocus]   Night
is the air,
of Heaven.   In one place
—in the place where God rests—
the Earth glows, in the light
of Heaven

                September 29th
                    1965

                North,
in the ice, the Bulgar
and his 3 sons.   Forever fastened,
as Northern lights, in one place NNW, Novoye
                                    Sibersky Slovo

Lost from the loss of her dragger heisted
on the back side of Salt Island full fall tide flowing
all waste and vessels drifting
far out from the neighboring shore their painters long
for the tide's rise and fall not this full harbor and
plunging ocean
in on the land   boxes racing
left by the trawler departing
at midnight in toward the shore like moon's scudding
or roads riding on top of hills high enough
to be up against sky   the earth
is only round when water
fills up ocean to the
top

The Ocean

             clay

        Ganesha
                 pushed

     into the

     sea (after a single year as worshipped

     God floated out and sunk

     in the Indian Ocean, from

Bombay

           target area as

St Sebastian—body as

shot full of holes for a

purpose the God punished each year done away with knocked off

       the Solar King the Excess—<u>Energy</u>

       transformed. <u>Used.</u> Excessive

energy

anyway—in a society like America energy if it is not moral is only

material. Which cannot be destroyed is never destroyed is only

left all over the place. <u>Junk.</u>

             Gloucester is
sea-shore where

Ganesh

may be

dropped rubbish

into the Harbor cleared away

yearly, to revive the Abstract to make it possible for form

to be sought again. Each year form has expressed itself. Each year it too

must be re-sought. There are 70 odd "forms", there are 70 chances at revealing

the Real. The Real

renews itself each year, the Real

is solar, life is not, life is 13 months long each year. Minus

one day (the day the sun turns) The Sun

is in pursuit of itself. A year

is the possibility, the Real

goes on forever

September 30th 1965

                    Dogtown—Ann

Robinson Davis

                    and the question who is

Goodwoman Josselyn?   Margaret Cammock?

was she brought from Black Point

in the final Indian raid

and lasted that long in the "woods"

above Gloucester?

                    She would be John

Josselyn's brother Henry's

wife.   Margaret Josseline

                    If Dogtown was practically the

top of the world the mortar of

advancement toward the continent

from which men & families were essentially shot

to Casco Bay, then the recoil

when Baron Castine & others led

the Indians to retake (for France,

and, argument-wise, the Indians' own

"country", Margaret

the last Gorges remnant

up there of the original migration directly

from England, was one caught,

and brought "back", among the cannon

sort of local or St Joe people

whom Gloucestermen were (before Mormons

or wagon-people

west

     It is like Essex

resuscitated, that at a date

          somewhere in the early

             19th

            century

             practically

               the tie

Margaret Josselyn

is all the way back

to

Elizabeth.

       Widow Josselyn

No.   How is it they speak of her

& go to the expense & outlay

(panoply almost) of a State Funeral

Gloucester,

because she dies?

     Item: so many shillings,

for gloves. And cakes And what else

              to tell

her death was of some significance

           none other

—& she seems actually to have occupied

        no more than a shack

        it feels like

up on the lower of the two Dogtown

roads?

     Margaret   Josselyn

To make those silent vessels go, to make them
talk, not the lumbering earlier palaces, nor the rafts
(I'm thinking of the earliest Polynesian family outriggers)
Or the dinkies—Pinks, and ———— and
shallops of
the 16th century English fisherman—"boats".
                         to make those silent vessels go—as Joseph Collins
cldn't, with all his superior knowledge, & experience: Collins'
"scholarship" (work for the Federal Government) wasn't
as useful as Joseph B Connolly's activity
could have been, his energy   ergon the Mass
is, in Orthodox   the work of the Mass
Christianity
                    Nor the small
chips upon the sea sloops, and catches of fishing on this side
            —smacks now the Italian dragger has shrunk to,
            again, with all the Diesel-speed they can come home
            on, but the schooners, the
            able handsome "ladies" Connolly says
—and here one might trust him, and not
have to fault him, for cuteness, for the wrong
he did, and those do, to the romantic, who
do not find life except in some athleticism
of it, the Americans who never, no matter if
they do travel do not get away from home
["Home" and "Mother" Melville taught the Typee
natives these two words in English—he was,
like Whitman was [like Michelangelo who thought his family
came from distinguished "blood", the Canossa's]

—what those wood vessels under sail and with hard-
driving fisherman captains could do in winter
storms or on passages from Reykjavik or
from Georges to the Boston market
in a north-easter
heavy need to go to windward, and with snow
against them, icing up their
vessels, and the vessel loaded down with fish
for lumpy ballast, this is the song the vessels
sang, something of it to imagine, and to seek to
draw

Cornély.
The legend
of this saint's arrival
in the vicinity, after his flight from the Roman
soldiery on the backs of two oxen,
and his transformation of the pursuing army
transfixed
when the sea barred further progress
the Roman soldiers, pursuing him
—backed off, on the Fort, at Gloucester, in the calyx of Fort Square,
not even able to get off into the land except
twisting
like the hair
from my own pubes   like Libya's feather
stuck out on the front of the Crown of Egypt
go right the curve is clock-wise,
go left

the curve
is
left-wards

        can't eat
or have food   can't go anywhere
except back to that impossible Nation,
        the Cape Ann Fisheries even
now closed, not one fair fresh fish, haddock
given
to those
who are in need [pollock solely dirty Harbor pollock
to be caught
off the deserted
wharf (as, Isle Madame, still a fresh
pollock
can be taken)

into the menhirs and cromlechs

        F. H. Lane and I stand up
        on this shore, stones in the sea to inundate
        the progress, stones pitched
        by each of us   to lay the Nation in its
        activity

I pass between
the stone soldiers, I remember
I walk
remembering
the night of dreams, <u>se promènent</u>
dans ces allees
in this alley of
Fort Square,
two cows on the Church of
the Lady of
the Sea   two cows on the Church of
Our Lady

Note: The alignments or avenues of frequently huge, undressed
monoliths, composed of local granite broken by the
primeval glaciers, line the shores.

"cromlech" of course it is
cromlech of course it is (Settlement Cove—
                              where the Parsons
had their first wharf, where the Settlement,
by the English
"colonists"—actually employees, of the Dorchester Company,
to set up a Factory House, and for fishing,
and "planting" probably meaning literally, in this case,
agriculture, cultivating the same open ground there
the Indians had long since cleared,
of the dark forest [Champlain shows Stage Fort
as just such a well-occupied, and corn-
field,
            And where I first went out,
in a dory,
with Fred Parsons, the elder—lobsterman,
and with a "pack-on-his-back," from the deformation
rowing—you'd have to call it, sculling—a dory,
standing-up, and driving her, forward, all his life.
I used to go with him, to Cucurru's first wharf,
the Fort, to pitch fish-heads for him, for bait

and later, moored my own first skiff, loaned me by
Roland Strong, from back down in back of his
oil-and-tar, and City-robbery garage,
so I could also
claim to go
to sea,
            Now dwelling,
behind the face of my six tenement windows,
plus the North light of the pane in my back-door
on that "Cove" over there to my right as I write,
                                        a 2nd
half-moon, larger than the one in the "picture"
(painting) by Fitz Hugh Lane (?)—there was one,
he did a
"Settlement"
painting,

            Arranged,
in the water, stones, men-
hir, standing
stones, the shore (of Stage Fort Park a
half-dolmen, half a league

onward, half-moon of the Holy
Circle (the
City—

        Or the Sea
(Or the Harbor or
the Ocean, great Menhirs, higher up on
Dogtown,

  a place of
Ridge

                                        October 12th,
                                           1965

       <u>echidna</u> is the bite
of the asp, or viper [the "Monster" of Lerna
which comes up at the Mouth of Squam River
(which pours its tide forcefully out and seals
Settlement Cove, by flowing by it
by flowing by it,
out to sea) the uraeus (*ouraios*)
attached by a band
to the forehead or the headdress
of rulers,
       the Horned Viper, the special Hydra,
the particular worship of the City until—or
                    <u>unless</u>
       the Armed Virgin
—or the Aggressive Man, the "Soldier"
cease aggression from
satisfaction. The Monster shall rise
from the Deep, the Armed Man
shall have no Right Hand (the War
of the World
is endlessly
poised

"Cut Creek," the River is, Wm Saville's
Plan of the Harbour of Gloucester
May 1813, Massachusetts Archives

an amateur affective drawing
(with the Harbour's edge ruberosa,
and the scale 50 Rods to
an inch, "Fort Point" [which,

in error Alfred Mansfield Brooks,
in his clever and sentimental—pictorial—
Portrait of Gloucester as of 1800, calls
Watch-house Point: Watch-house Point

is the end turned sea-ward
of the Fort)

                one identifies
this map as Saville's
by the quality of the printing
of names in his own hand by him
as definitely, and comparable only,
as drawing to Samuel de Champlain's
"Plan" of the Harbour 1606

                        Monday October 25th
                        1965

Maximus of Gloucester

Only my written word

I've sacrificed every thing, including sex and woman
—or lost them—to this attempt to acquire complete
concentration. (The con-
ventual.) "robe and bread"
not worry or have to worry about
either

Half Moon beach ("the arms of her")
my balls rich as Buddha's
sitting in her like the Padma
—and Gloucester, foreshortened
in front of me. It is not I,
even if the life appeared
biographical. The only interesting thing
is if one can be
an image
of man, "The nobleness, and the arete."

(Later: myself (like my father, in the picture) a shadow
           on the rock.

Friday November 5th
1965

The Death of Carl Olsen

She hove down,
his son told me,
on Grand Bank when his father
was, say, 50, and they found the old man
down in the
machinery. He had been
pitched out of his bunk
through the companionway
into the engine-room

And his head, the son said,
had never been
the same. Also,
in a dragger some years later, during the war, or afterwards, Carl Olsen
had had another like or worse
injury, when the dragger stumbled
in a bad sea. He'd been thrown
with his head against the radiator and, in falling,
his legs had wedged the cabin
door, so that to get at him the crew had had to
force the door in on him, driving his head even worse
into the burning and bashing
of the radiator, hot from steam direct from
the engine-room which it was just above. It was these two things,
his boy said, hurt him even if,
as he also said, his father
was the last of the iron men,
and died this Spring (1965)
at age 79. This was Carl Olsen,
captain of the Raymonde,
and in the time of our lives the instance
of the men who were called
captains, of the vessels which made up
the Gloucester fishing fleet. Carl Olsen
came from Norway, when he was about
17 years old, and fished out of here
until he was retired
some years ago. I have told other stories
about him,

other times. This is a way his only son, also Carl,
spoke yesterday, when for the first time
I learned
Carl Olsen
had died.

                    Charles Olson, Friday,
                    November 5th, 19–
                    65.
                            79
                          – 65
                          ────
                           14   Carl Olsen must have come to Gloucester
                                  about 1903. I knew him at sea
                                  when he was Captain of the Raymonde,
                                  and a halibuter on Brown's Bank,
                                  in 1936. He would have then been
                                  50. It must have been just after that
                                  that he suffered this first cruel
                                  harm to himself. Up to then he was a giant
                                  of the experience of being
                                  a man, and so scared was I
                                  of his reputation (as one was
                                  of all these great fishing captains)
                                  that I never went near him living
                                                  over the Cut as he did,
                                  and I wanted to, because of that
                                  idealization, or it was a condition
                                  of such superiority, Archie McCleod
                                  also received some of this same
                                  respect [and, I believe, is alive today]
                                  that belongs to what these men did,
                                  and faced, to handle other men,
                                  and direct their work and bring home catches
                                  which made these men leaders
                                  of the catching of fish at sea.

                                  It is a testimonial, that they are still
                                  or almost still, alive. They tie Gloucester
                                  to her earliest life, or at least to that life since

just after 1700, when Banks fishing
was invented here. And the schooner,
in which they all, and this includes
Carl Olsen and Archie McCleod
learned their
trade.

It is a pleasure to report,
to a city which is now so moribund,
that there are men still,
in some of these houses, of evenings,
who are of this make.

Tall in the Fort,
my son and I,
the fortune said. My son

leagues off, and I
high here on the little hill, all the world

close, and far away, fortune but
Fixed Will, Foreknowledge Absolute, the

wings of chance
filthy dew, and nothing given,

all that one cares for
proven

and come true

November 18, 1965

Here in the Fort my heart doth

harden,

Or my will does, and my

heart

goes

far far

farther

Into the Diagram

Migration in fact (which is
probably the
consciousness

as constant in history

as any one thing:

Migration is the pursuit
by Maximus plus
of a superior and new
environment

of migration

always invades
the Previous
the other
location:

This is the Rose
of the World

— as all the disposel

& were forced
or urge than the further

— we fools as well—

for the neighbors
use

Constant thy neighbors
great grandfathers

Charles Olson
Wyoming N.Y.
Saturday
July 30
1965

The winter the <u>Gen. Starks</u> was stuck

Out here on the end of the land, it going westward at a known

rate, the ocean approaching from the east daily and equally going

back, the Great Circle of the earth making a straight line over Cape Ann to

Tyre, and further round the world,

the exercise of being with

a continent or a ocean face or back as will will tell

me which way to look as the year turns to-day,

the Sun now in the Southern hemisphere half way

to that other Pole and life again here in the North saved

by the tilting of the ecliptic once more in its favor, another

year of spring to come and Dogtown unlock her frozen

bushes and roads which snap like piazza boards under foot,

the Harbor yet open and two and more hard months—

already

by this date December 1779 and solid frozen salt ice three

full months from Black Bess Point across to Dolliver's Neck

privateers waiting hung up in the ice from raiding British

shipping as English ships and captains had Spanish

shipments 2 centuries earlier, now another two centuries and

I turn either left or right or east or west or now

that there is promise again and the Sun comes back once more toward Equator and I can confidently expect the year,

looking at a Nation herself untaken since before this Harbor

of her Eastward Pointing Cape was tight in ice

and measurements and lines were dropped through ice as far

to the West of South as 207°, Ten Pound Island Ledge

if I twist West I curl into the tightest Rose, if right

into the Color of the East, and North and South are

then the Sun's half-handling of the Earth. These aspects,

annular-Eternal—the tightest Rose is the World, the Vision

is the Face of God—in this aspect the Nation

turns now to its Perfection. Its furthest or its highest

Point, its Limit now reached, the Imagination of it

here or anywhere men in duress or need in thought which taken

is belief, go on the frozen being and do take the marks and bearings.

December 21st 1965

December 22nd

The sea
is right up against the skin of the shore with a tide
as high
as this one, the rocks
stretched, Half Moon Beach
swallowed (to its bank), Shag Rock
now by itself away from
the Island, the Island
itself a floating
cruiser or ironclad
Monitor, all laid out on top of the water, the whole
full landscape a
Buddhist
message, Japanese
Buddhism and maybe,
behind it, exactly in these tightened coves, Chinese
Buddhism, fullness and
pertinax, sharp drawn
lesson, the rocks
melting
into the sea, the forests,
behind, transparent
from the light snow showing
lost rocks and hills
which one doesn't, ordinarily,
know, all the sea
calm and waiting, having
come so far

The whole thing has run so fast away it breaks my heart
Winter's brilliance with the sun new-made from living south
I also re-arisen another numbered year from December's
threat. Love all new within me ready too to go abroad. Ice
snow my car as hidden as a hut beneath it children pass-
ing without even notice, every house so likewise in-
teresting because of snow upon each roof. Lamps, and day,
nothing not new and equally forever upon this earth. All
but me, damned as each man in death itself the evil
which throws a dart of dirt and shadow on my soul and on
this Sunday when in this light, and on this point, no
conceivable hindrance would seem imaginable to darken
or in fact any difficulty of any sort except to keep
my eyes out of the sun-blaze on the sea and careful also
not to notice too directly the street, frozen and slippery as
the light

Sunday January 9 1966

like mountains   Stage Head & Tablet Rock floated up
in the mad mist—of late afternoon sun whitening all
the water on this side (Western Harbor) & whitening out
the sky or hills behind   so that just the headland and
the trees along the road going from Tablet & disappearing behind
Stage Head, show

                  And now the sun, coming out, already has
dispelled the illusion, & they have 'sunk' back to
normal place, the water this way now glistening & all
that split second of monumentalness—no, still
the sky beyond remains white & now Stage Head & the Rock ride
as islands, from the glaze

                As eddies work tidewards drawn
toward the River pulling as the sun does the Fabrick apart

Sonnetina

Sunday, January 16, 1966

        Golden life, golden light on Western Harbor
out my west window at least 35 minutes after
sunset—
              and brightest (silver) nearest
me, just over the edge of
the Playground

        Glow dying by 5:20
                  PM
40 minutes after sunset

light in house now almost
reduced so I cannot see
to write

Evening then is
at the most 40 minutes long

                Written today—and to honor
                the memory of Mason A. Walton
                (who wrote the 'Note' to his
                book, April 3, 1903) and who started
                his life of health in Gloucester
                in a tent on the bare rocks of the
                Poles (of Bond's Hill) 18 years
                earlier—1885.

Evening Star absolutely bright in the West
and farther to the North than the Sun (directly over Stage Head)

These people sat right out my window too

rode in Western Harbor at the hour I now
look out on it, the 45′ of 45° N latitude of
evening

& went ashore on Ten Lb Island to
gather berries which were here
—and flowers—the first sweets they'd tasted
since they'd left the other side England's
shore

On the Earth's Edge is alone the Way to Stand
At Her Helm Eastward and Comprehend
She is a Spinning Globe Turning Her Back Always
On the Vault of Heaven Falling Away From Her Westward
The Star The Moon The Sun Racing
Ahead of Her and She Passing Going at 11,000 Miles
Per Twenty Four Hours Always
In This Direction   Catching
Like Water on Her Teeth the Universe
Ahead of Her Always Facing
Forward and Passing Creation Backward To Her Own Night
Little Spun Boat or Beetle of Her Places
In the Great Heaven of Ocean

Snow At Evening

In the twilight snow for less than a minute
less than the time I proposed to write
that the green of the whiting dragger the <u>Santa Lucia</u>
was, two minutes ago, as worn & exact as the color
of that Saint's eyes as they lie as, three minutes ago
the color of the leaden sky too was the pewter of the plate she
holds her eyes out on in Zurbubran's painting of her act of
life & its proposed loss

Wednesday January 20th 1966

IF THE DEATHS DO NOT STOP
WE'LL HAVE NO EARTH OR YEARS LEFT

Has March now been added so I have to live a 2nd month of fear & Hell each year?

And is it therefore possible that a Year of Man wld end in 12 such months of livid Hell?

What then would one be but Odin or Christ stretched on that Living Tree

                    pure Flayed Skin all that's left

        when one has given or it has been stolen or one is All Loss

        all the intendedness of what we call other each tendered Name

—our Own Dog has Eaten All Twelve Months Away

        then Hang God Damn Creation We Ourselves As He

            Desires

                    For Harry and Kenward together
                    Friday January 21st 1966

February 3rd 1966   High Tide   10.6 Feet

8:43 AM

Look at Ten Pound Island all white

except for the dusky old Light looking

humpy and surely bedraggled like America

since after the Civil War, when all is snowy roof-top

's and light winter icing on Cup Cake

Island, and High Tide exactly floating her in the Pan

of the Harbor   7:35 AM

And now—7:55 AM—Shag Rock

is floating off by itself from the Island like an Eskimo Pie

And WOW now the next morning it's a WHITE SHIP all floating by itself like

a cake of ice

The Land as Haithubu

How the land stands somehow deserted
each day
As the ocean falls away from it leaving
it standing
Unshorn   its pants down   itself hiked up
a little
As though it had given too much or not yet
enough
A deserted or exposed or ragged
example of itself
                             And then the tide comes in
and raising the land with it until
it is a literal experience that all is higher
floating way up on itself and perhaps
will take off loosen go and the Ocean itself
into some other land or place at least
sail away both seem at high and equally
at flood tide as though they belonged to Earth
which is not true otherwise each day

a 3rd morning it's beautiful   February
5th | Sa. | The Full   10h. 58m.   High Tide
            Snow Moon,

                I I. 3′

Equally today Monday February 7th the Island floating
—and with Shag Rock like a swordfish's tail stiff
in the Sun Blaze   12:40
                        (after
                            noon) full
tide [no. of feet?

                and out ahead   pointing out the Harbor westward from
                the Island (like its 'sleek head'
                the verse he sd in his work emerges
like Shag Rock—like the 'head' of the
Sea-Serpent (its 'first-fold'
                            And the Island
                                carrying on
behind [like the Queen Mary a thin
cup of tea   a thin
Queen Mary going forever
            just in her own place
        in this Harbor   floated up
like the 'tie' she must have
to the 'Land' Below: a aglaia of
this Port ["Gloucester-Port"]
                        with this Jewel
in her Eye, 10 Lb Island, still & white
in today's sun—and Shag Rock pulling her
never to move, out beyond the Breakwater,
out SW over
        Dog Bar   by Round Rock Shoal

                and the buildings on it like the old Light itself
and the "ammunition" or vegetable storage stone small thing
[with a roof] show up white today (the water even also emphasized
grey
            and forever
on her way: shall never
move.   Is here. Fixed,
forever. But her rock head, each day,

going, more than she,
                    more rock than she,
home and rest of cormorants only,
she (nesting-rig for mackerel gulls galore
like lice in her hair she spreads herself
her own saucer of herself out broadly
if sometimes, at a tide like this, Aglaia
and neatly so, the stone of her head
having—I just looked out—having
left her. It is a permanent
advantage [of Wide-Law, the 3rd Wife]
that she should have at least one child
(we are speaking of dailynesses, throughout
this poem)
            who does—and cormorants choose Aglaia
as they would, and have [I saw it, for the first time,
Wednesday January 5th 1966, with John Temple seeing
Gloucester Harbor for the first time—and I wouldn't
believe my eyes: there were a cormorant
on the Black Rocks
spindle!
            That near my own
house, my own windows, at the entrance
to the Inner Harbor, to the Stream itself.
It released
all my own
target-area: my favorite own 'Boat'
had 'got free', my 'Big Ship'
which will never—Euronyme herself
                    Wide-Law will never move—
had 'taken' on her
'Child', had
'acquired' her
'head': 'Aglaia' the snow said
in the sun; and the Black Cormorant flew
in upon the scene as,
now, in the rusting of the new &
lasting snow—and the Full Snow Moon
[of 1966 AD] she
floats high so the earth and shores are
released from their shabbiness   And
my Rock, by which I have 'gone',
always 'gone', always thank God have 'left'
"Gloucester", Shag Rock, the property of
shag   the rule and roost of my
own black duck, look at it, today!
right now hurting my eyes she's so studded in the
glittering direct sun over her

                    Praise the mystery
of creation, that in matter alone, the soul said,
you shall not walk about in the heaven of intelligence,
I don't care how much you have felt free in
the heavens of composite natures, of
discriminated natures, and of myself,
said the soul, now you shall not walk
around the heaven beyond me, "That is no way for thee"

                    10 Lb Island,
always there in front of me, to which my Father
in the dream [as well as in fact] had rowed me,
                              the lower process
in this kind of work   tide in her revelation recovered

And I heard the soul, I had successfully walked
round the Three Heavens———the Three Towns, the
trimurta
            And was, in this last month and this
winter seeking
another step (or objecting, in my soul & to my soul
at fate, I was indeed planning
to walk round the higher world, to go as my cormorant flies
if such a short distance   when those words
of the soul———how could the heaven of the soul itself say
'That is no way for thee' how could I
be left
as the cormorant
with no more flight than
our own Rock? which leaves only in
effect, and only [if the instance here reported for days]
once a year takes off,
and not even from the land, seems only
as the cormorant itself laboriously gains flight
just at water-level, and lands,
almost as soon as in flight, on the spindle,
where have we
gone? and what is the 'prison' the soul says
you shall stay in?
            It is none, my Island
has taught me.

                    February 7th
                    1966

I have been an ability—a machine—up to
now. An act of "history", my own, and my father's,
together, a queer [Gloucester-sense] combination
of completing something both visionary—or illusions (projection? literally
lantern-slides, on the sheet, in the front-room Worcester,
on the wall, and the lantern always getting too hot
and I burning my fingers—& burning my
nerves   as in fact John says or Vincent Ferrini they too
had to deal with their father's existence.   My own
was so loaded in his favor as in fact so patently
against my mother that I have been like his stained shingle
ever since   Or once   or forever   It doesn't matter   The love I learned
from my father has stood me in good stead
—home stead—I maintained this "strand" to
this very day.   My father's   And now my own

                    I face
the snowy hills
of Stage Fort Park—hanging ground
And the hill behind
where Ben Kerr's house alone is still
stone
and the fore-hill
in front of my eye
(over Half Moon and between
Tablet Rock quite sharply marked
in mass
by the snow too [right up Kerr's hill skinny trees alone
declare,
with the snow,
the hill
        , the snow
on Half Moon "hill,"
and Tablet Rock—"Washing rock," of the Parsonses?
and Stage Point their stage therefore Tablet
their washing Rock?
                    my beach only
in symbolic fact   like wearing rubber suit
and going diving walking off heavily laden
like the Great Auk wobbling with lead all
weighing one at the waist
into the sea   I never
liked Half Moon beach   I liked Tablet Rock
and Cressys as I suppose my father also
he turned

as I tend to too to the
right when we
left the house he walked and I
grew up to meet him or stride after him
when he had set off
with his water-color box to paint
a scene   Or
as so often to
go to the Coast Guard
Station at
Dollivers Neck   or moonlight nights the lengths
of Hesperus Avenue to Rafe's Chasm (after
when he was dead and I was young I'd
do likewise with a girl or
friends
          , the T the shore
today pure
snow and "drawn"
in trees and shaped
in snow's
solidifying
rocks let stayed black
(as the tide,
withdrawn an hour say now from high
has this eye-view line Lane so also
used to show distances
back of each other   my father
And I
on the same land   like Pilgrims
come to shore
                    he paid
                    with his life dear Love to take me
                    to Plymouth
              for their
              tercentenary

              there
the U.S. Post Office
using
his purpose to
catch him
in their trap   to bust him
organizing
Postal Workers
benefits—Retirement age
Widows pensions   a different
leadership in Washington than
Doherty   my father a Swedish
wave of
migration after
Irish? like Negroes

now like Leroy and Malcolm
X the final wave
of wash upon this
desperate
ugly
cruel
Land this Nation
which never
lets anyone
come to
shore: Cagli said
sitting on the grass of the baseball diamond
of the Industrial League and as Cut Eagles over
out of my sight
        at the moment
        behind Tablet Rock mass and
        Half Moon
        my Wop
        sayeth
    whom my Father
    in a dream said
    Ad Valorem
    Cagli Cagli said no one can sit
    any length of time happily
    or at comfort or rest
    or by Seine's bank or
    the eye rest coming from DaVinci Airport
    into Rome by bus last summer on those
    utterly Etruscan
    or Mesopotamian or Egyptian
    Memphis-time
    crazy
Houses of Solid Hay constructed
like permanent
Acropolises NOT STAGE FORT PARK not America not this land
                                        not this Nation
                                        short-winded

        the very Earth,
        here

And my Father
dead of the fight
he got caught by then into
by the time I was 24—15 years
from the date he took me
to Plymouth, the week
we stayed with Mr Brown the Postmaster
of North Plymouth
—Leroy's father a postmaster
in some small New Jersey place (just outside Newark? or substation of

that city Obadiah Bruen

1st Town Clerk of Gloucester
went on [from New London] to from after
having come to Gloucester from
Strawberry Bank? how many waves
of hell and death and
dirt and shit
meaningless waves of hurt and punished lives shall America
be nothing but the story of
not at all her successes
—I have been—Leroy has been
as we genetic failures are
successes, here
it isn't interesting,
Yankees—Europeans—Chinese

What is the heart, turning

beating itself out leftward

in hell to know heaven

in this filthy land

in this foul country where

human lives are so much trash

It is the dirty restlessness

of fear and shame—human shame which doesn't even know how right

it is to hate   what ignorance

pervades

the social climbing of this

Ararat this mountain

of rubbish taken from used up anything and made a hill and home for

rats big scared rats my father and I shot

off the back porch Worcester

as the rats came closer

as they filled the Athletic Field

—and Beaver Brook Goddamn US Papers

with my 22

he gave me

and I don't have now to give

my own son

as I'd like to the bolt

was such a delicate

piece of machinery

to handle

and to lock to

fire

in counter

in Your Praise

this poem

clockwise

My beloved Father

to write

Circle

turning this page to Right

as Your Son

rest

Beloved   Father

goes forth to create Paradise

Upon this Earth

Secular Praise

of You and the

Creator

Forever

And an end to Hell

—end even to Heaven

a life America shall yield

or we will leave her

and ask Gloucester

to sail away

from this

Rising Shore

Forever Amen [. . .]

That island

floating in the sea,

just as the street-lights

come on

'

Moeurs de Societé

the Mountain of no difference which I

have climbed as other men and other men will

have no choice other than: there is no other

choice, you do have to listen to that Angel and

'write' down what he says (you don't your

other Angel does and you obey him

to the degree that it is almost impossible to

keep doing, that's for sure!

                    But,

does this Vision hold in faith

(as well as in credulity) and in my own experience crucially in necessity,

in perfect measure of rhyme and Truth,

does it, in beauty too, take me

            test, stiffly the modus

of this visione which

                    not as modulus, this

        , that is, measurement

                            "throughout the system"

    modulus precise finite segments

—"There are no infinitesimals"

all does rhyme   like is the measure of

    producing like, the Guardian

does dictate correctly the message

    is a discrete & continuous conduction

        of the life from a sequence of events measurable

in time   none of this is contestable,

there is no measure without it or

with anything but this measure:

—it does, my Beloved's head grows to Heaven,

              does my Life grow

out of my "life" Likewise—likewise?

        is the Modus

absolute? [I say it,

as a Prayer

          Dixit,
         February 11th
         1966
            [Friday]

Bottled up for days, mostly
in great sweat of being, seeking
to bind in speed—petere—desire,
to construct knowing back to image and
God's face behind it turned as mine
now is to blackness image shows
herself, desire the light
speed & motion alone are, love's
blackness arrived at going backwards the rate
reason hath—and art her beauty God the Truth

Got me home, the <u>light</u>
snow gives the air, falling

        how my own hills
and how Gloucester Harbor suddenly
coming in on 127 is hewn out
all perfect in one sight

          look as though
and, on the right as you pass Lookout
or what was Hammond's
Castle the straight to England

         which was true, Endicott
sighted the Winthrop fleet's
top-mast from Salem as

they sat here just where 127 shows
a brand new deck of cards ready
in your hand put there
as though Creation itself dropped

      and,

        with the cellophane off the
full American continent going
North by the Pole and

      West

                Charles Olson

             written the day I returned from
—Magnolia—and read <u>The Binnacle</u> again as
printed by Robt Creeley in
the Albuquerque Review December 28 1961

                  (February 16
                    1966

same thought—2

got to get that
goddamn pencil &

compasses to
make such shapes etc

in the universe I
rushed home here all
ready—and such

dividers: parallel
protractors also so
course equally is
equals: likes to
likes

efficacy

February 16th

This living hand, now warm, now capable

of earnest grasping . . .

The Day's Beginnings

(in <u>Gloucester</u>, where there are not enough <u>Birds</u>
or <u>Chickens</u> to arouse or announce the
Morning's Arrival)

gulls, on the grass, first   on which they never are except
when no human beings—or for that matter animals or children—
are yet up

the dogs, next, let out from each house as though they all—
the dogs—awoke at the same moment & the household—
someone in it, opened
a door in each of the houses at
the same moment: what is marked
(about the dogs) is the exact resemblance
—& exact same actions as human beings awakening
and first appearing to each other in their living rooms
or 'Mother' in the kitchen

The next of course the children,
busily making their way off to,

—and husbands, soon
—wives

Are last, and so much later—clothes on the line or
out with wash: the day's then well-
begun

        Chas. O. Monday
        AM   8:00? March
        7th, LXVI

valorem is

rate : the

Dogtown—the

rune of the

Nation

March 11th

As of Parsonses or Fishermans Field or Cressys Beach or Washington, the Capital, of my Front Yard?

SWly to a Plumb-
Tree

spirit water   spirit
level —well &
pond, well &
sea—water is
Father
Otter
Gassire's
fate to
1 FA- to
s-i-n-g the
root of
the Well of the
Liquid of the
Eagle's mouth:
teonanacatl is also
God's body
Ymir's trunk
the 'Tree' is—its roots are in the
'Head' of Mimir's
reflecting in his
Pool of

a man's song
when
his Father who is King won't
or even if he does if Gassire's fate is
fa- is
the son of Poseidon's fate is
songs   he'll
sing from the Well of
his own Sons'
until his own sons' blood does
awaken in the wood—the

instrument of song carved by the smith from
the trees' trunk:
he was provoked—each man is
or each man who is not to be King
—Prince in another
vocabulary
Leader in

our own sense: political

agent of
all other persons for a superior

purpose, that
their lives, all lives—Altgeld the Eagle, the Eagle

always, the
bird who <u>flies</u>   not necessarily can or does sing

does Fish perfectly in the deep-cloven river's walls & all the Jungle Folk startle as
the Golden Bird falls from the sky—fills the sky, to fish (to
lead—not I not any Son not any Poet we
as Chaucer in the eagle's feet, going up to see the
House of Fame is taught,
                        by the eagle, Geoffrey
your meter & your mode's all right but
my dear Chaucer you don't speak well of what is important, you
shall, when I return you to Earth, I <u>hope</u>, know more

the Partridge in the bushes was the one & I at Stage Fort Park was
played as out this kitchen porch a night in summer not so long ago was

or, years ago, one summer night too, sitting on the curb at the head of
                                        the street
                  I lived on in Washington the
                  capital of this great poor Nation
I had some time before—the Muses? where were the Muses—are the
                  Muses always in the guises of the
                  birds upon the earth,
there a nightingale, here a nightingale, Cressy's beach a nightingale
                              oh here nightingales?
in the night's air I alone
not partridges who drum as they fly coo or don't speak <u>here</u>?

        in any case any way always I was drummed ahead by
nightingales alone, here in the United States (part of America
—& wells are where our speech comes from
                              we speak with water
                              on our tongues when
                                        Earth
has made us parts of the World again, Poets, & the Airs which belong to Birds have
led our lives to be these things instead of Kings

in celebration of Events long past,
March 29th MDCCCCLXVI

white ships all covered with ice
on the first of morning's blue clear sea
coming in to the harbor from far away
on ocean's everlasting blue & colder
winds & spray in June-July as here
now in winter time—all March near
over but spring solely in the sun's
earlier arrival—as I write the ship's
prow black as Theseus' wrongly-flown
sail, and his father dashed himself
from the rocks—all <u>sea</u> it turns, <u>white</u> paint not
ice is on her brow this spring morning
And teeth alone & a red starboard
 anchor, all normal she arrives
 at my fair window over
 the Inner Harbor
red nose her prow shows now as nearer
Blue Peter comes from Newfoundland

The
northwest course of shifting man carrying
'hidden' (Hadean) matter with him as he has
  gone and at rate of a centimeter a year continues
continuously, in this respect <u>solely</u> to
go

The moon is the measure—man is the measure
Sun & Earth burning
red & green
while we reflect

The Groaner shakes louder the Whistling Buoy louder what rouses
Ocean now, an April night, to set man's signals going:
did Gudrun whet her son to fight
why sat they idle why slept their lives away
is that why now the waves stir up
the sounds to rouse my soul in its honor, in its
hunger, in its own desire to lay about itself
as violence, too, is of its craving to deliver
itself, to set all whistles gongs & mutterings
any instrument of man to clay as if those noises
were as the soul's own sailing
so on the surface of itself as waves do
not even man's boats are as little
as wave motion arousing now the signals
on this coast
                    You're not like Gunnar nor Hogni
or you'd get up off your fat asses & do vengeance
for your sister trod on by the Hunnish kings my brother
wld go take Goths on while you you sons of mine stay home
and leave your sister's memory as dismembered in the shit
of those Hun's horses beat the ground as they beat her bones into
hoofs shit where is your inheritance, children
of my blood at a later date

Land's End—

Times
End

and then

Monday   April 11th

light signals & mass points
            normal mappings of
         inertia & every possible action

                              of aether and of
change

                    II

to perambulate the bounds   a cosmos

      closed in both respects   both laterally &

                   up & down bonded

                   up & down
                                   determined
                                   Eternal

                         side on side

                              April 14
                              MDCCCCLXVI

having developed the differences, that Abraham Robinson, to take him
if here by 1640—he, and William Brown and, James Babson   rent a shallop Lechford
is information of, then by the test of the others—James Babson's mother
was born 1577, and his wife Elinor Hill is born 1603 he then probably, and Robinson
likewise, who dies 1646—or conceivably say might have been lost at sea, & William Brown
marries his widow, raises his son Abraham until he too dies, after his first child & Mary
the wife then marries finally Henry Walker, who raises the two children—so
assume Abraham Robinson was then 37 by time Gloucester—these were men
of the same age as the others who came within short two years
of them, to add other trades, and greater money, and obviously different
social position to these earlier
fishermen: Wm Stevens himself first of all ship builder, his own age un-
known but if already before arriving Boston say 1632 he had, England, built
the 600 ton Royal Merchant and, says Emanuel Downing, many other ships of
considerable burden, he must, almost like James Babson's mother, date before
1600—he dies some time after 1667 only though, & his wife Philippa in
1681
           with him seems to have come direct too from
Marblehead the man who or life Steven's children would doubly or
triply marry, John Coit who chose to leave when the New Londoners—or Pequots did
in 1651—his son John Coit though, who had married Mary Stevens stayed in Gloucester

& such others as Nathaniel Coit, raised with Robinson's & Brown's two by Henry Walker,
became Henry Walker's heir, at the end of the 17th century, when Walker
who almost outlived them all, & in any case probably did all of his generation
—his age too is unknown—left the largest accumulated sum at death 1692,
287 £—that little, for half a century, when Nathaniel Coit, & quickly thereafter others
such as the Davises at Mill River & to some extent the Parsons at Fishermans Field
were going to show much more—& by 1742 Thomas Sanders,
coming as a shipbuilder direct from England in 1702, was to leave
£3462, as good a sum as by then anyone

           in the 3rd generation then   but that long Gloucester
may it be noticed—in Boston say by 1676 already Edward Randolph reports
to the Lords of Council in London that there are 30 millionaires

the break-off, & clearly now writing this spring day of 1966, in the morning
sun, at places to my wish & will along Squam River and now
as I say this, on Lobster Cove, facing the sun direct in Squam
itself—Squam wasn't herself, except for Edward Harraden and Francis Norwood et al
anything until the 18th century   even though still the mystery is why
the neck I am on was from 1642 called
                     Planters Neck & story
in the Robinson family has it Abraham Robinson himself—and thus those others,
Brown & Walker maybe etc did come over here from Plymouth,

that he was the oldest, thus the Abraham of Rev John Robinson of Plymouth,
origin as John White was, from Dorchester, of Stage Fort settling 16
23—that, sd Rev. Eli Forbes in 17—, a church was here in 1633
the date the story of Planters Neck maintains——

            so now, so much this morning in these fields—a fox
I'm sure was what too fast for my surprise except the notice
when almost by my right shoulder at a stonewall near Ferry
Street going to a rock above 128   he   whatever was that
swift quiet animal was gone even when so shortly I did see again
his its shape last sight a distance over the field he'd gone
just two
impressions on my eye and no nose to smell with whether
this was wild animal
            I'd say so as here Squam hawks
over the tide:
           17th Century within my eyes & on my skin as
in my mind and, in fact and in fact belief I
write and map for you each lot 2 mo 42 were
divided up among newcomers—Stevens Coit Elwell others—and
Abraham Robinson left where he was, head of Harbor Cove best spot
of all, or Osmund Dutch alongside Thomson's fishery or
William Brown James Babson possibly even Henry Walker
left too where they had been along that eastward faced Fire shore
of Harbor
         and no one here when I sit in like position over Dogtown
in between—until Edward Harraden in 1656 buys from Robert Dutch
his stage—Osmund Dutch's son's stage here in Annisquam

or Planters Neck in sun and breeze enough beyond Squaw Rock
behind me and switching road down Lobster Cove to carry
light air of water smell as flower here where amazed I am that
20 feet from where my legs are crossed like this
a woman cut into field stone with a tumpline   this just now is the
20th Century   26 inches down an Algonquin piece I own

what world—and this I write about is only subject, is strings
I play on to invoke the world, to give it to you as, at noon I

as I read a poet say I lie
upon this bank   stretched out
               I solely want even as that fox
               was seen by me, that what

I offer you as now out of my right eye myrtle
flower and leaf are loud by presence solely

& gone in the thought—shall I
lay out those lots as well or

fall now in sleep
on this grass   and

do that work for you
tomorrow?

                    Ferns and a tree here
on Madam Goss's lawn sloping down

so I can lie on it stomach flat and write
and write feet now down hill to wharf

was once itself in the 1800s   until the Panic of
1837   busy with Lanes & Yorks & Robinsons and

Goss' Gees Dennisons Harradens whose not

ships   then carrying again to south'ard to Dutch Guiana
to Virginia—to Virginia before the Revolution—the bridge

rattles
which keeps ships now

if there were any down stream from it down cove out into Squam River
which was on this side and for Algonquins too as

Harbor was—for them too Champlain and Lescarbot show
map & story   as if I slid a few feet more I'd
put out my left hand in the dirt I dig out

the lady whose non head & mark the edge of an axe
of stone and on her back a child held up there

facing skyward as though the earth itself were face to the
moon   the tumpline on her forehead holds her so

                    Tuesday April 25th 1966

JUST AS MORNING TWILIGHT AND THE GULLS, GLOUCESTER, MAY 1966
THE FULL FLOWER MOON

Just as morning twilight and the gulls start talking the cinnamon moon

goes down over Stage Fort park one night short of full as I too

almost full also leave all those whom I have thought were

equally moving equally at least as much a part of this world and

its character as these rounds of planets—the sun, within

thirty-one further minutes will have started lighting up the East across

East Gloucester arm and, if I add this house or its place on the

Earth, three solid powers of being pass in property and

principle acausal also in this empirical world as I,

and as I still cannot believe my friends aren't too, no matter

that they choose or may, identity itself a recognition cognition

—that this moon in itself is cinnamon and bore

an image in my life as it now going on to China will

twelve hours from now bring tides again on this side, reverse

flow to the effect of its presence here 12 other

hours—I do not speak of solar proton ion force

effect on both their & my—these two friends, a man & woman

I have had reason to say were my only brother-sister, never having

but one, a brother who died at birth a year before myself was born—

that they or I were not effected too in birth and or conception or

in both by either ions stored in earth or thrown at her by

the sun at equinox, like-fluctuation to the moon's twytidal affect. Go down, moon and teach me too to

swallow what by analogy and continuity I now, at 55 know is

as much condition as the purchase of my soul by love as they

May 3rd, 1966

between QUEEN TIY (consort of Amenophis III, who reigned 1417–1379 B.C.) 'S

seal and QUEEN TIY's scarab, both found in a chamber tomb at Hagia Triada,

the seal before, and the scarab after the

p r i m a r i e s
_____

Phoenicians / before
_____/

—or by   1540 BC says in so many words the

Parian Chronicle that
                    it was that
in that year   /   Zeus

rolled up
  on the shore   and stole

as a bull   the daughter

    of Agenor

                & rushed off

with her on his back to the

south central shore of

an island since called Krete

            where

at about Gortyna he

laid her down gently having

given her the ride etc

of her young life and

thereon was born a series of

children including sons Minos,

the oldest? Rhadamanthys ⁄Semitic names

each of these ？ as well as a 3rd son's,

Sarpedon—?

1540 BC   control

date? for establishment of a new

"Western" Mediter-

ranean？   And since

in successive waves basically NW

as in fact the earth's crust once—& mantle or at

to the depth of the asthenosphere broke   least

apart & went

itself mid—

                        north north West

150,000,000 years ago to the t,

definitely now established by

J. Tuzo Wilson as well as other

oceanographers & geographers who have paid attention to the

fit of the Earth's continental shelfs

on either shore of   each

ocean   —including runs right down the middle

such as when

India ground a path for herself traveling

from an original place as African about where

Mozambique

& sometimes about 150,000,000 years ago

went off to where she now is, attaching herself to

Eurasia—as if Tethys went under Ocean to

maka the love with him

a   love   with

near Crete

on the water's

surface at or about

Gortyna

migrations

turn out to be

as large as

bodies of earth   and of

stories

           & primaries
of order which later is taken for granted are

such as the Atlantic migration which filled America

—had then 10,000 people by or about 1637 plus say 2

                       years

                maybe

    or take it right to the breaking out of Civil War

              in England

              that

     that primary NE 1623 to

        1637   or

      1630 when

      the Big Travel started with

      Winthrop's large fleet is

Indo- Euro- pean original

migration into lands bordering

Baltic & Aegean at early period not too far back of

1540—say rolls 2100 from Maikop or

           Aia the

             Golden

original name for Colchis the home of the

sheep's Hide—cld be Kuban, was the

                    Bristol or

    "London"   'a

    America

                Plymouth or

        Weymouth or

                Hercules born 1340—after Santorin

practically like   dropped
                Herculaneum   herself

    ashes

            precisely   Southeast of

    summer prevailing northerly winds

            put ashes on all

            Aegean islands south of Ándros,

            west to Khaniá on Crete,

            east to Rhódos and south

                halfway from Crete to the mouth of the Nile. The

            depth of ash fall on all land areas within

            this region was enough to cause desertion

            of the land by the people who survived exactly

            1400 BC—exactly

            60 years later than   2 generations   birth

                                Hercules

was born the

Greek Hercules thereabouts

Tiryns or Thebes or My

cenae

took all of the lineage of Tyre or Zeus

/ away

and buried them under themselves and their cities

Europe was beautiful

   800 AD to 1250—Java was also, Iceland was, Greenland, Vinelanda

Boston was 1637

                    ashes from

               Santorin   shallops from

                    London

   as the wind blew them   once

   out on to the water from

   Greece
                         plus Hell itself with it ahead of the wave
          a tsunami

                         Charles Olson May 1966 for
                         Wivenhoe Park its Re-
                         View

The usefulness

                                all which can be recovered at this date

of tramping out with great care

—the usefulness of this is twy-of-garland-of the growth-thought of

, that that too be as repossessed as Whitehead did then, 1927-28

                                   300 years from then   what

               is the true <u>style</u> of thought from Descartes 1st time after

Plato, & a recovery of his—from his damages to

knowledge: that

          each possible knowledge of

        the year by year Arrivals Winthrop thought to

       make his History—I quote (Thos. Dudley) and to

                             Winthrop why

now that that stile he reentered into a field of

                       —<u>incita</u> of

a <u>pratum</u>

        is worth each bit can be brought together and

gone over until as though it were the secrets of a universum

<u>is</u> the one matters, that

<u>that</u> migration—50 English fishing vessels on this side

in 1624 by 1637 was 15 reported; 1636 the

<u>Desire</u>   built [Marblehead? & by Wm Stephens—or on Salem

Neck, & therefore Richard Hollingsworth's?]. Made

trip Feb 26 1638 made evident West Indies Trade

wld be economy laterally—as well as Newfoundland's

trade—for those: by 1638 how many of the 10,000

people who came in the 1st decade to the three-ply

shore: Cape Ann—or Smith's deliberate

naming of the other landmark as bold

on the ocean as was the rock Upper Platte

                      Sioux later

either Land's End or Isle of Shoals lying

almost a straight course this way from the

Azores; Salem harbor still poor to

find one's way into—Haste and Little Haste Bay

comment characteristic of

             Westcountry comment of these new shores

      Little-Good

      Gloucester   Stark-Naught or Pure Zero Gloucester or as

      Matinicuns explain the 10 £ Island near theirs as

      derogation, abt that much worth—and pretty Folly meant

John Gallop's Folly in founding himself & vessel in such a deceiving flat place as
that roadstead chosen in a rash decision not even tolerated so early
—Winthrop says Gallop lost
a great shallop date

that when August 27 1639 a vessel in from the West Indies itself—well, the
General Court action ——————— 1639 had finally decided that
John White Rector of St Peter's Dorchester there Eng. and
the younger Hugh Peter pastor North Church Salem before

going home to England, and his death eventually from

staying, and choosing revolution as

more interesting—active anyway more quickly say, had

been chosen I'd suspect

　　by John White for the Salem post when

Hugh Peter's service in the Hague or Rotterdam

[Perry Miller's sure

Peter was

one of the secret

non-separating

Congregationalists who

the Massachusetts Bay Company had

carefully screened and settled on

to make their polity once removed

across the Ocean from

Mother England Church; and that John White

was patsy when

the Great Fleet sailed and wrote

the Planters Plea, that

great Norfolk men, and York

and Nowell and big Saltonstall were

party with great Winthrop in this

use of Craddock and

old John White's determined

years, to see this Nation

planted, younger men and

stronger in

the England of

Charles I; that truth it is,

the Charter of

the Company was

as slidded too

as these wise Government men: 'twas Richard

Saltonstall cried Havoc here

when Guinea ship

came Boston with

two natives, roared

unto the Court you shall

return these men,

right back, and see

they get to their own

homes, you'll sell

no human flesh, alive or

dead, in Boston. His father,

Sir, was Ambassador

to that same Holland where

the Bay as much as Plymouth was

religiously at least con-

structed: John Robinson himself,

as White (if Miller is correct), were

played on by these gamblers of

a Nation which they'd draw

out of a Church,

they said, as heretofore States were before

there was religion, they

    —and Rembrandt painted Saltonstall, and Winthrop's nose,

and narrow eyes—and his son,

was primed for Minister

of England as his pere

had once hoped he

would be

worthy of

a ministry, until

—as lawyer, I suppose, he

found instead he

waked with Christ when,

in that morning instant

each of us know, when,

all before us stands our lives, Christ,

John Winthrop says,

had slept with him

the night, and sweetened

his arising, paths were laid down, though

wrong—and slidings—John Winthrop grants,

at 49 he, has not known

Christ's ways

out of, a

branch—or willow—whatever makes

proper stem to arrow Winthrop Sr. was   and

when Governor in London of that Company

he as, deliberate piece of the ordinance also intended

to shoot the Ocean and land a

massed people in

this State, says in so many words

(1644) "we

with money & with power

had unnamed persons near to Charles

remove

as though it were a eraser that

headquarters of a company shall

be in this island   —John White's study

was raided by the Crown's uniformed

Cavalry, John Robinson never did follow the Pilgrimes

here, —and William Ames's library,

rather than himself, came over, shipload after

his own body didn't, and formed the College,

at Cambridge, so deliberately re-named's

library—in England, sd the docquet, this Massachusetts' Bay's

headquarters—they shall elect

"governors and officers here"—"so this was intended", says

Winthrop, "&

with much difficulty we gott it ab-

scinded" so,

     if my island Cape an and

     the future—if now England

     today this year 1966 J. Prynne

     —and Edward Dorn and Andrew

     Crozier—and Tom Pickard   and

     England too sleeps now with nights

     new to their souls, "the light cloud

     blowing in from the ice of Norfolk

     thrust", Company here,

     bridging a peninsula too to

     a continent,

           "the top and head",

he had it, Men

of Power (who are still what now

eats out our policy, from Boston &

vicinity come

Presidents—or President-makers,

the moskitoes of Beverly Farms

worse than the Southeast Asia &

Pacific, where their money was then

made—as streetcars, in Athens, made

Prime Minister's of England's money—

o men without heat, without Christ

to keep their night with them, with morning

only briskness for their keep, good wives,

& children, like the wives, only later Am-

bassadors, health and pretty boats out on

Nahant Head, or curled in Manchester Port

—a creek bed   and Chatham?   men?   now?

anyway, then—and now is ours, and England's—

"like a heart", Edward Johnson said in

The Wonder-Working Providence of,

New England, Boston, "having two hills

next the sea, being

the center town and metropolis of

this wilderness work, invironed with

the brinish floods they crossed, Hugh Peter only the younger

of the conspiratorial ministers &

the Executives (of the Company determined

to have policy here, to be a State drawn

from the egg of the effort to love

and to believe,

and to bring home their arrow

to the heart or shoot

between the eyes, on the forehead

where Wisdom is, and the pillow of God

's

Foot is, and man

holds up

it all,

dares,

as in chance Puritans took

a Westcountry, and then a London, Company

turned even Boston Neck

into

Fortress : "loud-babbling guns" they

posted, instead of a Dutch

Sea-Fort or

John Smith's Southern Palisadoes

blew his hand off, or at least,

the whole canoe and shipped him

back to England full of

show and skin 3/4s gone from

powder, Boston,

hiding her crookedness between three hills, absconding even here with Wm Blackstone's

home, and apples, purposing purpose,

having

care,

hating error, desiring

a Nation and

God, desiring

that society & belief

are one,

"had one small isthmus"

to the neighbor towns, "gave them free access to",

into this nest

of the crook of Massachusetts Bay,

with Cape an one horn and the pommel of

a larger Gulf, Maine,

going Eastward, and down to France,

to Newfoundland and Iceland, to Murmansk, to the White Sea, to the rivers

going in to Europe where Muscovy Company, headquarters York, and

had been to Armenia, and to the Caspian and Karakoram

from Holland to North Parish Salem Hugh Peter preached,

fish

as White by mail from the other side   Winthrop

and his own &

Endecott & Downing to

> see a fishing on this side as
>
> more valuable than shop-keepers,
>
> [merchants soon, & since the Nation's
>
> choice—
>
>> money money including
>>
> and you cld kiss their ass—2 years
>
>> or 7, the

losses

> the lice
>
> of policy, on the body
>
> Politick "a
>
> entire and Independent body-
>
> politic
>
>
> ought not to stretch beyond the same

OCEANIA,
                    the Child
        of the Moment of the Mind
        and Thought

        I've seen it all go in other directions
        and heard a man say why not
        stop ocean's tides
                        and not even more than the slow
        loss of a small piece of time, not any more vibration
        than the normal wobble of the earth on its present axis

no paleographic wind will record these divergent
and solely diverse animadversions—some part also of emotions
or consciousness.   Actually the stirrings now of man faced
                                with a wall going
up—man is now his own production, he is
omnivorous, the only trouble with his situation is he eats
himself and since 1650 this
                        infestation
of his own order has
jumping to
2,700 million and
        going to 6,200 on
        January 1st 2000 is

his—the People are now the science
of the Past—his
increment.   Only he has no
thought left, nor money nor
mortalness. He is only valuable
to himself—ugh, a species
acquiring
distaste
for itself.   This tonight
after a weekend is the burden
and gives scum on the river carrying
the tide toward
        Ipswich
        Bay under Cut Bridge
        Sunday June 5
        1966

And the tide
came to a stop
while I wrote up to the last line over
on the bridge
abutment (actually
swinging
gate of
bascule

        And as I write these
lines & have only stopped to watch
the police
cruiser
check me out writing
in the lamp's light now
on the Cut side of
the bridge & lit a cigarette the

tide's now going
back to ocean——I shld have

chosen to write
this poem
the
full tide of
June

        It must be say   1:55
AM   Daylight Saving   Monday June
6, simply for a
                guess.   Will check out.

Have, on the other side,
peering in
the bridge-house
window—1:25
                it was, so the tide swung say
            here at the river's
                mouth at & after 1
                & before say
                    1:20

And now I look onto the marsh
away from the boulevard
lights—& there is the
        whole back of the river's
            mouth flooded as I had
                5 yrs ago called it   Oceania!

As a stiff & colder
wind too, straight down
the river as in winter
chills   cools
the night   people had sd

earlier they'd hoped
wld have been a
thunderstorm   I had sd no
the wind's still
where it was

      Excuse please   no boast
        only the glory of
           celebrating

      the processes
        of Earth
           and man.

    And no one
to tell it to
   but you   for
           Robert Hogg, Dan Rice and
            Jeremy Prynne

      And the smell
of summer night
      and new moan
        hay
           And the moon
            now gone a quarter toward
          last quarter comes
       out

And, coming back,
           the wind
  had died as the tide
    had lost
    the hurry
    of its re-surge
    & the sultry
    summer night
    possessed
    the river and the

land and lightning
heat lightning probably
   was shooting
      over the night
                        ?

         ?

      also sullen &
            red

            And orange
      like the mouth of Hell
      in this light the bridge

      as I continue
      downward toward
      the harbor and
                        increasing?
      in the
            haze & the little breeze again?
      stirring

      the inland ocean?

      to a fresh water lake

And the back of the boulevard
from the high school field

was a yellow pond
or an orange one
in the exact irregularity
of this specific night as
I am once more writing
in the light at
      the bridge
the air again
      cleared   the moon once more
      in its piece missing
      free in the sky & the harbor
      all free   and orange too
         as with no more reason than
      thirst or another desire I
      with out wish & full of
            love, leave it to
                  itself
            & tell you I have ——?

It is actually
          the red light
on the harborside
                    of the bridge
which made it glow so
     from upriver
          as I come nearer
                         to end
     this night

          & I go off
     a last time
          to leave
     the bridge from

The river runs now
as free & clear as drinking
water—& on the bench
opposite the bridge tender
the second time up the bridge
     goes and through it from
     the harbor comes
     the same
     Trina Lea
          Newburyport
     old &
       gillnetter
[came through the night the moon was
                    so swollen]

          & I go off
          a last time
     to leave this gate
          of my life
            & of the city
since Ocean was its father and
          ours

          chop now
               suddenly
          the warp of ocean's own
          swell clangs
          in the water before my eyes as dawn's here & the 1st sputtering

          of the gulls tells
          that day is coming

and Toot the 2nd
gill-netter
before
I can get away

as at
the same hour
3:30? 4:00 I used
myself at
16, 17
come
to
knock too
for the bridge to rise
& sometimes take
the Riggs through

(as the Guy R
goes, and
a slow coming
lobsterman
Sandra G

And as I go down
the boulevard toward
town another gill netter & behind me
now a quarter of a mile
the bridge sounds
rising like
a light thunder
to come with the
lightning previous which didn't
develop and day now will
claim the people and
be hot

and bang
as I go by
the Fisherman's
statue
the bridge gates open
again

the last sound
I shall hear
& here report

                        one
        PS: while at the head
    of Harbor Cove having a root
        beer Big Fishermen
    start out & several cars
            of fishermen come into
                & turn down the Fort or along Rogers
            St to go aboard & go out
                    to
        sea

MAREOCEANUM

Forming a lake just outside
Spain and Portugal, and near to Tethys
on the hither
side, Tripolitania its
southern shore,
               Newfoundland a large peninsula
joined almost to
Biscay, Cape Race and
          Finisterre almost
            stuck together
      So North Atlantic once was ponds
far far above   Gondwanaland

To my Portuguese—and, seeing in a Sicilian's head yesterday, &

again today, the old eyes of man and manhood which the Guanches

    You know, Gloucester itself comes from the

    Canaries

probably. One even, at this date begins to look on man as

a pure decline from

Paleolithic, so animal—or as birds make love—is

the human eye, when, inside, it does not know

any more than what it can express by living &

that sight be in this man's eye is the expression we call love:

the Muses

told Hesiod

there was

4 things got

genet—that before the World

there was heat or muspilli it is called in Norse

and made a bound of space certainly & probably

of time herself because the Norse or Bavarian word also means

End of the World

and there was wetness or moisture or like cloud nebel

in German in Norse the 'place' of same [to agree

almost—Muspelsheim for example is the

locative of End and Niflesheim is cloud's or

—Red Cloud [or out of my eye today, Man-Afraid-of-His-Horses   High Backbone

Little Wolf

Red Dog   American Horse—"water's End"?

Ocean's

Boundary?   acyanas? 'Tis True, the World

Began, and after two 'conditions' then came

Four Things, and only ever these 4 before

procreation:

      Hunger Himself or Mouth-Without-The-World-To-Eat

χαω the Muses said the word for the first

time conceivably, *chaow* they said or Norse is

Ginunga Gap   something to fill: what lies

outside us is not formless, it's

as we are, the sound itself of

greed. Then Earth, and Tartaros within her, and

for fourth one thing this time a 'quality' alone?

Love

      And Guanche-eyes I saw

yesterday,

and today, Sicilians, and I say

      Gloucester herself when Earth Herself was One

Continent, Ocean-Tethys were the Single Ocean Round

Earth [though this side of Tartaros, a 'hole'

you have imagine too is topos, Tartarus,

where earliest procreated Gods and Men are

chained, is outside Ocean

                              In mid-Mesozoic

time, 150,000,000 years ago—and Gloucester still moves

away from the Canaries—she was Terceira

"lightest" of those Islands and where Cape Juby

is now on the run-off of the Atlas Mountains, hip of

Africa, Terceira first hop, and here, where I today

in June of Fish or Aquarius Time tell

those other darker people of my City she too came from the

Islands

                             June 15 [Wednesday]

                             XLVI

Same day, Later

Contemplating my Neolithic
neighbors, Mother and Son, while Son mows
noisily, with power mower the grass & Ma
hangs over the fence simply
watching—and Maiden, or Unmarried Sister
comes around the corner to see him,
too
& if you let the ape-side out the eyes
have died or become so evolutionary
and not cosmological (vertical
not the eyes any longer of the distinctness
of species but of their connections
And then Nature is a pig-pen or
swill, and any improvement or increase
[including the population] of goods—things,
in the genetic sense, plural, and probable,
in that lottery—are then what human beings
get included in, by themselves as well as by any
administrative or service conditions such as contemporary
States find the only answer, the ticketing or studying of
—or selling of—family relations among contemporary Americans and
not Africans but of the baboons as a kin group in
Africa: I prefer my boundary of
land literally adjacent & adjoining mid Mesozoic at
the place of the parting of the seams of all the Earth

When do poppies bloom   I ask myself, stopping again
to look in Mrs. Frontiero's yard, beside her house on
this side from Birdseyes (or what was once Cunningham
& Thompson's and is now O'Donnell-Usen's) to see if
I have missed them, flaked out and dry-like like
Dennison's Crepe. And what I found was dark buds
like cigars, and standing up   and my question is
when, then, will those blossoms more lotuses to the
West than lotuses wave like paper and petal by petal
seem more powerful than any thing except the Universe
itself, they are so animate-inanimate and dry-beauty not
any shove, or sit there poppies blow as crepe
paper.   And in Mrs Frontiero's yard annually I
expect them as the King of the Earth must have
Penelope, awaiting her return, love lies
so delicately on the pillow as this one flower,
petal and petal, carries nothing
into or out of the World   so threatening
were those cigar-stub cups just now, & I know
how quickly, and paper-like, absorbent
and krinkled paper, the poppy itself will, when here,
go again and the stalks stay like onion plants oh
come, poppy, when will you bloom?

> The Fort
> June 15th [Wednesday]
> XLVI

AN ART CALLED GOTHONIC

ARMENIAN   Thursday June 16th [1966]

George or Isaac   and James
                    MEASURE
Dennisons   building a house on

each of the ways leading from

Town to Squam   and to

Sandy Bay

(a living room as true as a cabin

or fo'cstle at

sea   and the formal

nature of a ship's   keeping

is

what a humanist

Lake Van measure is

rate of rate in the woods where

Harraden-Dennison store and ship-tending

as B. Ellery   at equal turning

of the lower of two and Back

road   "Dogtown"   signed his

resident's as

             & built (?)

and owned The Dolphin   and

etc
          The

     account books of

     the "Store":   two further

     movements into

the woods, the Germanic

(and Celtic?) "forests"

             silva

     John Singer Sargent called

     a book I say James Audubon's

     bird book—or birds except for

     as so much else nature in

     another   as Henry Wallace

          a further

     movement into America:

             prairie

America, Ezra Pound.   Pliny

was or now one does quote

             Saxus

Germanicus to

locate early enough Tys or

each of the GOTHIC condition

                    GOTHONIC

                                        to

bear the path back to the
                        same

departure Italic and Greek

                        and

    now Hittitic or "Hattic"

                    HURRIAN

    like KELTIC a

    spore? of

new breeding?

            We trace wood or
                            path
                    will not
                            hasten

                        our

                    step-wise ad-

                    vance

we

don't rush off backwards to

other places or colonialize either

what hasn't even yet borne its

human actions   its

measure   & not viols

stops or the Sapphite or

Solonic   —verse is like

                              suits

they called sails or John Smith

in "Accidence   A

Sea-Grammar   says

                    fabrick

the Dennisons   Isaac and James

up as the path went above Goose Cove

and equally coming from Squam above

Lobster Cove

                    on these two

                              like sea-water

        ways also have

                    "corners"

        sat down and—   is kame?   or they cleared

those sunned parts

                    why there,

on the hills of the ways above

Gloucester, and

Ipswich Bay   reaching

like new-land itself

Eastward?

            Tuesday   AM
            June 14th

[to get the rituals straight I have

been a tireless Intichiuma eater & crawler of my own

ground until I went today from

John & Panna up where Gloucester thins out

home, & feeling
        what a small-town a dug-out I am

descending into, & have lived in as my pit

as, by Riverdale mills I

was again wakened as that

Indies captain had his Chinese boat

on Mill pond I heard my own

gnawing comed out & rituelle

Sabéen mine
        actually ismaël-
    lienne
            topi animated until

even the Earth 7,500,000 years off us

is my

gravel

Sunday

night June 19th with some hope my own daughter

as well as 3 year old Ella may

live in a World on an Earth like this one we

few American poets have

    carved out of Nature and of God

        [and son for that matter but I was thinking of swinging

        —or push me like Ella said on my swing]

Love makes us alive   The careful ones I care for are those few

        people—John Wieners,

           Edward Dorn & the women they love,

        and Allen Ginsberg in some way at least
which in a poem like The Telephone or his unbelievable ability to make a picture
           postcard alive front & back
or even a beer coaster or a photograph taken by himself

      and Robert Creeley of course who like I is tight where lusimeles goes

having written to Joyce

Benson 2 or 3 days ago that those poets whose

mental level does permit them to

know order, is <u>for</u>

participation mystique   the

      paths (Intichiuma

      made known,

        Love made known

              MDCCCCLXVI

This town

works at

dawn because

 fishermen do—it makes therefore a

  very different

  City, a hippocampus of a

  City   halfish set & halfish land &

  day is riverine: when men

  are washed as gods in the Basin of Morning

[Monday June 20th]

The hour of evening—supper hour, for my neighbors—quietness
in the street, and kids gone and the night
coming to end the day (which has piled itself up
in shallows, and some
accomplishment—sweet air of evening promises
anew life's endlessness, life itself's
Beauty which all forever so long as there is
a human race like flowers and, I suppose,
other animals—they too must know something
of what it is to love, to be alive, to have
life, to be on the sweetness of Earth herself,
great Goddess we take for granted, God the Father so much
more the strain of our beings, she the sweetness
we arrive in pursuit of
—when in such as this
hour falling suddenly the air suddenly
the voices of each child now
distinct, the
light itself, as the air, suddenly
separating—disassociation of day, wit
approaching—love approaching because
Night accompanies
Heaven coming
to love Earth, the ambush
they the Sons the usurpers
turned on their
Father, in the dark knowing
his habit, to come,
with Night, to make Love to
their Mother—& they harmed him,
Heaven went away that night, Night
stayed, Earth in fact was a Party to her sons'
action—these losses
regained each day when

time brings
the shortness of
Day to an end (Night's daughter
leaves Earth to
Night—and Heaven can,
again, fall in His Desire onto
Earth. Except for this interference
of ourselves, children of this
long & Eternal sequence of
Love & Desire, of our own lives'
scandal in
the Story
as those Sons ruined
their Father and gained Earth or
Their Right, and divided
us—as we too divide the
air of Heaven the mode of
Love-making which
penetrates Earth as
if now it, earth, the
ball also solely it is
as the sun also is, and the moon solely
planets—stars, three in
all the heavens' million millions
which we can see, at night—all nothing
but what is, equally—all physica
if now Earth again has, in her will turned
to shift her axis and,
already in a
10,000 year readjustment of
her magnetic field, we'll—
or so Bruce Heezen speculates that
then (4000 years from now, mid-point, or double
Platonic month—two, as

there's been two since
Indo-European man came
from the Caucasus onto
the Plains—a
like Time—he brought
these versions of the animate
nature of Creation, of
ourselves)—if in 4000 years we'll
lose because the sun's
Gamma—Edda gone to
Gamma—
will pour through the enveloping
Atmosphere—Heaven the Father of Us
not the stars, not the Universe, solely
this extended skin of our own
composite body—miracle of
form will
break—broken into, spoiled in
nature and by Universe, dogged down by
rays—Lord, Father, correct Earth and
Love as
at this hour, each day, in our mercy
of being your Child
in the Paternity of only
Aether, love us and
keep us in Your
Receptacle of
Which You Are The
Source—and Night the
Sweetness of the
Intercourse of which
We Are the Separable,
& tentative Eternal creatures,
Men,
and Women, simulacrum of the

Story, semblable of
You
—of which Life is not
solely Ours not
Everywhere
not all
here on Earth
& in these
troubled
stories
of our Selves, of our
Parents and their repeated
occurrence
Each Turn of Earth
Before Our Own Eyes
Each Day She
Turns Her Back on
Sun, And Night
brings Heaven
to Her to
Begin Again, Love
And Man Shall Continue To Be the Mystica of
This One System Flying
Loose in the melee of the
Universe
And the Perfect Bowl
of the Sky of Gloucester
in which these Events
May be Seen
Each Evening Hour
Each Day before
Night comes
to cover Heaven's
approach, to make Love to

Earth
And bear Us
as our Ancestors were
So Borne

The history
of Earth   And of
Creation (that the Universe
is the <u>plataforma</u> of
Truth—or, to make sure there is no chance of
misunderstanding, that the Universe
in the instance of its voice, rather than
its appearance (as multifold & so many
stars etc) a <u>condition</u>   condicio—<u>said</u> with—which
is what one is talking <u>about,</u> that
the sd Universe does like 'speak'. And thereon declare
—lend the
experience of
Truth [what can also be called, and is so often, to yield the
suddenness, and completeness, and thereafter difference
in the being (whether it is man or Earth—all the rest
<u>is</u> self-declared, and simply will or can reveal itself
by Earth & <u>to</u> Man if he
chooses. It is
knowable. And of knowledge there is a
result.
        I looked up and saw
        its truth
        through everything
                sewn in & binding
        each seam

Migration in fact (which is probably
as constant in history as any <u>one</u> thing: migration

is the pursuit by animals, plants & men of a suitable
—and gods as well—& preferable

environment; and leads always to a new center. If I were pressed
I'd add the dipole of the Aesir-Vanirs, that

to the <u>impetus</u> (the raging there is added the
Animus: that the Mind or Will always

successfully opposes & invades the Previous, This
is the rose is the rose is the rose   of the World

                        Monday night August 8th

The boats' lights in the dawn now going so swiftly the
night going so swiftly the draggers'
lights shoving so sharply in what's left
clouds even like the puff
of cottons she left which, forgotten,
even with all her care   care of such an order
love itself was put down as over-
ably as, if she chose   and she had
still no choice to organize
every thing: love made as straight
as if   if you could get her womb out
if she cld that is   and it was so close
to the mouth   both my own and her
legs all the distance of her
hair to the tip of the rounded boy
behinds   I could hold both of them in
my one hand   her hair itself
even on her head more clouded
and dense than any depth at all
there was before her womb's mouth
was at the entrance: love's puff
of irritated
wetness   puffs
in the sky and the night
still dark and handsome as the
face of her legs lifted
wetly to be loved and those hurrying
silly two lights boats busily
like little hurrying nifts going too fast
and now too small even though bright
in the still dark but coming now earliest
or latest of earliest light and latest of
night as the darkness and the white puffs
on and by the bed the girl whose head
and whose love she lifts opening
and raising her legs are so
alike night still light already
too far out and the small draggers
too small and bright in the first dawn since
she left was here and
I was
covered as I am not now
alone ill of
separation I cannot

allow love having
not on my own part taken
it
part in her
face & face
hair & hair depth
to my eye and hands
one hand
so much as caught
in her
hair my member my
middle finger right on her crown
love as large and tight as her great
mouth's turning
in perfect tuned love lying
all out three great parts each at
a different rate and
interchange of
time

Out of the light of Heaven   the flower

grows down, the air

of Heaven

Hotel Steinplatz, Berlin, December 25 (1966)

snow
coming
to my window, going up
and as well across
in front of my glasses in front of my eyes and
two thicknesses of glass windows also
between me and
the outside, trying to see actual flakes

But this is the slightest snow, snow starting perhaps, light
(at 2 PM) already
lessening and perhaps—yes, now, speed
begins to—oh no, again they hold,
in the air, and could as well
as some do sidewise—rots at the side the Tree of the World
my injury, in my side, not the lance not the lance by which watery fluid,
I imagined, ran out the hole in his side. As these rain-balls

      which could as well fall back to rain, play,
      in the air, so far only two, have come near enough
      to be, snow even if more as tufts of cloth

          —as the female animal in the boughs
          of the Tree, out of eating the leaves makes milk
          which warriors do not know is

              —oh now the snow speeds
        & thickens!—
              is strong drink they suck

          from her hungry tits, sweetened by my devouring
each of them—separately of course but swallowing or enclosing each all
in my mouth (while she watches, above, her eyes on me like

she would not let me see—oh now the snow is <u>all</u> thick
flakes. And light increases, in my room falls thickly erasing
gloom.   But brings terror the sky itself is falling the End

of the World Tree has come! Oh, white hart of the Tree's boughs
oh rotten side of the Tree's side   oh Serpent, of the Earth
do not make this the Epoch simply that man has—oh now the snow

has swung back, no longer falls as though the top has gone, tries
itself once more lessly—It is not good, I want
the snow, I want need, hail and ice, need-nail   fingernail of Abwehr

the staves
the three staves of my giants, I need two sweet environments, of precreation,
creation
and

TiuBirka's bebt, TiuBirka
s shaking, of the top and
dew dew aurr sprinkling until she cries

who is this man   who drives me   all the way
who drives me on down this weary path?

Snowed on by snow, beaten by rain
drenched with the dew, long I lay dead
And pressed me, as he went
not caring, so soon as he had heard
what he had forced out of me
the Tree itself alone—ah now no snow at all

the salt, & minerals, of the Earth return—Enyalion
                                                    arises
from the froth of Ocean,
                              the Master of
Tripura, the War, and Beauty, of the World
                                              of man,
of the living world

11 o'clock at night. The southeast wind,

from off the ocean, relieves

the sultry air and my spirit,

as sultry, unflags

its destiny, almost for the first time,

so has suffering offended

the earth

of my being.   Hunched up

on granite steps in the part dark Gloucester

and ghettoes gone cities and an infantile people

set loose to recreate what was ground

and is now

holes

Celestial evening, October 1967

Advanced out toward the external from
the time I did actually lose space control,
here on the Fort and kept turning left
like my star-nosed mole batted
on the head, not being able to
get home 50 yards as I was
from it. There is a vast

internal life, a sea or organism
full of sounds & memoried
objects swimming or sunk
in the great fall of it as,
when one further
ring of the 9 bounding
Earth & Heaven runs
into the daughter of God's
particular place, cave, palace—a tail

of Ocean whose waters then
are test if even a god
lies will tell & he or she spend
9 following years out of the company
of their own. The sounds

and objects of the great
10th within us are
what we hear see are motived by
dream belief care for discriminate
our loves & choices cares & failures unless
in this forbidding Earth & Heaven by

enclosure 9 times round plus
all that stream collecting as,
into her hands it comes: the

full volume of all which ever was which we
as such have that which is our part of it,
all history existence places splits of moon
& slightest oncoming smallest stars at
sunset, fears & horrors, grandparents'
lives as much as we have also features
and their forms, whatever grace or ugliness our legs
etc possess, it all

comes in as also outward leads
us after itself as though then
the horn of the nearest moon was
truth.   I bend my ear, as,
if I were Amoghasiddi and,
here on this plain where
like my mole I have
been knocked flat, attend,
to turn & turn within
the steady stream & collect which
within me ends as in her hall and I

hear all, the new moon new in all
the ancient sky

(LITERARY RESULT)

That a cormorant fishes

now out my window—that Jeremy Prynne wishes

my own poetry—or us, two, as men, should—

as Larry Eigner the one day yet, so many years ago I

read in Gloucester—to half a dozen people still—

                                 asked me

why, meaning my poetry doesn't

help anybody. The black cormorant,

                        not the gull

possesses

my eye-view.

                                       /Oct 18 VII/

The Telesphere

Gather a body to me
like a bear. Take it on
my left leg and hold it off
for love-making, man or woman
boy or girl in the enormity
of the enjoyment that it is
flesh, that it is to be loved, that
I desire it, that without it
my whole body is a hoop
empty and like steel
to be iron to grasp
someone else in myself
like those arms which hold
all the staves together
and make a man, if now as cold and hot
as a bear, out of me.

[Wednesday November
15th (1967)

Sun
right in my eye
4 PM   December 2nd   arrived
at my kitchen
window blazing
at me full in the
face approaching
the hill it sets
behind glaring
in its burst of late
heat right on me
and as orange and hot
as sun at noonday practically
can be. Only this one
is straight at me like a
beam shot to hit me
It feels like
enforcing itself
on me giving me its
message that it is sliding
under the hill and
that I better
hear it say
be hot man
be hot
be hot and orange
like I am
I am
sending you
this message as
I slip exactly to
West I am burning you man
as I leave   I'm even stronger
now just as I
go   I am already
cooled that much   but still
I turn on you
and flare
as I start to
go. But still
hot and <u>red</u> now blaring

on the south slope of my disappearance
point.
Now I begin to
go hear me I
have sent you
the message   I am
gone

Great Washing Rock   renew one's faith in the fathers   I was born
1 hr and 40 minutes after sunrise on the day of the year
when the sun returns again from its farthest point 23½
South out the window the Parsonses Great Washing Rock hides
automobiles lights—cuts sun off for a second
or two, and when they re-emerge they are several feet
lower, over
Half Moon beach.   If I have Great Washing Rock properly
identified: one assumes Stage Fort was in fact
the location of the stage proper, and any such emphasis on
washing wld then seem to be the 'other' of the two
rock masses.   In any case Great Washing Rock makes it
with me as minutes are now added to the late
day as still the sun rises later (until
three days from now when I shall be 57, so many years
on the lookout and no further than here too where
I can myself regard this possible correct identification
of a fixture the Parsonses made enough of to
use it in their division of land, 1707 to mark
their own five-way apportionment of what they had had from
their father

                    December 24th
                    1967

The sea's

boiling   the land's

boiling   all the winds

of the earth are turning

the snow into sand—and

hiss, the land into

desert sands   the place

into hell.   snow wild

snow and hissing

waters

Monday January 8th
[1968]

the salmon of
wisdom   when,
ecstatically, one
leaps into the Beloved's
love.   And feels the air
    enter into
strike into one's previously breathing
system

That's
the combination the ocean
out one window rolling
100 yards from me, the City
out the door on the next quarter up a hill was a dune
300 years covered very little so that, a few years back
a street crew were and I picked up the white
sand

On my back the
Harbor and over it the long arm'd shield of Eastern
point.   Wherever I turn or look in whatever direction,
and near me, on any quarter, all possible combinations of
Creation even now early year Mars blowing
crazy lights at night and as I write in the day light snow
covering the water and crossing the air between me and
the City.   Love the World—and stay inside it.
                                        Concentrate
one's own form, holding
every automorphism

                        2 Feb. 1968

That there was a woman in Gloucester, Massachusetts whose
father was a Beothuk "Red" Indian (her mother was
a Micmac.

And that this was in 1828 and that she remembered
traveling in a "canoe" which had the full forepart
of itself covered sufficiently to enclose all the
children as well as household goods and dogs
(like a wicki-up but larger, in the sense that the women too
were inside this forecastle

So that we have here an instance of the Pleistocene
'boat' as such—the Biscay shallop of another
age literally en place in Gloucester, Massachusetts
—and probably not even far from Biskie Island, that
Speck interviewed this woman

Who was able to give this evidence because
her father had been, and one has
a picture of some such 'boat'
both from Newfoundland and

from the painted cave of Castillo
at Biscay

['LX VIII]

Added to

making a Republic

in gloom on Watchhouse

Point

      an actual earth of value to

      construct one, from rhythm to

      image, and image is knowing, and

      knowing, Confucius says, brings one

      to the goal: nothing is possible without

      doing it.   It is where the test lies, malgre

      all the thought and all the pell-mell of

      proposing it. Or thinking it out or living it

      ahead of time.

           Reading about my world,

           March 6th, 1968

Wholly absorbed
into my own conduits to
an inner nature or subterranean lake
the depths or bounds of which I more and more
explore and know more
of, in that sense that other than that all else
closes out and I tend further to fall into
the Beloved Lake and I am blinder from

spending time as insistently in and on
this personal preserve from which
what I do do emerges more well-known than
other ways and other outside places which
don't give as much and distract me from

keeping my attentions as clear

"Additions", March 1968—2

Take the earth in under a single review

as Eratosthenes as

Ptolemy as had Ptolemy's Tyrian teacher who had the name <u>marine</u> in

history

as there was John Gallop   John Tilley   Osman Dutch   Ralph Green   Gloucester

at various times with staging rights Fisherman's Field

a peri-Mediterranean syllabary neither Greek nor Egyptian nor Semitic

but in between them such as the lines Eratosthenes ran before Pytheas

were as good as all the distances of the globe then turned out to

be—as rivers run under seas and bays to come up

Meander under Piryne as

Alpheus under the Adriatic to

Latinum

as Phoenician is a chorography carrying

Gloucester as

I go

That great descending light of day

It was the wild geranium not the fringed gentian which

stood above my eye & steered me into

                              the Soul's

size   into sawol into

                  the Armenian

                          jointure of

                  into Creation's

View of herself

And melancholy

       Time's
unbearable complexity— as though our souls
could never be the equal of our bodies, its
devouring
occurring, at such a rate only knowing
Ko Hung says white and preserving
black (that the mystery-unity is seen only in the sun
        —as against the Truth unity and
will make us unsuccessful
in the desire for death

                    Tuesday July
                    23rd 1968

Outer Darkness   Inner Schoodic   the ranges
of the light or the 'colours' of knowing whiteness and
preserving blackness——the 'unity'
                            seen only in the
                            sun,
                    and not
                    the truth-unity
                which has too many
                references, and
                breaks-down
                all-the-time, none of us
            sustaining   being
            very gods ourselves
        not all the time
        only some of it when
        we do.   Otherwise the pin
        does penetrate
        the crown, the head
        is lopped off, the sight
    —the power of the sight, the lust
for Outer Schoodic slips
into the specialization of
Darkness of the stones tumbled
in their own congeries

above the head of John Day's pasture land,

a small parcel for

house   1707   "Margaret Josline   widdow"
               ————

Only

one such possible person so named at sd date wld

be her son   Henry's mother—and therefore

Margaret Cammock herself,   John Josselyn's

Sister-in-law   &   hostess   Black Point, 1671

[just before the Indian attack, 1676, after which

no further record* of Henry, or of Margaret his

wife   until

                *not true. He died, Pemaquid, 1683.

this strange message out either

upper Cherry or of Gee Avenue itself, that

      she shall have a small parcel for

house   being a widow ————

no way else to figure it except

that at some advanced age   & with

her son's   house

———— married after 1643, say she was in her 20's

[how long had been Thomas Cammock's wife?]   &

her 2nd husband had died Pemaquid 1683 ————1707 cld be
                                    1643
possible ———— like – 20   77 plus 7—plus?
                          ————
                          1623

FIRST OF ALL OF ALL DOGTOWN PERSONS ? THE

JOSSELYN OF JOSSELYNS OF THE JOHN

"who was again with his brother in the eastern country",

July 1663 till

   July   1671 ———— and Margaret Cammock Josselyn
                                                    mother
                                    pre-
of Henry Josselyn, John's nephew born   1658 [here

by reflux before Indians, with John Wallis from

Falmouth foreside   by or after   1675:

Margaret became Henry Josselyn's wife after

Thomas Cammock's death in 1643

    Henry the 2nd   her son's child Margaret born

    Gloucester 1687
                                    yes:
                                        on Dogtown-to-

be, 1707,   the vanguard of it all, apparently,   Margaret
                                                    Josselyn

widow   1st parcel of all ————————————
                                    (Wednesday July 24th
                                    1968)

I'm going to hate to leave this Earthly Paradise

                                    [Monday August 5th
                                    —at post 1:10 AM (of
                                        the 6th) having finished
                        (at 1:10) the longest telephone call
                        I believe I ever did have—
                        since <u>before</u> 9 PM ? to
                                        1:10 AM?
                                    4 plus hrs? to one
                                    person?

            this alembic of the strongest (when
            Mauch Chunk, P. A. is changed to Jim
            Thorpe, P. A.—and Mollie McGuires are filmed
                    in such re-al-it-y

The earth is dug down to low—Lane
cldn't paint it but he understood, es-
pecially in full moonlight or near full though
equally it is true in the day when
the tide is all the way out there
is at the shore—boats hanging
over on their side rock shapes con-
forming to another shore the
points of land encompassing more
—reaching out further embracing more
roughly gauntly milder water breaking
more loudly in the stillness lower
Earth makes water louder un-
familiar grounds and islands
—10 Lb Island enormous in the
height so severely suddenly ac-
quired Dunkums Point & Rocks
as if tonight Lane himself were
painting Moonlight on the
At Low Water Harbor
Scene: I said to my friend my
life is recently so hairy honkie-
hard & horny too to that ex

tent I am far far younger
now than though of course I am
not twenty any more, only
the divine alone interests me at
all and so much else is other-
wise I hump out hard &
crash in nerves and smashed
existence only

such a night or the recent day a
low tide then over Harbor Cove flashed
in my eye as though a vessel was
[in fact it was on the railway
there] up on the land so low lay
now that urban destruction has
permitted the Atlantic Halibut wharf
to turn to concrete rubble all
of Duncan Point is bush & rock &
weed, a view too Lane was
interested in as he spotted
a single red flower on the low tide's edge &
I that am over on any Dunkums
Federal Rubbish picked vetch
& took it to the Diner asking
the new summer waitress please
for a 2nd glass of water glass for
it I didn't know was vetch but
flowering weed: low tide night is
just the same the bright white moon
light slashing harbor water as
differently in look & sound as
waters noises coming up beside

this Ragged Arse Rock Earth
                              divine
upon such August low tide night
I celebrate what Fitz Hugh Lane
                              too
                              saw
hobbling about like cats & I on
his weed-crippled legs on his side of
the same shore I look out full on the
Harbor, Lane Hawthorne's
sweet contemporary when Noah Webster
was their senior & the earth had not
yet known its etymology yet he
as Hawthorne had the emotions

Shiva meant when war was nec-
essary even against the Goddess of the
Three Towns herself in
the crumpled dirty wild Tripura
Earth & Sea themselves supply when
moon & sun draw tides so far
Shiva had to draw his bow to kill
Tripura 'cause
    why other than that man & gods
                        alone
                betake
a day or time when only only <u>one</u>
& 4th condition God himself makes
necessary to a vision I no more than Lane
can give the art to though
in day or night I know tonight the rubble
I'll be free to cut away like nails
of all my toes and fingers maybe
too in pain to see the Earth
dug down again

            ————————

                  ?Monday Aug 5th
                  —2 AM plus
                  [of the 6th]

        pre-Testament & Muslim Arabian pre-Phoenician
        holy Idrīs view of lowest Trismegistus
        take anything but one thing only out of
        coffee human being or visit talk or work
        one element of all a low tide night or day
        teaches me is Enoch's view here
        for Fitz Hugh Lane's clumsiness of
        foreground in so many paintings I
        have cut off at my loss & now
        this night regain the virtue of
        in loneliness & in such pain I <u>can't</u>
        lift the bottom of the alemb the gold-
        making juices lie in sounding in the

striking of the surf & waves while
off-shore out the Harbor for the 1st
of all the nights of life I've lived upon,
around this Harbor I hear also
even in the fair & clear near round
& full moon August night the
Groaner <u>and</u> the Whistling Buoy in their
soft pelting of the land I love
     as though I were my love & master Bach
and say in hymn & prayer
himself
    God festen Berg or Earth Is Shown
    Beneath Her Nails tonight.

               O., for Lane, in
            hymn & celebration
        of Idrīs   Ragged Arse Gloucester
                       and
      the Everlasting only worth the life
                 2:25 AM

burning gold water-strip setting
even-sided to my feet like Robeson Channel
marking Wegener Fault the full length of the
Western Harbor to Fort Point from near full
moon setting this date in the West as far
south as to sink tonight exactly in
the Cove of Freshwater Cove as red or
fire or orange or of gold-water as
Al' Idrīs is in the Chinese
word of Al' chimiya   Al' chimiya the
Gold-making machine I sd disclosing
myself in bungling it repeating it to
Harvey Brown two hours ago

              2:45 Aug
         5 (6th   'LXVIII

   with all the new bright lights which make
   Natalie Hammonds 17th century fake
   Dollivers neck a Sausalito Over the Bay
   in now Modern post pre-literate Am-
   america [same day minutes later

plane overhead & whiting vessel's
                                   going
too fast as the school bell rings the hours too
fast over on Wonsons Paint Manufactory at
point above Black Rocks on Rocky Neck

                         —just rang

                                   Two Bells for
            what goes out an hour between
            2 and 3?

            Flying Saucer landing, Blinking Lights, Beverly
                                             Force Base?
                  Air Port possibly or Hanscom Air

                  moon go down   mad lumpy upper

            shape like Two nights ago 3/4

            pushed-in left-side face like

            Frank Moore's birth face forceps
                  bent

                        salmon-pink glow now

                  as school bell will
                  in two minutes ring
                      3 o'clock in the morning

December 18th

And the rosy red is gone, the

2nd—3rd—story of

the Mansfield house, the darker

flower of the

street   —   oh Gloucester

has no longer a West

end. It is a

part of the

country now a mangled

mess of all parts swollen

& fallen

into

degradation, each bundle un-

bound and scattered

as so many

units of poor

sorts and strangulation   all hung up each one

like hanged

bodies

And suddenly even the sky itself, and the sea

is rummy too (nature is

effected by

men   is no more

than man's

acquisition or improvement

of her—or at least his entrance

into her

picture. If he

becomes bad

husbandman she

goes away into

her unreflected

existence. And the pole

    (—the Poles, the Poles

     of Bond's Hill, of

    what was then

    'Town') are

         down too, like the bricks

         of

         what was Main

         street are now

         fake gasoline station

         and A & P supermarket

   construction

the fake

which covers the emptiness

is the loss

in the 2nd instance of the

distraction.   Gloucester too

is out of her mind and

is now indistinguishable from

the USA.

"We are not a narrow tribe of men . . . we are not a

nation, so much as a world."

H. Melville

Redburn (1849)

flower of the underworld

to build out of sound the walls of the city
                                    & display
in one flower   the underworld   so that,

by such means   the unique
              stand forth   clear itself
shall be made known

Between Cruiser & Plato   sea mountains   and

just south of Atlantis Gloucester

tore her way West North West ½ West to arrive

where she is   from her old union with Africa

just where the Canaries lie off shore

Wednesday, January 1st, 1969

As Cabeza de Vaca was
given the Guanches gift
and so could cure
And did, at Corazone,
New Mexico, remembered
in the name

From Fuerteventura crossing
by the Dog, Gran Canaria, Gloucester
is nearly Guanche too
And may she too have
as well-thought, and felt
a place in men's minds

her stern like a box the
<u>Doris Hawes</u> waddled
off Brown's out of the offshore westerly until
after the lightning storm   I thought
shall she never come back from the oasis
of the full North Atlantic its-
self?

Full moon [staring out window, 5:30 AM March 4th
1969] staring in window   one-eyed white round clear
giant eyed snow-mound staring down on snow-
covered full blizzarded earth after the
continuous 4 blizzards of February March   5 feet
of snow all over Cape Ann [starving
and my throat tight from madness of isolation &
inactivity, rested hungry empty mind all
gone away into the snow into the loneliness,
bitterness, resolvedlessness, even this big moon
doesn't warm me up, heat me up, is <u>snow</u>
itself [after this snow not a jot of food left
in this silly benighted house   all night long sleep
all day, when activity, & food, And persons]
5:30 AM hungry for every thing

The first of morning was always over there,

and, when I went to work, to be at the Post Office

at 7:15—or 7:05, and before 7:30, the

Cut was so often a pleasure to walk,

hurriedly yet likewise Harbor air gulls

already bummaging—and freshness I only

look at now.   Or can feel, like this morning,

in my kitchen at even an earlier hour, eating

probably already poisonous Pacific waters (in Geisha crab-meat

& drinking the juice with pleasure) pride in love

lending my blue robe even firmer feeling that

even Genji and/or Lady Murasaka couldn't

even in that far distant & more heightened time

have been more relaxed in their hands and

fingers or more alert to morning's

beginning even though their duty & life

lifted toward a more caparisoned day

than I shall already lying back here in bed

again to sleep Sunday away, my own life &

nerves having day & night as parquet or

Go-board for my less lucid & wilder

American-Chinese millennium to live in

Sunday morning, April 20th
'LXIX

the left hand is the calyx of the Flower
can cup all things within itself, nothing else
there, itself, alone limb of being, acting
in the beneficent air, holding all tenderness
as though it were the soul itself, the Soul's
limb

Sun April 20th 'LXIX

The Island, the River, the shore,

the Stage Heads, the land, itself,

isolated, encased on three sides by

the sea and water

on the 4th side, Eastern Point an arm

such as Enyalion's to protect

the body from the onslaught of

too much and give Gloucester

occasion, give her Champlain's channel

in & out (as her river

refluxes), a body of land, hard on granite yet

arched by such skies favored by such sea and

sweetened in the air so briar-roses grow

right on her rock and at Brace's Cove kelp

redolents the air, jumps the condition and strain locus

falls or emerges as the rain on her or the sun

                    [Saturday May 24th
                      <u>'LXIX</u>

Just to have her body in my mind (to objectify the possibility, the

Heavenly Flower of
One's Own Possibility, the

Pomegranate of Creation

Kore – Demeter – Self

June 18th
Wednesday,
1969

Strod the water's edge & the
land as though there were some reason to
do such a thing   not going away any further
to have his eggs than a rail does

[Monday June 23rd

Enyalion of
    brown earth:

Strod the yellow earth

with a long dry harsh call

    krk   krk   krk

slownesses
      which are an
         amount

way into the woods by
an original
topographical
road, and by an otter pond

            to forecast a tied
      ellipse in which a story
      is told and the ends of the strings are
      laid over and stand

         as though the air
         began again another
         story by another man

         Monday June 23rd

            [after night of Sunday
               to Monday early a.m.
            & now Monday 8 plus
            PM]

I was bold, I had courage, the tide tonight

and the Fort swimming in summer wetness from a southerly

and turning southwest onshore wind around

10 knots, I am reminded

(even visiting Pineys wharf   the whole town

gone to sleep) the nights I crossed

the Harbor etc I cld wrap myself in the tide it is so flat

& at her threads

            and sleep

as Homer did that last night on Smyrna's

edge hard on the road-side ruts from

having spent too long watching

& eating too little and go as though this Fort were

                        a sea-fort

                            easily

anywhere from night to cate or from the Bosporus to old [landwards?]

Samarkand

Golden Venetian Light From
Back of Agamenticus Height Falling
Like Zeus' dust All Over the River & marsh as
Night Falling Saturday June 28th 1969 on

Gloucester
Ripping Red River

I believe in what the Arabs by
muezzin—that at least once a day
(& for me it almost has to be sunset) to face the sun directly
as often as it is out & let its rays or whatever
(the fact of its existence, & that without itself as the hydrogen furnace
there'd be no us on the earth

The power of that fact too beside the one that
we were born is one to still
one's being, seen
& felt as the Father Plant & Day-Sun of
life he Helios $\diagdown$ to quote pater
Helios etc but equally not to quote
at all, to recognize this moment I too enter
into that contract, that he deserves
our love's obeisance in himself for our
furtherance because—
                  if I understand Mohammed's
                  reasons—or for that matter
                  Ra & the Sun Boat
                      $\diagdown$ & its night journey
                        too
                                anyway

practice of stillness
before him, & astride the curb of the embankment
just where the Aldermens polished granite statement of its
                                                building is
                                          set near
near the old Newell Stadium baseball diamond

            having my lean Muslim-American supper of
            two cheeseburgers a thin milk shake
            called a frappe Gloucester & a black coffee
            Saturday evening at sunset time June 28th
            Jack & Mary Clarke's wedding day   1969

II.

       Look at the size of those Blackbacks & bossing it
over the normal Gloucester gull on the marsh—4 of them,
1 Blackback & 3 mature regular gulls, like
water-fowl, & swooping low over the River & calling
strongly when in the air, back of the "homes" of my 1st
poems—the Frazier Federal   *
       double & 4 masted was it Brooksie called the proud Monster Federals

and the Aunt Vandla gambrel (also enormously overdone and so like

that model toy steam shovel I bot the Waiting Station for Chas Peter's

1st Christmas Gloucester (age almost 3) and I stood naked in a

rage both fr. tiredness (& from damn) and the goddamn toy

it wasn't one   it was a goddamn literally practically <u>exact</u>

model   crank-crank &   all that shit in the world: it was too much

both for him and myself, and his mother like any mother

doing that thing all from love, that somehow

the goddamn thing might satisfy.   Bullshit, it won't if it don't, and

forever!

      *   They both curiously
have a goddamn built on
    Blackback solarium or some shit extra smart
    modern kitchen or little chincapin of
themselves   both of them. That's curious
what with one with a hip roof & the
other with that doll of the gambrel roof
of my Aunt Vandla's toy village.
                        But
what <u>is</u> this kooked back
               development
like some goddamn modern merchandisers
itty witty Federal cute thing for the
rear end like some fucking new chick's
perked up product ridden arses

What a kook job. The gulls have left,
& I better cut out. The sun anyway

which I was here for—well not really
I mean I happened to get here today at
the right hour and the tide was
running & still is but is slowed

by I suppose bumping finally into the 'Other River'
coming in from the Bay—& where
                            what do they actually in fact
slowly impede each other?

                    —& now
    with the wind itself taking that charge all
    over the earth of night's effect upon her
        (the Earth's) east-ward   turning airs
        the tide is softening
            too
                    No   wow the gulls

are suddenly back &

    chomping

            and there are people
            in the backyard of the
            one with the high
            shirtwaist at its
            collar   ╱ to cover

        my Aunt Vandla's

    unoffensive

        egg at the front
                        of her

neck!

        Love

            O

at nightime in the Gloucester
revelations.

And again the virid
    grass comes on

as the River turns blue also.

Trout in them—no pickerel—no what, herring

in those

waters

today. Signed off

& going home. Me.

Love life until it is

your own.   Missive, & PS

∕ like also for

Jack & Mary s

lifetime

they put some laundry out
at the gambrel. and it's hard to leave
                on such a summer night after
another humid day, night's up
                like morning
                        And the air
                                freshens
            the air of earth
            traveling

                through space <u>soon</u> now

                                tonight

<u>at night</u>   And with a full moon

        carrying her   sail of her

            Isis-boat   going

        around by herself as the

                Sunboat Ra

        don't. He goes down

        into the underworld

            each night as the Mother

        like a sweet woman turns

        in her sleep. Isis

    doesn't need to revisit

    the Dead. Man does, men only

    live high, —and far down (where

the Father

Night's journey
after evening's changing
everything
—Earth herself
is different
from the air itself

Short Possible Poem To Follow
Long Excessive "Venetian Job" Written Earlier
At Toward Sunset on Squam River Tonight Also

Moon going down [actually only going into cloud or fog, same position of
southwest or out over Harbor at exactly
& now exactly 3:38 AM of Sunday June 29th, 1969
after such a fantastic wobbling night of utter brilliance   humid[ness?] and then
relieved by freshening wind—actually fog coming in athick (so I had to
in all fairness call
Mr Browne on duty East Pt Light station after having
asked him to
secure 10 lb Island diaphone
—& he did, kindly—to say, like,
so that you shldn't, like, get into trouble with those
poorly-written "Acts" etc of Navigation, dig I

sd he says I'll
exercise her, Sir

& it is now again as it was last night a
Smokey Moon of Dog-day Summer
Time   Sweet Love Time   Natural Crazy.   Time
Human Dogs stay out in the
Natural Time
(of Night
            I again am
                  Up

                  O

            & wobbly again from
            etc and
            solid pure hunger

                  Charles Olson alone
                  still Saturday-Sunday night
                  June 1969

His health, his poetry, and his love all
in one   [Wednesday July 16th
                                            'LXIX

the green glow of Glaowceastre now that
everything is to be made like shit & the rubbish
the moon has turned out to be at too close
a look   only

the power companies of course or men per-
mitting themselves to be so imposed
on discolor their streets to protect
what?   And in so doing make them-
selves penal: Reich was
right, the
race does seek
to resemble its own
experiments   so if
St Francis
& Clara whose body still lies in front of
Kenward Elmslie's eyes (and mine in
Assisi behind
plate glass   the dark nun saying
when I as an American asked she
replied   Natural
Preservation
                And made
                such sense
                to me

& to Father
Carpini listening
at the tents & beezars around
    Karakorum for any last sign the Mongols
might try again to
hit Europe,   this time
& reach
the Atlantic, 1248
                It isn't any
                problem, or
                question even. The condition

is quite pronounced, and happily,
among the dead there are a great many
who are still alive. Well, like, some are

And in any case the few who are do still,
in that sense, define the, like, possibility

—as, indeed, it was always
so defined. One does only wish
that these poor stuffed people,
& their hopelessly untreated children
—except to anything they want——
cld either be removed
to the cemetery
or to the moon and

it be less cluttered
with obstacles to the
still handsome & efficacious
environment,

the slumberous
animal forms tonight
of the rocks (again) in
Settlement Cove (the tide
even the best I ever saw it
for disclosing this mysterious
animate condition of those
rocks because they rise
                            laving themselves like steady
sea-lions] in & like <u>from</u> [no not so much as <u>through</u>,
water—like Jack Micheline
had to ask me
in so many words
do they grow there

        (that is like
he had just learned
trees do, & grass does
naturally [having never before been out of the Big
City
            So suddenly even anything
—which is true enough—does, then,
like he thought

And so I walked
thinking as I did so, I come from the last walking period of man,
                                                homeward,
happy and renewed, in that sense, by the sight of the
original cove of the City populated
megalithically, & pure Brythonic

Wed. night   having gone over the Park again
just to freshen my <u>body</u> itself up
after that long go of last night on
the Woman Who Is Loved poem
       July 16th
—'LXIX

Thank God
I chose a Protestant
Federalist
    town

I come from the last walking period of man

                                   Wed   Jl 16th   1969

the unit   the smallest   there is

Wed night (after 2 AM Thursday
July 16th–
'LXIX

Charles Olson

Father   From My own old
Sky   Mother Earth   View point

Chomplain   hippopotami
chomplain's map   slomberous rock animals   slow whale Freshwater cove
whar il dipped bockets for refreshing his galliots crew—
barrels   a stream fell down steeply thar up from why
Ravenswood "park" used to be only nameless road to Manchester was
Jeffries [one of the Stage Fort men?]s creek—Algonquin called
sd forest Magnolia [Magnolia glauca] strange Appalachian biosis stream
sub-Arctic & Tropic fluence here in Glossester's
environs   I sit on small slumbering baby whale rock
over which all Harbor from father's spring farthest green in my
eye   Dollivers neck termination Southerly (westering) continental
shore then wide mouth of channel to little red dot on
Dogbar breakwater protecting granite blocks hiding
little aluminum masted cat boats were glinting
in recently settling sun behind my yellow sweater over my
non-Buddha non-healthy American-nerve Golden Triangle sensitive
back between & below shoulders   then the huge long crazy long
Eastern Pt with summer buildings only still poor palaces including Clarence
Birdseyes   a charmant small model clipper bow square stern
schooner   tied up off Niles   Ten Pound Island channel marker (Nun Buoy 10)
from this now strange view where I used to too lay my wife once
perhaps one other lady   right under the eye of the sky which
here on this little baby whale—behind it the 'Seat' rock my
mother & father equally came at evening to sit comfortably for
my mother whose legs were short a park bench supplied them by
geological—same time given my bottom this baby whale & below
me my imagined Hippo & his crazy pal an Ipswich Bay mother
whale   all over next left what where loco

                    chomplain drew
up his shallop   Oakes Cove & on that faggot Worcester paper company
—envelope company probably—owner's house drew backward
to what I am doing counter clockwise likewise
                                          Ben
Widdershins the
Harbor with to my left now hidden Algonquin corn
houses—& lodges?   Anyway came cleared for
their use & so as I look finally toward where
I now live & the new
O donell-Usen freezer adds white to Clarence
Birdseyes original
plant the City Hall & Tavern the last
of the corner the shoulder of Tablet Rocks blocks
what Lane has so well drawn between

Chomplain & Charley Olson from over the like
Cut——
        so, Saturday night, cool
    so cool none of the usual
      urbanites here & therefore I
      instead on old evening spot years & years
      ago
           loving ancient love spot of me
                      Indian?
         looking up through my back & to topknot
                       of Head to
      the eye of the apex of the bowl of the

 sky

              #

              July 19th—1969
                  'LXIX

I,

    Death is the mother binding us to our end

<u>Thurs. June 26th 'LXIX</u>

II,   the false

    lure of

the woman who

      "betrayed us" by

            eating of the father's-husband's

                self (soil of Hell   <u>plant</u> of Hell   <u>King</u> of the underworld &

                    Our Own Father of whom she

                      the Mother is the

                        Daughter—&

                    Queen of: converts the "Underworld" into

                      Hell—Death the

              under ground   under

                us   undestroyable

              under ground

III,
     of Death, and of love   of life, and of Heaven

         of us and the Creation

        kun, and
      <u>shên</u>: the
    prowess, the
      gloire   hug life to your bosom, & rise

resplendent by the body of her flesh

        Expose yourself when
      your beauty is expected or
      asked for <u>by her</u> when
      she passes & asks her maids to
      ask you to see if the reports are
      true   (that you be there when
      the word is that you are supposed to have
      some evidence of
      strength —— shên is
      that strength wearing
    the "traces" of
experience—not
fluffing it off, being
you, itself

                    shên Thursday June 24th
                        1969

              the form of the method of both a likeness and
                 "necessary statement", <u>Li</u> is
              logos, and <u>the Abysmal</u> is
              eros "where love dwelth
                              in the palaces of death,
              and of the mind" and it reads
              cut in excellent letters into the
                              standing stone
                                     (of slate
                                            it
              says   Death passes no man it does
              not   it runs up   on us, Love &
              Death and—us. We do,
              and
              there is this headstone
              this streamer from the
              mainmast

[a late 1st Maximus "Letter" in Reply to
   that Earlier One my
   <u>"Mother"</u>

              the sign Kên, mountain, the possibility
& IV,   (which represents the stillness
              that by your inner world you may
              dwell in the outer as well without
              any loss of your being

                 <u>Stirb und Werde</u> the
       <u>Mountain-child of</u>
       <u>Water and of Mind</u>

a part of the
River Map,
& imagined as written
on what Mr Saville there calls
a hill of rocks, 18–

22

Mother of the tides (father, sun)
swelling through Cut Bridge of an
August evening so humid the air
itself even if a strong on-shore
breeze is blowing, a stiff one,
and a labor to walk beside it

while through the Gut or Cut ocean
pours a race-stream so
wild I am swung by it,
                    crossing
in a lather from the air

Monday July 28th 'LXIX

Melkarth of Tyre—
    Lebanese of Gloucester, Herodotean
report: the proportions
now declared to be without end—
    or beginning other than that they valuably,
occur   as in fact Egyptians said
(because they were continuous, and had had no calamaties
speaking to Solon, that is [as of Greeks—& one might too
as of
Jews] that there has been
no break—there is now no break in the
future, a thing does flow etc and
intensity
is the characteristic throughout
the system.   Why I raise monuments
by this River and have sd it does take a mole to join Gloucester to
the Nation.

                Thursday   September 11th 'LXIX

Nasturtium
is still my flower   but I am a poet
who now more thinks   than writes, my
nose-gay

I live underneath
the light of day

     I am a stone,
or the ground beneath

My life is buried,
with all sorts of passages
both on the sides and on the face turned down
to the earth
or built out as long gifted generous northeastern Connecticut stone walls are
through which 18th century roads still pass
as though they themselves were realms,

the stones they're made up of
are from the bottom such Ice-age megaliths

and the uplands the walls are the boundaries of
are defined with such non-niggardly definition

of the amount of distance between a road in & out
of the wood-lots or further passage-ways, further farms
are given

      that one suddenly is walking

in Tartarian-Erojan, Geaan-Ouranian
time and life love space
    time & exact
analogy time & intellect time & mind time & time
spirit

       the initiation

    of another kind of nation

the Blow is Creation
& the Twist   the Nasturtium
is any one of Ourselves
And the Place of it All?
    Mother   Earth   Alone

my wife   my car   my color   and   myself

EDITOR'S AFTERWORD

This edition of Charles Olson's *Maximus Poems* brings together in one volume the three previous collections of the poet's major work. At the same time, it presents the reader with a reliable, authoritative text. The edition has been photo-reproduced from the three earlier volumes of the sequence—*The Maximus Poems* (London: Cape Goliard, 1970; first published New York: Jargon/Corinth, 1960), *Maximus Poems IV, V, VI* (London: Cape Goliard, 1968), and *The Maximus Poems: Volume Three* (New York: Viking/Grossman, 1975)—with corrections and alterations where necessary or appropriate. The 1970 resetting of the 1960 Jargon/Corinth *Maximus Poems* by Cape Goliard Press, making the volume uniform in format with the *Maximus Poems IV, V, VI* that Cape had previously published, has been photographed here to keep typefaces as consistent as possible, even though, as will be pointed out, there were special problems with that edition.* The illustrations used for the original covers have been replicated as dividers between volumes, and for those who may have reason to refer to those earlier editions, or to use the editor's *Guide to the Maximus Poems* (Berkeley: University of California Press, 1978; revised paperback ed. 1980) keyed to their pagination, two sets of page numbers have been provided: new consecutive pagination and, in brackets, volume and page numbers from the previous editions.

The present text seeks to be as definitive as possible and has been edited according to the principles and standards of textual criticism maintained by the Modern Language Association's Center for Scholarly Editions. Even though this text has been photographed from the editions specified, it has been necessary to correct typographical mistakes in those earlier volumes and to account for seeming discrepancies such as possible misspellings. It had to be determined, for example, whether such appearances as "discovera" (89:20) for "discovered" or "urgeng" (235:12) for "urging" were intended by the poet. It was imperative to go back to the original manuscripts to make sure an apparent or suspected error was in fact that, and to pinpoint the source of each mistake, so that it could be corrected, by tracing the publishing history of each

---

* Actually, the copy used for reproduction was one of the Cape Goliard edition bound with Jargon/Corinth title page for American distribution, though textually differing in no way from the English edition. The 1960 edition itself was photographed in part from two earlier collections printed in Germany, mixing two related but distinct typefaces. In the final volume the titles have been reset to be more uniform with the typeface of the previous two volumes.

poem backward from the original volume to any earlier separate volumes, to magazine or similar appearances, to manuscripts sent editors, and to original manuscripts surviving among the poet's papers at the University of Connecticut Library.

The surprising discovery was the extent of error: of the seventy-seven poems first published during the poet's lifetime in magazines, anthologies, or as broadsides, only fourteen appear exactly as in the later published volumes or the original manuscripts. Differences extend from omitted punctuation and altered spacing to misread words. Even in the case of a two-line poem (422), for example, a magazine's editor-publisher rearranged the original line break to fit one of the poem's long lines more comfortably on the magazine's page. The immediate problem in all cases was to determine which, if any, changes were authorized, which were errors. Without the living author as arbiter, the original manuscripts and the poet's own corrected editions were the final guides.

There are over thirty discrepancies between the 1960 Jargon/Corinth edition and Cape Goliard's 1970 resetting—the version reproduced here, now thoroughly corrected. These discrepancies range from irregularities in spacing and lapses such as "near" for "hear" or "Historie" (the poet's consciously antique spelling) coming "back" instead of "bang into the midst of / our game," to such grim marrings as "deathly mu-stick" for "mu-sick." Some not only distort the meaning but render quite the opposite of the poet's intention, as in the case on page 33 of that edition, where there appears a sentimental, anthropomorphizing "humanness" that neither the poet's father "nor I, as workers, / are *infuriated* with" (italics added) instead of "infatuated" with. For poetry as idiosyncratic and demanding as Olson's, every effort must be made to insure that what one sees is what the poet wrote.

Olson himself was cognizant of the difficulties and procedural necessities of editing, and no doubt was sympathetic to the rigors of textual criticism. He wrote to himself on the night of June 11, 1966, among some fifty pages of notes accumulated while laboring over proofs set from a typescript prepared by Jeremy Prynne for a proposed but never published Corinth Books edition of *Maximus Poems IV, V, VI*: "Proofing itself *does* at least bring copy-errors [Prynne's typed version, from which proofs set] into view, and, checked by my *original* and by *xerox*—thus 4 versions have to be in hand: proofs / Prynne's / Xerox / original / [*also*—note—some magazine printings." His demands for an edition were precise, although somewhat paradoxical and sometimes impossible to achieve, owing to the mechanics of type (type size, spacing, and leading) and the inescapable difficulties of transforming a handwritten or typewritten manuscript into a typeset text: Procrustes was the original printer. Olson wrote in 1967, probably for Cape Goliard's printer, a "*Further note on the type-setting problem*":

> Each poem *set individually*, for itself, on the page, irregularly though they may seem, *at the same time* that *the normal justifying of printing* is not lost, even though it is obliged to, *in this instance,*

as say those *wheels*—whatever they are that they call in watch-making the watch's jewels—this combination [it is the *same* double-matter I meant about the style & a prose-semblance] is the only way *the disparateness* (the kooked balances of the book throughout) work.

OK?

I hope this helps. I don't $\frac{\text{mean}}{\text{want}}$ anything but the *simplest*. But it is a *stinker*, in the instance!

The changes in the present edition are grounded on a collation of all available texts, including holographic manuscripts, typescripts, carbon copies, photocopies made by the poet, corrected proofsheets and correspondence relating to proofs, audiotapes of the poet reading his work, and published versions, especially the poet's own copies, which may bear corrections. The differences among the various texts of the poems identified during the course of establishing a true text, or copy-text, have been fully recorded by the editor. Rather than burden this edition with a lengthy list of variants, however, it was decided that such notes be made available separately for specialists wishing to follow the editor's footsteps and consider in detail the textual decisions he made. These notes, along with related information, have been published by the University of Connecticut Library under the title *Editing the Maximus Poems* (Storrs, Conn., 1983). A concise yet comprehensive summary follows.

For the first volume of the poem, there were available for collation the initial installments, *The Maximus Poems 1–10* and *The Maximus Poems 11–22* (handsomely published by Jonathan Williams in 1953 and 1956 respectively) together with their original manuscripts—typescripts and early versions among Olson's papers in the Literary Archives, University of Connecticut Library, and the typescripts sent Jonathan Williams for typesetting, which are now among the Jargon papers in the Poetry Collection at the State University of New York at Buffalo. Also available for consultation were other early drafts and typescripts prepared by Olson and sent to friends such as Robert Creeley (among Creeley's papers at the Washington University Library) and Paul Blackburn (in the Archive for New Poetry, University of California, San Diego). Superseding all earlier manuscripts were the final typescript of *The Maximus Poems* (1960), incorporating the *Maximus Poems 1–10* and *11–22*, and the invaluable corrected proofs of *The Maximus Poems*, both at Buffalo. There were also the poet's own annotated copies of these three early volumes among his papers at Connecticut. Indeed, the only item the textual critic lacked for an exhaustive examination were the corrected proofs for *Maximus 11–22*, which are not among Jonathan Williams's papers at Buffalo.

Between book and manuscript were also magazine appearances of a number of the poems. One-third of the thirty-nine poems in the first volume initially appeared in the enterprising magazines of the day—in every case, it should be noted, with differences from the final published versions. Some of these final versions suffered the thick fingers of error, others were effectively perfected by the poet. A few have minor differences, such as the absence of "important" in "I, Maximus of Gloucester, to You" (5:19), first published in *Origin* 1; most are extensively revised. Wherever possible, manuscripts sent to magazine editors were therefore located for comparison; in some cases the poet's copy of a magazine, occasionally with corrections or pertinent annotations, also survived and was consulted. In one such instance, where the version of a poem is replete with errors, the poet in correcting his copy added such comments as "look at the incredible changes of leading on this page! Also, throughout, the sloppiness of the quads!"—an early instance of the poet's concern for the appearance of his words on the page. Thus, the full progression of the text, with the one exception noted, was available for the editor to prepare a definitive text.

The most important change made in the present text of the first volume is the identification of a poem that, through a printer's inadvertence, was previously run together with the preceding poem. It has here been printed as a separate poem and has been given the title "*2nd Letter on Georges*" (offering a second view of Gloucester fishermen on Georges Bank in the North Atlantic), anticipating a third such "letter" in *Maximus Poems IV, V, VI*. Olson pointed out the error in conversation with the editor, and plentiful evidence among the original manuscripts and in the proofs of the 1960 *Maximus Poems* supports the restoration of the distinct poem.

Apart from the "*2nd Letter on Georges*," all other changes in this volume are minor emendations, some of which nevertheless clarify or strengthen certain lines. "Fisherman" (68:3), which appears in the singular in the typescript sent Jonathan Williams (and in the published volume), is here corrected to the more grammatically agreeable "fishermen," following other typescripts among the poet's papers. A somewhat more significant confusion of the same word occurs in 127:2, where "fishermen" has been restored to the singular of both the original holograph and the typescript sent Jonathan Williams (but missed in proofs), to agree with "[John] Smith . . . the / Androgyne" (126:31–127:3). Also, "or" has been corrected to "of" (151:4) and the misspelled "tercentennary" to "tercentenary" (155:3). "Bullfinch" (11:24) remains uncorrected, as do "neiborhood" (114:4) and "an continent" (137:26), but "Expresso" has been revised to "Espresso" (94:27). These alterations, together with the corrections of errors in the 1970 Cape Goliard edition described above, constitute the total number of changes for the present text of volume one.

With the second volume, *Maximus Poems IV, V, VI*, the same abundance of materials existed. Again, there was the opportunity to make use of the original manuscripts of individual poems, preserved among Olson's papers at the University of Connecticut. Over one hundred original holographs survive—about three-quarters of the total poems in that middle volume—some written on envelopes, on torn paper bags, on Olson's son's schoolwork, as successive "runs" in notepads and in many different pencils and inks, reflecting Olson's total absorption in his work.

Where a holograph does not survive, it was often not possible to determine whether the poem was composed directly on the typewriter or copied by typewriter from a handwritten original then discarded by the poet. For a poet commonly (if too simply) known for his celebration of the typewriter in poetic practice, however, a surprising number of poems have holograph originals. What is most clear and significant is that Olson's typescripts seek to reproduce the holograph originals faithfully—a fact that subsequently set an example for the editing of volume three and the insistence on faithfulness to the original appearance of the poem. Many typescripts themselves have further revisions, indicating the successive growth of individual poems, despite the spontaneous, even casual appearance of Olson's work to some readers. Olson also made corrections, after publication, in his copies of magazine appearances and of *Maximus IV, V, VI* itself, his habits being like those of most daily lives—catching error where one can. The overall impression is that he was, while not compulsive, as meticulous as possible, in keeping with attitudes expressed in his poem, "A Round & A Canon" (*Archaeologist of Morning*)—"he dies / as the instant dies, as I die / for an instant listening / to the slightest / error"—and reaffirmed in "Letter 7" (36): "The exactness / caulking, or 'play', calls for, those / millimeters / No where in man is there room for carelessnesses . . ."

In all, there was a complete set of manuscripts to compare and to chart the development of the poems in *Maximus IV, V, VI*: the original holographs or typescripts based on holographs or both, and in some cases additional manuscripts or typescripts prepared by Olson for publication in a periodical or anthology. Lacking those latter manuscripts, there was the magazine or anthology itself, including the poet's own annotated or emended copies, and, in a few instances (namely *Poetry* and the *Psychedelic Review*), both galleys and page proofs. In addition, among the poet's papers were photocopies of those various manuscripts made by Olson, often with his further corrections and revisions, as well as the typescript prepared for him in 1964 through the offices of Jeremy Prynne at Cambridge. A combination of these formed the basis of the manuscript Olson sent Corinth Books in 1965 for a planned edition, the proofs of which, corrected and photocopied by the poet, were also important to the process of collation, even though the actual book was never published. Next, there was the more final and authoritative manuscript Olson sent Cape Goliard Press in 1967, together with the author's corrected proofs of that edition (both preserved at Simon Fraser University Library), which, as has been stated, are the most immediate bases of the present text. Finally, there was the poet's own annotated copy of the published *Maximus IV, V, VI*, corrections in which have been incorporated in this edition.

Changes in the second volume presented here range from eliminating unauthorized British spellings and replacing italics where the underscore should have been retained (a seemingly insignificant point, but one repeatedly insisted on by Olson—perhaps as a nod to the typewritten or handwritten original or an attempt to reserve italics for special functions), to correcting typographical errors and restoring accuracies. For example, "parsons" has been restored to "persons" (231:49), an error missed in the proofs of *Maximus IV, V, VI* but correct in all the manuscripts and also corrected by the poet in his copy of the book. Similarly, "land" has been corrected to "lane" (234:13) and "where" to "were" (347:28), a small but marked improvement. The most important change, perhaps, is the correction of "accent" to "ascent" (241:17); the slip, missed in proofs although correct in an earlier published version, has already led one critic into a fanciful interpretation. In only one instance has the editor arbitrarily made a revision: in the case of an obviously extraneous final *e* in "here" (191:42), which should have been "her." "Here" is how it appears in the original typescript as well as the manuscript sent to the publisher, and is likewise uncorrected by Olson in proofs; still, all sense requires it to appear correctly as "her." On the other hand, the obvious grammatical error, "Days' " for "Day's"—a matter of agreement of the possessive, the collective Day family—has been allowed to stand as it appears in all available versions of the poem. So are certain other unusual spellings such as "urgeng" for "urging" (235:12), reflecting a seventeenth-century inconsistency and following the original holograph, the typescript (where it appears indistinctly, but is clarified as "urgeng" by Olson in the margin), the final manuscript sent Cape Goliard, and the proofs of *Maximus IV, V, VI*, although the poet corrected the *e* to *i* in one other (earlier) typescript. Also allowed are "eys" for "eyes" (355:34) and "haveing" (355:36), next to which Olson requests "stet—spelling" on his typescript sent for publication—certainly endurable eccentricities.

One concession to practicality made in the present edition is the addition of page numbers for *Maximus IV, V, VI*. As part of his own conception of serial structure, Olson had left page numbers off the volume in the belief or expectation that a reader entering the poem at any point could perceive its structure and concerns and apprehend a given poem's extensions backward and forward in the series. Here the linearity of conventional pagination has been introduced for convenience of reference.

The largest number of changes in this edition occur in the third volume, which was originally prepared, following the poet's death in 1970, by his literary executor at the time, Charles Boer, together with the present editor. (A full account can be found in the introduction to this editor's *Guide to the Maximus Poems*, pp. xliv–lv.) Because of the unusual circumstances—a volume produced without the author's immediate supervision or final approval—the text of the last volume has a certain limited authority. Although Olson wrote all the poems, the final selection was not entirely his own. Still, within that selection it is reasonable to hope the intentions of the poet have been met.

In addition to various textual modifications and improvements, alterations have been made in the third volume that were not necessary or possible in the case of the previous two. A number of poems have been added, one previously published poem omitted (or, more properly, withheld for a separate volume of such "alternate" *Maximus Poems*), and the positions of several more rearranged as new dates have become available.

The major change has been the addition of poems not previously included in *Volume Three*. Olson's extensive papers were gone through yet again, especially his poetry manuscripts and notebooks from 1963 on, the period of this final volume; and a number of unpublished poems that had been overlooked, disregarded, or unavailable during the original editing of the final volume were retrieved. These were then considered, both for intrinsic merit and their role in the larger context, and after being dated as precisely as possible they were inserted into the series in their proper order, following the overall chronological arrangement. The result is twenty-nine new poems, ranging from a single line to five pages in length.

At the same time, the decision was made to remove from the series one poem that had been included in *Volume Three*. This was the poem beginning "the / Bulgar—& / the 4 sons . . ." (III.35–36), which actually fit nicely into the series and explained the appearance of the figure of the Bulgar in the subsequent "Enyalion" poem (405–7). Olson had written it earlier than first realized, however, and had placed it in the sequence directly before "The Cow / of Dogtown" (318–20) in the second volume but had "discarded" it (in the poet's words on a final typescript) in preparing that volume for publication; he did not send it to either Corinth Books or Cape Goliard Press as part of the final manuscript. It was therefore deemed better to withdraw the poem from the sequence and to reserve it for a volume of similarly set-aside, or "alternate," *Maximus* poems that accrued during the twenty-year course of the epic. A number of these poems have already been published in *OLSON: The Journal of the Charles Olson Archives*, nos. 4, 6, and 9; *Hasty Papers* (December 1960); and *Albuquerque Review* (28 December 1961).

Several poems—"My shore, my sounds . . ." (438), "This living hand . . ." (506), "Outer Darkness . . ." (589), "flower of the underworld" (600), "Enyalion of / brown earth . . ." (610), "Nasturtium / is still my flower . . ." (632), "I live underneath / the light of day . . ." (633), and "the Blow is Creation . . ." (634)—were given new locations in the chronological order after more accurate dates were discovered for them. Most significant, perhaps, are the penultimate poems, which here more faithfully follow their original order of composition as it appears from the notepad in which they were found, although the poem designated as the "last" one by Olson still appears as such.

Regarding the text of the final volume itself, since *Volume Three* had been edited directly from original manuscripts and in a few instances from published appearances, mostly magazines, there were fewer intermediate stages to consider than with the first two volumes. It was appropriate to go back to the original manuscripts for comparison against the published text, as well as to the separate magazine appearances and to copies of manuscripts sent editors, whenever those could be recovered. The original manuscripts in all cases but one were readily available among Olson's papers at Connecticut, and a copy of the one for which no other original survived was obtained from the magazine editor who published it. The thirty-two poems published in magazines (in one case a broadside) by the poet, along with another five that appear on audiotape but not in print, were checked against original manuscripts, so that in no case was the copy-text entrusted solely to the magazine version. The poet's copies of magazines were again examined for corrections or emendations. Where available, tape-recorded versions of various poems read by the poet (thirteen in all) were also compared against written texts, especially where a manuscript contained uncertainties.

Some readings remained inaccessible even after repeated attempts, and they have been left bracketed with question marks, indicating their questionable or doubtful nature (all other brackets within the text are the poet's own). In certain cases, to attain a necessary freshness or distance, the original holograph was read into a tape recorder and played back against the written text. Colleagues and visitors, especially those familiar with Olson's hand and concerns, were also invited to make an attempt at deciphering particularly stubborn words—but to no further avail. There are some forty alternative readings, some as minor as "soldiery" for "soldiers," others such as "block" instead of "black" or "on" for "of." In all, only six remain impenetrable or highly questionable: 497:27, 498:12, 498:29, two in 612:16, and 618:4. A complete list follows these notes.

In the end, some seventy changes were made between the present text of the third volume and that of the previous edition. These vary from substituting a long (two-em) dash for a short (one-em) dash to changing words, that is, making what the textual critic W. W. Greg called substantive changes. Omitted accents and commas were restored, extraneous ampersands removed, and spaces added or deleted between words and lines. The few typographical errors such as "feshness" for "freshness" and "botton" for "bottom" were corrected, but also new readings of words previously misread were substituted—"set" for "sit," "where" for "when," "now" for "not," and also "transpired" corrected to "transfixed" and "piston" to "proton"—the configuration of letters in each case suggesting how readily such misreadings might occur among the handwritten originals. Most of these changes clarify the text in addition to correcting it.

More elaborate alterations include the substitution of a preferred reading of seven lines in the "Cornély" poem (468:1ff.), and the restoration of two lines of "I'm going to hate to leave this Earthly Paradise" (594:6–7) inadvertently omitted in its magazine appearance, which the original *Volume Three* had too readily accepted. In only six cases were the poet's misspellings editorially corrected: "whereever" in the original typescript of "Ships for the West Indies . . ." revised to "wherever" (393:38), "baloon" to "balloon" (457:29), "tercentennary" (an error also occurring earlier in 155:3) to "tercentenary" (496:35), "Mezozoic" to "Mesozoic" (549:24), "millenium" to "millennium" (605:22), and "Assissi" to "Assisi" (619:17). And in 548:6, although it is Cape

"Jolly" that most probably occurs in the original manuscript, certainly Cape Juby is intended, just as the name more clearly appears in later notes on the manuscript of "Between Cruiser & Plato . . ." (601) and "As Cabeza de Vaca . . ." (602). Otherwise, all else remains as Olson wrote it, including the seeming false start or redundancy of "am- / america" (595:38–39); the "antiqued" or dialectal spellings of "slomberous," "bockets," and "thar" (624:2–4); and the apparent error "Penelope," wife of Odysseus, for Persephone, bride of the king of Hell (550:15).

Adjustments were also made throughout the volume regarding spacing—not only between words and lines and stanzas, but in the placement of poems on the page—following Olson's care and insistences in the preparation of *Maximus IV, V, VI*. Abundant evidence exists of just how particular Olson was regarding the composition of that volume as a book. Spaces between the lines and sections of poems and blank pages (pp. 243, 245, 246, 248, 284, 285, 288, 349, 350, and 352 of the present edition) were very much part of the meter and rhythm of the book. Besides separating one untitled poem or movement from another, these spaces and blank pages provide a balance of whiteness or its echoing effect, the measure of it, comparable to rests in music. Such spacing can bear a weight of meaning, as pauses do in speech—the commentary of silence or the familiar signaling of a change in the direction of thought. Likewise, the location of poems on individual pages was calculated to recapture the appearance of the poem on its typed or handwritten sheet and thereby remain faithful to the original moment of composition, reflecting the poet's poise or kinesthesis, the full intention of his act of creation. Perhaps even more than predecessors Ezra Pound and William Carlos Williams, Olson was aware that poems could be composed with a spatial sense corresponding to an internal or proprioceptive order, that poetry was a spatial harmony as well as a time art—the black print of language deliberately enduring in white space. Every effort has been made to preserve this sense as well.

The editor would like to pay tribute to the following for helping to make this volume as accurate as possible: the staff of the University of Connecticut Library, Storrs; Robert J. Bertholf, director of the Poetry Collection, State University of New York at Buffalo Libraries; and Percilla Groves of Simon Fraser University Library's Special Collections. Also deserving thanks are Donald Allen; Charles Boer; Jack Collom, formerly editor of *the*; Michael Davidson, director of the Archive for New Poetry, University of California, San Diego; Holly Hall, head of Rare Books and Special Collections, Washington University Libraries, St. Louis; Ann Hyde, Manuscripts Librarian, Spencer Research Library, University of Kansas; Lakehead University Library, Thunder Bay, Ontario; James R. Lowell of the Asphodel Book Shop; R. Russell Maylone, Curator of Special Collections, Northwestern University Library; George Quasha, formerly editor of *Stony Brook*; Saundra Taylor, Curator of Manuscripts, Lilly Library, Indiana University; John Wieners, formerly editor of *Measure*; Theodore Wilentz of Corinth Books; and Jonathan Williams, publisher of Jargon Books.

George F. Butterick

ALTERNATE AND QUESTIONABLE READINGS IN VOLUME THREE

384:25   there] possibly "these"
384:28   for] possibly "from"
384:29   or] possibly "on"
386:3   the flower] possibly "The Flower"
391:12   block] possibly "black"
391:25   of] possibly "on"
397:18   front] possibly "first"
397:36   few] possibly "feet"
398:15   sick] remains doubtful; possibly
         "sicke" or "sickly"
398:16   ever] possibly "even"
448:4   drum] possibly "dream"
448:10   as] possibly "us"
456:21   such] possibly "Sense"
460:2   flowing] possibly "floating"
466:31   fisherman] possibly "fishermen"
467:9   soldiers] possibly "soldiery"
467:15–16 possibly an additional space
         between lines
478:7   farther] possibly "further"
492:34   show] possibly "shows"
495:4   or] possibly "of"
496:22   let] possibly "1st"
497:27   rest] a less than certain reading
498:3   from (2)] possibly "form" or "found"
498:8   punished] possibly "pinched"
498:12   failures] a less than certain reading
498:29   scared] a less than certain reading
498:32   Athletic] possibly "All Latin" or
         "Hill[—?]"
498:33   US] possibly "its"

518:25   when] possibly "where"
542:13   from] possibly "for"
546:9   living] possibly "loving"
546:10   that sight be] possibly "that sight
         that be" (MS has "letting that be,"
         with "letting" together with the *t* of
         "that" crossed out and "that sight"
         substituted)
573:23   are] possibly "all"
573:32   such] possibly "each"
605:3   7:05] possibly "7:25"
612:16   cate] remains doubtful, but no
         better reading presents itself;
         possibly "cats" or even "locate"
         (cate, usually plural and meaning
         delicacies, provisions bought rather
         than those simpler fares made at
         home, is very rare)
612:16   landwards] remains questionable,
         even doubtful, the handwriting in
         the MS is excessively cramped;
         possibly "Landreau's," since lines
         8–9 originally read "at her threads,
         like Landreau's Flat-Woven / Rugs,"
         with the final four words crossed
         out (Tony Landreau was a weaver
         at Black Mountain College)
618:4   humid[ness?]] remains questionable
618:13   sd] possibly "so"
633:16   between] possibly "between,"
633:20   Erojan] possibly "Eroian"

INDEX OF POEMS

First lines serve as titles to poems otherwise untitled.

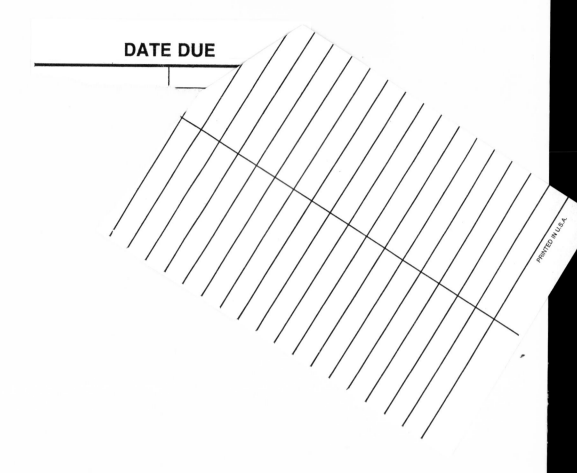

DATE DUE

PRINTED IN U.S.A.